Securing the Perimeter

Deploying Identity and Access Management with Free Open Source Software

Michael Schwartz

Maciej Machulak

Apress®

Securing the Perimeter: Deploying Identity and Access Management with Free Open Source Software

Michael Schwartz
Austin, TX, USA

Maciej Machulak
London, UK

ISBN-13 (pbk): 978-1-4842-2600-1
https://doi.org/10.1007/978-1-4842-2601-8

ISBN-13 (electronic): 978-1-4842-2601-8

Library of Congress Control Number: 2018966332

Managing Director, Apress Media LLC: Welmoed Spahr
Acquisitions Editor: Susan McDermott
Development Editor: Laura Berendson
Coordinating Editor: Rita Fernando

Cover designed by eStudioCalamar

Cover image designed by Freepik (www.freepik.com)

Distributed to the book trade worldwide by Springer Science+Business Media New York, 233 Spring Street, 6th Floor, New York, NY 10013. Phone 1-800-SPRINGER, fax (201) 348-4505, e-mail orders-ny@springer-sbm.com, or visit www.springeronline.com. Apress Media, LLC is a California LLC and the sole member (owner) is Springer Science + Business Media Finance Inc (SSBM Finance Inc). SSBM Finance Inc is a **Delaware** corporation.

For information on translations, please e-mail rights@apress.com, or visit http://www.apress.com/rights-permissions.

Apress titles may be purchased in bulk for academic, corporate, or promotional use. eBook versions and licenses are also available for most titles. For more information, reference our Print and eBook Bulk Sales web page at http://www.apress.com/bulk-sales.

Any source code or other supplementary material referenced by the author in this book is available to readers on GitHub via the book's product page, located at www.apress.com/9781484226001. For more detailed information, please visit http://www.apress.com/source-code.

Printed on acid-free paper

As Adam Savage from Mythbusters says: "Failure is always an option!" That's why this book is dedicated to the vibrant, tenacious, and global identity community who has been at it for 20 plus years and shows no signs of slowing down.

Table of Contents

About the Authors

Michael Schwartz is a domain expert on digital authentication and centralized application security policy management. Since starting an ISP in 1995, he has been directly involved in network and application security. In 2009, he founded Gluu Inc, a security software development company that has created an IAM distribution based on free open source components. In addition to his participation in several identity standards, Mike is the co-chair of the OTTO working group at the Kantara Initiative, which is developing new standards for identity federation. Mike has worked with organizations in many sectors, including finance, government, education, and enterprise. A graduate of Washington University in St. Louis, he currently resides with his family in Austin, TX.

Dr. Maciej Machulak is an expert in security, privacy, and trust in the Cloud. He works on digital identity and security at HSBC. In the past, Maciej worked for various companies in the identity and access management space. He also founded and became the CEO of Cloud Identity Limited (acquired in 2015), a company that developed innovative security software based on proprietary and open source components. Maciej serves as the Vice-Chair of the User-Managed Access (UMA) Work Group at Kantara Initiative and is one of the authors of the award-winning UMA protocol and of two OAuth-related specifications used in Open Banking. In June 2015, Maciej was awarded the prestigious MIT Technology Review Innovators Under 35 Poland award for his work on privacy and security. Maciej is a PhD graduate from Newcastle University. Outside of work, he enjoys various outdoor activities and sports with his family.

Acknowledgments

Thanks are in order! First of all, to Andee, Marzena, Zia, Brant, and Maya, for supporting the stressed out authors and tolerating our occasional absence! Thanks to Rita Fernando and Susan McDermott for supporting this project at Apress. Thanks to William Lowe, Sam Morris, Meghna Joshi, Chris Blanton, Michal Kepkowski, and the rest of the Gluu team for their contributions and support! Thanks to Thijs Schreijer from Kong for his work on Chapter 6; Radovan Semancik from Evolveum for the Midpoint content; Francesco Chicchiriccò from Tirasa for his content on Syncope; Martin Čížek from Orchitech Solutions for his contribution on Wren:IDM; Quanah Gibson-Mount for his help on OpenLDAP; Sixto Pablo Martín García of OneLogin for his help on PySAML and all his great federation software; Eve Maler from ForgeRock for her review of Chapter 8; Justin Richer from Bespoke Engineering for his sequence diagram on stepped up authentication; Nat Sakimura, from the Nomura Research Institute, for his great diagram on OpenID Connect security levels; Matt Moyer and John Wandelt from the Georgia Tech Research Institute for their contribution to this book and to the community on federation trustmarks; Nick Roy for his contribution to Chapter 10; Tom Smedinghoff for his insightful slides from Identiverse; Rainer Hoerbe for his thoughtful presentation at EIC that was included in Chapter 10; Rajiv Dholakia from Nok Nok for sharing his genius on FIDO; Igor Farinic from Evolveum for his support; Anil John for agreeing to share the results of the ERASMUS pilot; Mooketsi Regoeng and Roberts Lapes for their comments; to Kaliya, Doc, and Phil, who have tirelessly organized the Internet Identity Workshop for more than a decade; and last, but certainly not least, Colin Walis from the Kantara Initiative for his tireless efforts as executive director, and his support of this project. We are leaving out countless other people and organizations who had a less direct impact, but without whom this book could not have happened.

CHAPTER 1

Introduction

The goal of this book is to demystify Identity and Access Management (IAM). There are thousands of professionals around the world helping companies with IAM, but that's not enough. In this book we aim to increase the supply of IAM engineers by sharing some of the techniques and strategies developed over the last 20 years in a wide range of industries. Whether you are starting a small organization or deploying an IAM solution for a huge enterprise, the techniques presented in this book should help you deploy a solution based on Free Open Source Software (FOSS) to meet your needs. Nothing in this book is hard, and if you put the time into it, you can be an IAM professional too!

Each chapter of this book will provide both theory and some pointers to software. There is a lot of great Free Open Source Software (FOSS) for identity. This book will cover client and server software, web software and mobile software, libraries, and plugins. It is not a comprehensive survey of FOSS identity tools—there are too many to cover in one book! But hopefully, after finishing each chapter, you'll be in a good place to start your research.

Components of an Identity Service

If you're going to build a world-class identity service, you need to understand the components. It can be confusing because many identity vendors try to position themselves as a one-stop-shop for identity, and in the process blur the lines between what are distinct identity services. Figure 1-1 can help you visualize an identity infrastructure.

1

© Michael Schwartz, Maciej Machulak 2018
M. Schwartz and M. Machulak, *Securing the Perimeter*, https://doi.org/10.1007/978-1-4842-2601-8_1

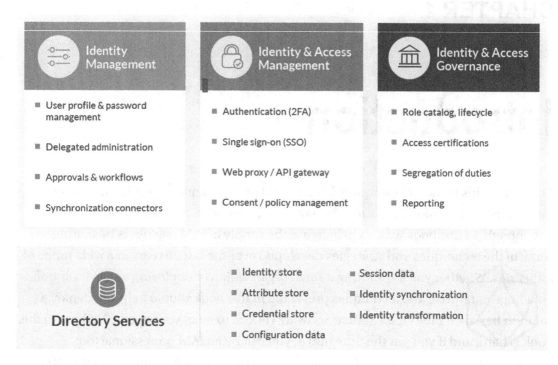

Figure 1-1. *Identity service components*

Identity Management

Let's start with Identity Management (IDM). This term is sometimes used to summarize the identity service holistically. However, professionals in the industry mean only one thing when they use the term IDM: managing how systems are kept in sync when information about a person changes. One of the most important IDM use cases is "provisioning" and "de-provisioning". Identity management events happen when a person's record is created, updated, or deleted. For example, when a person is hired by an organization, this may trigger a workflow where accounts are created in several systems, approvals may be needed, and equipment may be issued. Conversely, when a person leaves the organization, accounts need to be removed or inactivated.

When a person's information is updated, this may also trigger a workflow. For example, if a person's role in the organization changes, access to systems may be granted or revoked. Changing your password is also an example of an update. For this reason, many IDM systems include a self-service password reset website as part of their solution.

IAM is a "consumer" of information managed by the IDM system—meaning the IAM system expects data about a person to be already present and accurate. It's garbage in, garbage out. The access management is only as good as the quality of the underlying data. If you fire an employee, but never take him out of the database, it doesn't matter what kind of fancy authentication technology you use!

The lines between IAM and IDM can get blurred. You can have IAM features in your IDM. For example, two-factor authentication account recovery—you need to be strongly authenticated before you can reset a strong credential. You can also have IDM features in your IAM. For example, social login, where users are added on-the-fly the first time they are authenticated. Another example is forcing people to reset their passwords during a login flow.

Organizations have two options for IDM: buy or build. Many websites implement simple registration and account management—adding, editing, and removing records about people is handled by custom code. In larger organizations, where there are more systems and the business rules are more complex, an IDM platform may be more productive. There is some excellent FOSS IDM software out there. Although this book is primarily about IAM, IDM is covered at a very high level in Chapter 9.

Identity and Access Management

What is Identity and Access Management? A little history will help give you some perspective.

The original Internet IAM infrastructure was based on the RADIUS protocol. If you are old enough, think back to the days of modems (or if you're not, think of a VPN or WiFi connection, which still use RADIUS). These systems have three parts: (1) a RADIUS client requesting access to the network, (2) a network device that has modem ports or some other network resource, and (3) the RADIUS Server that provides the AAA—authentication, authorization, and accounting.

RADIUS was developed by Livingston Enterprises Inc. (now part of Alcatel Lucent) to control access to "terminal servers"—network devices that had a high concentration of modems. It later became an IETF standard. Today, the last A in "Triple-A" ("accounting") has dropped off from most modern IAM systems. In the old days, you might only have a certain number of hours of dial-up, and the RADIUS Servers would interface to the billing system of an Internet Service Provider ("ISP"). After authenticating the person, the RADIUS Server would authorize, for example, to allow either one or two channels, depending on which type of account the person had purchased. This is a simple example of the authorization capabilities of RADIUS.

Fast forward a few years. The next phase of Internet IAM started to take place when the World Wide Web achieved critical scale. Believe it or not, a ubiquitous web was not a forgone conclusion. By 1998 a company called Netegrity (purchased by Computer Associates) launched a product called SiteMinder. This was a new kind of AA server designed to control access to websites instead of network devices. The design was similar to RADIUS. There were still three parts: (1) a person using a web browser (the client), (2) a web server with the SiteMinder Agent installed, and (3) the central SiteMinder Policy Server. In the Policy Server you could make policies about which people could access which web servers. A new advantage of web AA platforms like SiteMinder was that you could achieve Single Sign-On (SSO). In other words, the person could authenticate once and access multiple websites in the same domain.

More generically, this pattern is commonly known as the "PDP-PEP Pattern." And there are a few other standard parts. Consider Figure 1-2.

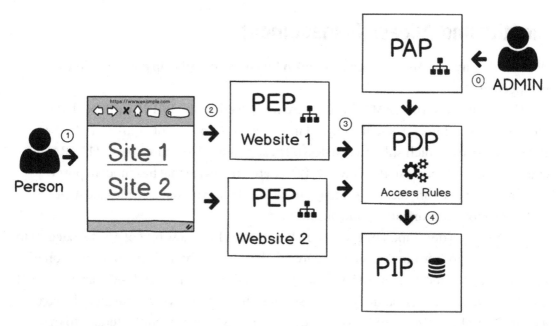

Figure 1-2. *PDP-PEP pattern*

Here is a brief summary of the components:

- **PDP** "Policy Decision Point"—Knows the policies which people, using which clients are allowed to access what resources. In a way, it's the brain of the system.

- **PEP** "Policy Enforcement Point"—Is responsible for querying the PDP to find out if access should be granted. There are usually many PEPs. For example, there could be hundreds of web servers in an organization, each relying on the PDP to grant access.

- **PAP** "Policy Administration Point"—This is some kind of interface that enables an administrator to define the policies in the PDP. It could be a website or command-line interface. Without a PAP, administrators are forced to manage the policy data in a database, or by configuring files.

- **PIP**—Policy and user information is persisted somewhere, normally in a database like an LDAP Server.

Let's go through an imaginary flow based on Figure 1-2. In step 0, the administrator for this organization creates the policies about who can access which websites. (It's step 0, because it happens before the person even tries to get to the website.) In step 1, a person using a web browser clicks on a link for "Site 1". In step 2, an HTTP request is sent from the browser to the web server. The web server either acts as the PEP or contains other software that intercepts the request and authorizes it. In step 3, the PEP asks the PDP if it should respond to the request. In order to evaluate the request, the PDP may need to know "who is this person," and thus the process of authentication may ensue. This brings us to step 4—in order to authenticate the person, the PDP may need to validate a person's credentials, such as with a username and password. This usually requires a query to a database, or the PIP. Sometimes the PDP may return information about the person to the PEP. This is also gathered from the PIP. If the person tries to navigate to Site 2, in authentication may not need to occur if the PDP can recognize the web session. In this case, the evaluation of policies still occurs—this website might have different requirements for access. But the user experience is improved.

So now that you know the history, what does an IAM system look like today? While the protocols and technology have changed, the basic pattern remains the same. Of course, older proprietary solutions such as SiteMinder have been replaced with open standards for web access management. These open standards leverage APIs for IAM. In the early 2000s, XML/SOAP APIs like SAML and XACML were introduced. This book will take a close look at SAML, which is still widely in use today. With the introduction of the iPhone in 2007, a trend toward JSON/REST APIs gained even more momentum—and this carried over to IAM APIs. New protocols based on OAuth (which are RESTful, if not one hundred percent REST) currently have the most momentum.

Identity and Access Governance

Identity and Access Governance (IAG) is the process of decision making and the process by which decisions are implemented (or not implemented). Identity governance is not entirely a technical challenge. It is a combination of systems, rules, and procedures that are defined between an individual and an organization regarding the entitlement, use, and protection of personal information in order to authenticate individual identities and provide authorizations and privileges within or across systems and enterprise boundaries.

A governance-based approach answers three important questions: (1) Who does? (2) Who should? and (3) Who did?. "Who does?" addresses reality: you need to have an inventory of the security process in your organization and compliance practices that are in place. "Who should?" is the process of mapping roles to resources, setting policies, and affecting automation to efficiently affect these decisions. "Who did?" requires monitoring and audit and involves activity collection, review, and alerting. Consider the diagram in Figure 1-3.

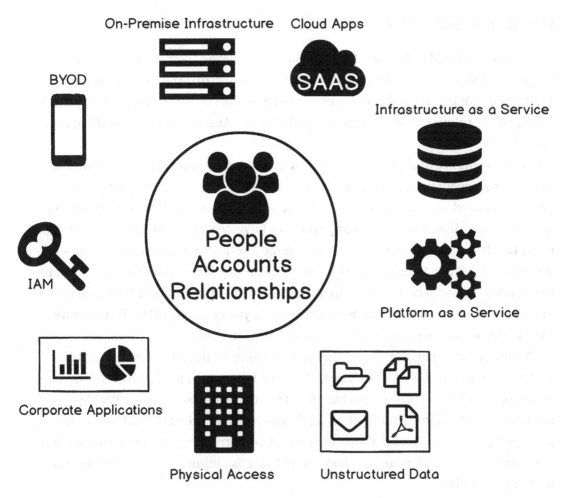

Figure 1-3. *User-centric approach to security*

IAG encompasses the totality of the relationship between the organization and all the digital resources of the company. You can think of the IAG system as the brain, while the IDM and IAM system are the body. Simply put, in IAM, we assume you already know what policies you want to implement! In IDM, we assume you already know which users you want to push to what systems.

Governance happens whether or not you have an IAG platform. In order to respond quickly, governance tools frequently provide convenient graphical user interfaces to increase productivity and to reduce incident response times. There are few open source governance tools. Evolveum Midpoint, introduced briefly in Chapter 9, has some governance features. It's a new area of development, with commercial software solutions arising within the last eight to ten years, and few open standards to implement.

Directory Services

The substrate of IAM is data; all that data about people and their privileges has to be persisted and retrieved. Technically, any database will do. And in fact, different solutions use different databases to solve specific requirements. However, many access management solutions use the Lightweight Directory Access Protocol (LDAP) to front-end identity systems.

Historically, LDAP databases were faster at retrieving simple data than relational database management systems (RDBMS). This may or may not be true anymore—properly indexed, many databases could be made fast enough. LDAP also has strong data replication features, which is important for large-scale identity systems. And finally, many LDAP implementations are able to enforce fine-grained access to the data—defining policies in a tree structure is easier because you can make rules about all data that resides "below" a certain node in the tree. Many people think of LDAP as being fast to read and slow to write. This is not always true anymore. Many LDAP Servers have write performance on par with other database technologies.

No matter what persistence strategy you are using for the directory service, it's a critical part of the identity platform. Configured incorrectly, it will inhibit all three components we have discussed so far. Also, if your directory service is really big—millions, tens of millions, hundreds of millions—you really need to think about the persistence layer. You should always benchmark performance with requirements similar than what you expect. One of the black arts of LDAP is optimization for a certain data or transaction profile.

Is IAM a Good Place to Start?

Now that you know the various pieces that comprise an identity platform, you may be wondering where to begin. Conventional wisdom is that you should start with IDM and IAG. This book goes against the grain and suggests IAM and directory services should be your initial focus. IDM and IAG tend to be long projects that involve business and technology. Understanding processes and workflows and negotiating changes to how the business operates takes time. By contrast, implementing an IAM platform is a shorter project. Doesn't it make sense to get the shorter project underway first? Furthermore, by delaying the IAM deployment, applications may not know about important security requirements. For example, perhaps a content management system does not support SAML or OpenID Connect, which will become important requirements after you implement an IAM. Not supporting these open standards may be a reason to eliminate this CRM from the pool of candidates. But if you haven't started your IAM project, you will not know this. It won't hurt to have the IAM in place when you discuss IDM and IAG with your organization.

Identity Standards

Identity services have to play nice with a diverse IT infrastructure. For this reason, open standards for identity have become increasingly important. There are several standards bodies in the identity ecosystem. The ones this book will focus on are the IETF, OASIS, Kantara, and the OpenID Foundation. However, many identity standards are built on standards governed by other standards bodies. For example, X.509, a standard for digital certificates, was developed by the ITU.

There are two types of standards: "build it and they will come" standards, and "let's work together so we don't all do something different" standards. The most successful standards typically fall into the latter category, but in the identity space, without some of the former, some of the latter would not exist. This book will cover old and new identity standards, in order of appearance in this book: LDAP, SAML, OAuth, OpenID Connect, and UMA.

LDAP is the oldest identity standard. Completed in the '90s, it has been the core competency of identity experts across the globe since that time. The standard includes a communication protocol between clients (who want information) and servers (who hold information). It also includes standards about the format of data, how data can be serialized in a text format easy for humans to read and write (called LDIF), and other conventions that improve interoperability between the clients and servers of various implementations.

SAML is one of the most important web-based federated identity standards. It's the most widely supported standard by SaaS providers who want to accept credentials from large enterprise customers. It uses XML as the data format, which has become somewhat problematic, as parsing XML documents has been fraught with risk (there are a lot of places you can go wrong). Like most other federated identity standards, it is based on redirect a person's browser to a website maintained by their home organization. Assuming the website is trusted (and how that occurs was quite innovative), the home organization then returns information about the person to the original website. It's quite a big standard, and this book will cover only its most widely used features.

OAuth 2.0 is still under active development. It uses JSON as the data format, and RESTful APIs to enable a person (or organization) to authorize access to resources. Loosely based on a previous protocol by Facebook and the experiences of Microsoft and Google, it was initially hashed out at the Internet Identity Workshop in Mountain View, California. OAuth is a delegated authorization protocol, not an authentication protocol. You've used OAuth if you're used Google login at a third-party site and approved the release of information.

OpenID Connect is the most prevalent profile of OAuth. In this protocol, you can authorize the release of information about yourself to a website or mobile application. The previously-mentioned Google login example is actually OpenID Connect. Google has no idea if it should release information about you to this website. Only you know if you want that, so why not just ask you? OpenID Connect is a collaboration of Google, Microsoft, and other large companies and a few smaller contributors. Google authentication and Microsoft Azure authentication is OpenID Connect. Many organizations are adopting the standard. Although similar in purpose to SAML, it offers a more modern API design and better support for mobile device authentication.

The User Managed Protocol (UMA) is another profile of OAuth. It offers a flexible protocol to enable three parties to collaborate on security: the Resource Server (which publishes the APIs), the Authorization Server (which issues tokens that grant access to APIs), and the Client (which is the website or mobile calling the API, sometimes on behalf of a person). UMA also defines a protocol to enable the Resource Server to register its protected URLs with the Authorization Server. Using UMA, organizations can implement a PEP/PDP access management infrastructure.

Gluu Server

At the center of our IAM narrative is the Gluu Server, which includes free open source identity components, integrated together in several easy to install and configure distributions. Gluu's founder is Mike Schwartz, one of the authors of this book. The Gluu Server includes a SAML IDP, an OAuth Authorization Server (supporting also OpenID and UMA), a component to handle social login, an LDAP Server, and an administrative web interface.

Gluu is committed to keeping the Gluu Server free. That means the code is available on GitHub, the binary packages are published for Linux, Docker, and Kubernetes, the documentation is available, and your questions will be answered on the community support forums.

The goal of the Gluu Server is to be the best free open source IAM platform and to have the lowest total cost of operation (TCO). This has been done by incorporating good existing open source components where they exist, and by writing software to fill in the gaps. By not writing 100% of the platform, Gluu has been able to deliver one of the most innovative platforms on the market.

Why Free Open Source?

Why base your organization's IAM infrastructure on free open source software?

The cost of commercial IAM software is prohibitive to many organizations. Many of you reading this book are looking for lower cost alternatives. There is a saying that FOSS is only free if you don't value your time, since it sometimes requires more time and effort to implement than commercial alternatives. But even if nothing is truly "free," FOSS is less expensive. Saving money is always good, right?

But why should you use FOSS if cost is not an issue? IAM systems are mission-critical, not only to the security of an organization, but also to the availability of its digital services. Most organizations are happy to pay money for the best technology if it gives them a competitive advantage or mitigates risk.

And interestingly, here's where the reasons for FOSS get even more compelling. Jim Whitehurst, CEO of Red Hat, has asserted that FOSS is the best development methodology—that it results in the best available software. Research in 2014 showed that open source software had 0.59 defects per 1,000 lines of code, while commercial code had 0.72![1] But FOSS software has also proven to be very innovative—with fast release cycles.

FOSS has been particularly successful at implementing Internet standard protocols. As of July 2018, more than 62% of the top million busiest sites ran the Apache or Nginx web server.[2] The services we enjoy from Google, Apple, Dropbox, and many software as a service (SaaS) companies could not exist without FOSS. This is even more true when you consider that most of these services are running on the Linux operating system.

---

[1]Steven J. Vaughan-Nichols, "Coverity finds open source software quality better than proprietary code," *ZDNet*, April 16, 2014, https://www.zdnet.com/article/coverity-finds-open-source-software-quality-better-than-proprietary-code/.

[2]*Netcraft*, "July 2018 Web Server Survey," July 19, 2018, *Netcraft*, https://news.netcraft.com/archives/2018/07/19/july-2018-web-server-survey.html.

Another reason to use FOSS is because there are more people who can use the software. It is easier for beginners to get hands-on experience with FOSS, which translates to more people getting trained. This means organizations can find more candidates, whether recruiting an initial team or replacing members of an existing team.

Publicly searchable support is another reason many prefer FOSS. Would you rather Google a question or open a support ticket with a vendor? FOSS communities offer an alternative to support from a vendor. And as a last resort, you can always look at the code. Developers are used to this process and are frustrated when commercial support is the only option, which frequently leads to less content.

If you pay a lot for one of the many expensive commercial offerings, won't that save your job if something goes wrong? You can say you advised the purchase of the best software the market had to offer. Your company can sue the commercial company vendor if there is a problem. But all open source licenses prevent you from suing. You get what you pay for, so FOSS IAM platforms must be worse—why else would people buy these expensive commercial platforms? In practice, suing a software vendor is a joyless, unproductive, and unpredictable way to recover wasted time and money. IT failures occur for complex reasons—assigning blame to the vendor is usually difficult.

Another factor to consider is reusability. People move from one organization to the next with surprising frequency these days. Will you be able to bring your tools with you to the next gig? If you master FOSS tools, the chances are good. If your tools are dependent on a large financial commitment and a long, drawn-out legal process, probably not.

Some sage advice: being great at your job is a much better plan than to "not get fired" when something goes wrong, and it's a lot more fun! The best reason to use FOSS is because it's the best software available. Don't make decisions based on fear. "You get what you pay for" is not always true anymore. Every one of your organization's digital services hangs off the identity system. The ability of your organization to meet the demands of the market is intertwined today with the IT infrastructure. You have a critical contribution to make. Be a champion of open source software at your organization because it gives you the best chance to succeed in the long term!

Where to Start?

IAM platforms consist of a number of pieces, integrated together. The Gluu Server provides an easy-to-install package of several popular FOSS components, including an LDAP Server, an OAuth Authorization Server, a SAML identity provider, the Passport-js Server for social login, and an administrative web interface. Binaries are available for several Linux distributions, including Ubuntu, Debian, Centos, and Red Hat. Docker and Kubernetes distributions are available, but you'll have to see the Gluu website for those instructions.

It's best to learn by doing. The Gluu Server provides an ideal environment for trying out some of the techniques described in the subsequent chapters, and many of the examples will assume you have a Gluu Server up and running. This section will help you kick start your effort to install the Gluu Server, so you'll be ready to get to work.

If you are using the Linux packages, the Gluu Server uses a file system container strategy called "chroot" to install everything in one folder in the /opt directory. Don't confuse this with new container strategies like Docker, which offers process and network isolation. The goal of chroot was to make the Gluu Server easier to install, uninstall, and upgrade—which is more difficult if the components are located in many locations on the host file system.

For development, you may want to use a local virtual machine (VM) running on your laptop. Use NAT networking to enable the VM to reach the Internet, and so that you can connect to it via IP. Make sure you give the VM at least 4GB of RAM. You should also allocate at least two CPU units if possible. The Gluu Server has a bunch of Java applications, so be generous! If you don't have a workstation that can host a VM, you may want to use a cloud server. You probably already have a favorite Linux distribution. My normal plan is to download the ISO for the Linux distribution to my laptop, and then specify that file as the boot image in the CD/DVD settings for the VM. I normally do a very minimal Linux installation, without X Windows and no services except sshd.

After you install the base Linux system and get the latest updates, you'll want to install the Gluu Server package. Check the Gluu Server documentation website at http://gluu.org/docs for the exact package installation process, which will vary based on your distribution (Ubuntu, Debian, Centos, or Red Hat). The basic idea is that you will add the repository, add the keys for the repository necessary to verify the package signatures, update your package index, and then install the Gluu Server using your standard package management system. This will take some time because the Gluu Server is large—around 500MB.

Once installed, you'll need to start the Gluu Server. How you accomplish this may also vary based on your distribution. For example, you may type something like `service gluu-server-3.1.4 start`. This mounts the file system, which will enable you to then "log in" to the container—for example, by typing something like `service gluu-server-3.1.4 login`. Again, check the Gluu docs for the exact syntax for your platform.

Now that you have the Gluu Server package installed and you've logged into the container, things become similar between the distributions. The basic idea is that you are going to run the setup program (see Listing 1-1), and then voilà, it is done.

Listing 1-1. Initial Gluu Server Configuration

```
# cd /install/community-edition-setup/
# ./setup.py
```

Installing Gluu Server...

For more info see:
./setup.log
./setup_error.log

** All clear text passwords contained in ./setup.properties.last.

```
    Enter IP Address [192.168.88.145] :
    Enter hostname [localhost] : idp.mydomain.com
    Enter your city or locality : Austin
    Enter your state or province two letter code : TX
    Enter two letter Country Code : US
    Enter Organization Name : Example Incorporated
    Enter email address for support at your organization : info@example.com
    Enter maximum RAM for applications in MB [3072] : 4096
    Optional: enter password for oxTrust and LDAP superuser [qXlNCzOo5xAS] :
    Install oxAuth OAuth2 Authorization Server? [Yes] :
    Install oxTrust Admin UI? [Yes] :
    Install LDAP Server? [Yes] :
    Install (1) Gluu OpenDJ (2) OpenLDAP Gluu Edition [1|2] [1] : 1
    Install Apache HTTPD Server [Yes] :
    Install Shibboleth SAML IDP? [No] : Yes
```

```
Install Asimba SAML Proxy? [No] :
Install oxAuth RP? [No] : Yes
Install Passport? [No] : Yes
Install JCE 1.8? [Yes] :
You must accept the Oracle Binary Code License Agreement for the Java SE
Platform Products to download this software. Accept License Agreement?
[Yes] :
Do you acknowledge that use of the Gluu Server is under the MIT
license? [N|y] : y
```

	:---------------------:
hostname	Albacore.example.com
orgName	Example Incorporated
Os	Ubuntu
City	Austin
State	TX
countryCode	US
Support email	info@example.com
Applications max ram	6000
Admin Pass	qXINCzOo5xAS
Install oxAuth	True
Install oxTrust	True
Install LDAP	True
Install JCE 1.8	True
Install Apache 2 web server	True
Install Shibboleth SAML Proxy	True
Install Asimba SAML Proxy	False
Install oxAuth RP	True
Install Passport	True

Note   Don't use 127.0.0.1 or localhost for the IP and hostname. You want to be able to reach the Gluu Server from your laptop's browser. Even if you don't have DNS set up for this hostname, you can edit your localhost's file to make sure the name resolves.

Once you're confident your browser can resolve the hostname, navigate to `https://<hostname>` (the hostname you used during setup). Your browser will warn you about the insecure HTTPS connection because the Gluu Server initially generates self-signed SSL certificates. It's okay—you would upgrade these on your production server, but for your test server, such self-signed SSL certificates are fine. You should be presented with a login form. The default username is `admin`. Use the password that either you specified or was auto-generated for you during installation.

If it's successful, you should see the Gluu Server login page.

Conclusion

You now know the components of a modern identity stack: IAM, IDM, IAG, and directory services. And hopefully you've installed your first identity component! Congratulations, you're on your way to becoming "identerati"—a guru in this emerging industry.

As mentioned earlier, digital identity is a growing discipline that needs more practitioners. If you're interested in continuing, you should consider joining IDPro, whose mission is to "foster ethics and excellence in the practice and profession of digital identity". IDPro is a community where you can connect with other identity professionals and share best practices. You can find more information on their website at `https://idpro.org`.

In the next chapters, we dive more deeply into the introduced topics. You can read the chapters in order or skip to the chapters that most interest you.

CHAPTER 2

LDAP

Directory services are a critical part of your identity infrastructure. Many components in the identity stack need to either read or write data. While any database could work, a popular choice for many identity projects is LDAP. This chapter is not a comprehensive guide to LDAP. If you are deploying LDAP in your environment, study the documentation for your LDAP Server of choice. Like other chapters in this book, the goal here is to give an overview of the technology and brief descriptions of some open source software tools.

History

You can retrieve data stored in a tree format quickly by ignoring data that is not relevant to your search. For example, think about your family tree. If you want to know the descendants of your parents, you can ignore all the family tree beneath aunts or uncles. Reducing the scope of the search saves a lot of time.

In the late '80s, the X.500 set of standards, developed by the International Telecommunication Union (ITU), standardized the storage and retrieval of data using a tree structure. X.500 infrastructure worked well for early messaging systems. However, the popularity of Internet Protocol (IP) lead to the need for a new directory access protocol. Collaborators from the industry released several related standards from 1993–1997 via the Internet Engineering Task Force (IETF), independent of any X.500 dependencies.

The LDAP IETF RFCs do not define a persistence mechanism. Nothing prohibits an in-memory LDAP implementation, or even a persistence mechanism based on homing pigeons (although you'd have to build many lofts, and the performance would be terrible). Today, each LDAP vendor has its own persistence strategy, and there is a diverse range of technologies. When you choose an LDAP platform, you always need to consider the underlying database with its respective tradeoffs. One of the most popular

17

© Michael Schwartz, Maciej Machulak 2018
M. Schwartz and M. Machulak, *Securing the Perimeter*, https://doi.org/10.1007/978-1-4842-2601-8_2

databases for LDAP is Oracle Berkeley DB. OpenLDAP uses LMDB. IBM's LDAP Server uses the DB2 database. Radiant Logic offers a commercial LDAP Server that uses Hadoop as the backend.

Where did the LDAP Servers of today come from? It may help to understand that some LDAP implementations are related. In 1993, at the University of Michigan, Tim Howes wrote the first LDAP Server. In 1996, Netscape forked the project and launched the Netscape Directory Server, which became one of the leading commercial servers. The OpenLDAP project started, also by forking the 1996 version of the University of Michigan LDAP Server code—today the University of Michigan directory project redirects to OpenLDAP. In 1999, Sun Microsystems and Netscape formed an alliance, called iPlanet, re-branding Netscape Directory Server. In an interesting twist, AOL became part of this partnership when it acquired Netscape. In 2002, the iPlanet alliance ended, but the parties retained the right to use the LDAP Server code. Sun rebranded the LDAP Servers as the Sun Directory Server Enterprise Edition. In 2004, AOL sold the LDAP Server code to Red Hat, who open sourced it as the Fedora Directory Server (FDS).

Sun continued to innovate the original Netscape Directory Server. But in 2005, some of the developers felt that they had gone as far as they could with the old code. Developers proposed to rewrite the LDAP Server from the ground up in Java. Refactoring and innovations in Java and persistence libraries would improve performance and make it easier to manage. The launch of OpenDS, a new Java LDAP Server platform, aligned with a short-lived open source movement at Sun. OpenDS used the same schema and access control mechanism as previous versions of Sun Directory Server, so the servers were relatively compatible.

And then Oracle bought Sun. There was overlap in the identity products. Regulators fussed, and Oracle agreed to divest some of the business. Some of the former Sun identity team raised money and acquired some of the technology—including OpenDS, which by this time was an essential part of the identity platform. Forgerock rebranded this new Java LDAP Server as "OpenDJ" and continues to release source code from time to time under the Common Development and Distribution License (CDDL).

One of the benefits of LDAP is that because your application uses a standard protocol to access data, you are not locked into one vendor's implementation. However, this does not mean that there are no switching costs with regard to managing the server.

One of the interesting results from this long, intertwined history is that some LDAP Servers share some important management conventions—particularly how schema and access controls are managed. For example, the same schema can be used for OpenDJ, Fedora Directory Server, and even commercial LDAP Servers from Oracle and Ping Identity.

No discussion of LDAP would be complete without mentioning Microsoft Active Directory (AD), one of the most widely deployed servers with an LDAP interface. During the development of Windows 2000, Microsoft recognized that the flat user management strategy from Windows NT 4.0 was not sufficient to serve large enterprise customers. Developers forked the directory component from the Exchange 4.0 email server and added many features. Since its first release in 2000 as an official part of the Windows Server platform, AD became one of the most common directory servers for organizations. For many identity and access management deployments, AD is an important source for information about people.

Why Use LDAP Today?

Today, some people wonder about the relevance of LDAP. It's not a protocol you want to use over the Internet to retrieve your cloud email or to access your cloud files. Even Microsoft's new cloud identity service, Azure Active Directory, does not support LDAP connections from the Internet. Some would even argue that the hierarchical representation of identity should give way to a linked data graph model, where people are interconnected, not subordinate within an organization.

The right persistence strategy depends on many factors. How big is your data—thousands or millions of entries? What is the concurrency requirement? Are read or write operations more common? Is multi-data center replication required? Does the concurrency warrant database shards? Can you use the database interface for in-memory cache? There is no "correct" answer—if data gets stored on the disk, any database can work for identity services.

But for many organizations, LDAP has proven to be a nice choice for the database in the IAM stack. Here are my top 10 reasons:

1. LDAP helps you avoid lock-in to one implementation. LDAP has a text-based format called LDIF—LDAP Data Interchange Format—so you can always export data from one LDAP Server and import it into another.

2. There are many free open source libraries and tools to manage data using LDAP.

3. Replication technology is mature for several LDAP Servers. For identity data, business continuity is critical. Many organizations want to know that a full set of data is available in two locations. While several other database technologies include replication, some implementations are "best efforts," which means you may need to compare data sets periodically to make sure the data sets are still in sync. In other database implementations, replication is not available in the free open source packages.

4. Many LDAP Servers support numerous algorithms to hash passwords and provide an easy interface for password verification.

5. Tools exist to generate large LDAP sample data sets and benchmark performance—ensuring that the database performs as expected.

6. Search performance is excellent in LDAP. By reducing the scope of searches and properly indexing, lookups are fast!

7. LDAP has excellent UNIX command-line tools that enable you to perform most of your day-to-day administrative work over a simple SSH connection.

8. There are strategies to scale LDAP horizontally, putting more disks and reducing replication traffic.

9. Binary and text backups ensure you never lose your data.

10. Enterprise customers have successfully deployed and operated LDAP infrastructure for many years, proving its reliability.

Basics

LDAP is a client/server message-oriented protocol. The primary operations defined in LDAP enable the client to read or write data, "bind" (authenticate a requestor), and "abandon" (signal to the server to cancel an operation). Figure 2-1 shows a typical sequence diagram of the LDAP protocol.

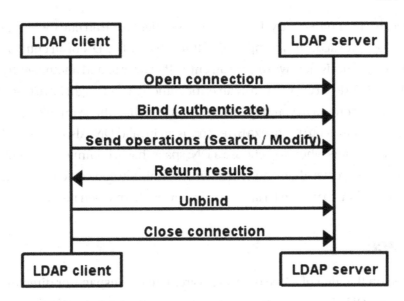

Figure 2-1. *LDAP sequence diagram*

LDAP is not a simple text-based protocol like HTTP. You won't be able to compose messages on the fly—you'll need the help of client software. LDAP on the wire uses a set of rules for encoding data structures called the Basic Encoding Rules (BER), which is actually a binary format for ASN.1. Binary encoding significantly improves performance, and high throughput has always been an important design consideration for LDAP.

If there is a need for a new operation, LDAP defines a standard extension mechanism called "extended operations." For example, the StartTLS operation enables a client to indicate that it wants to initiate an encrypted transport layer or perhaps to use cryptographic signatures, so the parties can validate that they trust each other.

In addition to operations, clients can include LDAP "controls," which can enable servers to implement extended behavior not specified in the core LDAP protocol. For example, the SimplePagedResultsControl, which is described in RFC 2696, enables a client to control the rate at which an LDAP Server returns the results of an LDAP search operation.

Entries, DNs, and RDNs

A unit of information in an LDAP tree is called an "entry"—think of it like a record in a relational database, or an object with properties (and no methods), like a Java bean. An LDAP directory is composed of many such entries, connected together to form a tree.

DN stands for "Distinguished Name" and RDN stands for "Relative Distinguished Name". The DN is the full address of a node in the LDAP tree. The RDN is the partial path of an entry relative to another entry. For example, we might have an entry with a DN of uid=foo,ou=people,o=acme. It is comprised of three RDNs. The DN of an entry must be unique in the tree, and it is how we refer to an entry. If you try to add another entry with the same DN, the LDAP Server will throw an error. Although you might have learned to leave a space after a comma in your typing class, don't do this when you reference DNs. For example, uid=foo, ou=people, o=example.com, is an invalid DN! Also, you should avoid several special characters when you choose a DN: space, hash, comma, plus, double-quote, backslash, less-than, greater-than and semicolon. Technically you could use these characters if you escape them, but do yourself a favor and just avoid them when naming entries.

Namespace

LDAP is based on the idea of a tree data structure. The namespace, or directory information tree (DIT) is defined based on how we name each entry in the tree. Over the years, some common practices have arisen in LDAP namespaces used for enterprise identity and access management. Let's just dive into an example. As you can see, the namespace in Figure 2-2 has three levels.

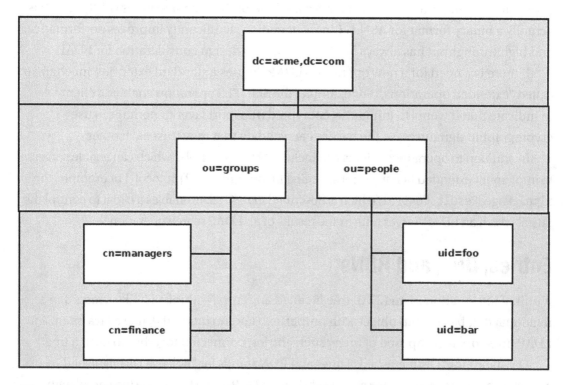

Figure 2-2. *Sample namespace for hypothetical company Acme, Inc.*

The first level is called the root node. It consists of one entry: dc=acme,dc=com. dc stands for domain component. It may seem confusing that this root node has two components. Shouldn't dc=com be the root? Perhaps, but a root node can start from a sub-tree. Another convention you might see is to use an organization entry as the root, for example o=acme.com. You might like this convention because it's less typing. The second level consists of two entries: ou=people and ou=groups. ou stands for organizational unit. It's a common container used to group entries, similar conceptually to a file system folder. There normally isn't much data in the ou, except for the name. The third level contains the leaf entries with the actual data. In Figure 2-2, there are entries for two people and two groups. The DN for an entry can be known by starting from the entry in question and traversing up the tree until you hit the root, for example uid=foo,ou=people,dc=acme,dc=com.

Schema

An entry in LDAP is composed of a DN and data. It may be helpful to compare/contrast LDAP to the more familiar model found in a relational database management system (RDBMS), where data is expressed in a table with columns and each row is a record. At a high level, one could say that the LDAP equivalent of a table is an "objectclass"; the equivalent of a column is an "attribute;" the equivalent of a record is an "entry." In an RDBMS you need to define your schema—tables and columns—ahead of time. Similarly, in LDAP you need to pre-define objectclasses and attributes before use.

There are differences. An LDAP entry can have multiple objectclasses. Such an entry could contain any of the attributes found in any of the objectclasses. Another difference is that LDAP attributes can be multi-value. In an RDBMS, you need duplicate columns to hold multiple values, or you have to serialize many values (for example in a JSON array) and stuff it into one column. In LDAP, it's easy. Consider the example in Listing 2-1.

Listing 2-1. Sample Entry with Multi-Value Attributes

```
dn: uid=foo,ou=people,o=acme.com
objectclass: top
objectclass: person
objectclass: organizationalPerson
objectclass: inetOrgPerson
cn: Foo Bar
```

```
sn: Bar
givenName: foo
l: Austin
mail: foo@acme.com
mail: foo_bar_2016@gmail.com
mail: luckyFoo@yahoo.com
```

This is the first time you are seeing LDIF, the text representation of LDAP data. Notice that the DN of the entry is on the first line. After that, comes the data. There is no requirement that the objectclasses are listed first, although it's a nice convention for human readers. Both `objectclass` and `mail` are multi-value attributes.

Another feature of LDAP schema is that certain attributes might be required for a certain objectclass. For example, the person objectclass requires `cn` and `sn`. A rule of thumb is not to use required attributes. Strict schema rules seem like a good idea, until you have an exception. If you make all attributes optional, you have some extra flexibility.

Attributes have data types, which impact the server's implementation with regard to searching and ordering. The most common type of data for an LDAP Server is text. However, integers, dates, or even binary data like photos or certificates may also be supported. For more information about data types, you should check the documentation for your server.

A quick note about object identifiers, or OIDs. These are used extensively in LDAP configuration servers to identify many different types of things, such as objectclasses and attributes. By convention, many OIDs are written as strings of dotted decimal numbers, like the ASN format. In some cases, the LDAP Server may accept any unique string as an OID. Some servers are very strict about OID using valid ASNs—this is up to the implementation. Organizations can register an OID in the IANA global registry, which makes the objects referenceable (or their owner discoverable). I'm not sure why this is necessary, but I guess it was helpful at some point, way back.

Filters

You will sometimes need to search an LDAP tree for a specific subset of data based on specific criteria. Filters are a compact and flexible mechanism to express which data you want to see based on conditions relating to the attributes values. Table 2-1 contains a summary of some of the most commonly used LDAP filter expressions.

Table 2-1. *LDAP Filter Overview*

Operator	Type	Example
=	Comparison	sn=bar) Find entries with last name bar.
=*x*	Contains x	cn=*manager*) Find all entries with a cn that contains manager.
x*	Starts with x	cn=*manager*) Find all entries with a cn that contains manager.
*x	Ends with x	cn=*manager*) Find all entries with a cn that contains manager.
<= or >=	Less than or equal to comparison or greater than or equal to comparison	(dob<=19950101000000Z) Find entries with a dob before 1/1/95.
=*	Presence	(memberOf=*) Find all entries who belong to at least one group.
~=	Approximate	(sn~=smith) Find all entries that sound similar, like perhaps "smith" too.
!	Not	!(memberOf=*) Find all the entries who don't belong to any group.
&	And	(&(memberOf=*)(l=Austin)) Find all the entries in location Austin who are a member of at least one group.
I (or symbol)	or	(I(status=dead)(status=alive)) Find all entries with status dead or alive.

Note   Certain characters must be escaped if they are used in a search filter: asterisk (\2A), left parenthesis (\28), right parenthesis (\29), backslash (\5C), and the null byte (\00). For example, to search for a group with the name 5* Staff, you would use a filter (cn=5\2A Staff).

It's a good idea to always use parentheses to contain the individual elements of a filter. For example, even though sn=bar is legal, you may want to get into the habit of using (sn=bar). LDAP filters use prefix notation. That means the operator is first and then the operands come next. Let's say you want to know all the entries who have the last name Foo, Bar, Baz, and Spam. You could make a filter like this: (|(sn=foo) (sn=bar)(sn=baz)(sn=spam)). However, if you wanted to know only the people (not any entry) with the last name Foo, Bar, Baz, or Spam, you could make a filter like this: (&(objectclass=person)(|(sn=foo)(sn=bar)(sn=baz)(sn=spam))).

One trick that I use is to set up the parentheses and operators first, and then add the attributes and values. For example, literally starting with (&()(|()()()())) then adding the conditions is easier because you know you have the syntax right from the start. If you're using a program to generate the filters, prefix notation is easy to automate (as LISP fans can attest). Once you get the hang of it, LDAP filters are fun!

LDIF

The LDAP Data Interchange Format, or LDIF, as described in IETF RFC 2849, is one of the most important and underrated tools you'll have in your toolbox. LDIF is a text format for representing data. It is returned by the LDAP Server when you use the ldapsearch command-line interface (CLI), and it can also be used to feed instructions to the LDAP Server when you use the ldapmodify CLI. Both ldapsearch and ldapmodify will be covered later in this chapter.

An LDIF file always starts with the DN of the entry, and then normally is followed by attributes. Each entry is separated by at least one blank line. Don't forget to leave a blank line after the last entry. Comments in LDIF are prefixed with a #. If an attribute has two colons, for example see the description attribute of the second entry in Listing 2-2, it means that the attribute is base-64 encoded. This may be necessary if the entry has characters that may confuse the LDAP Server. If you inadvertently leave a space at the end of a value, the LDAP Server will base-64 encode it. Remember that to an LDAP Server, "this" is not the same as "this ". Also note how an attribute may have multiple values—the description attribute in Listing 2-2, for example.

Listing 2-2. Sample LDIF Data

```
# The first entry
dn: uid=bar,ou=people,dc=example,dc=com
objectclass: top
objectclass: person
cn: Foo Bar
sn: Bar
uid: bar
userPassword: {SSHA}GeXnaWqROzNpzdHnL8QQ==

# Another entry
dn: uid=baz,ou=people,dc=example,dc=com
objectclass: top
objectclass: person
cn: Foo Baz
sn: Baz
uid: baz
userPassword: {SSHA}FaKPP5zK6xLkR5IxXyf6_z==
description:: TGFzdCBjaGFyIGlzIGEgc3BhY2Ug
description: Another note about this person.
```

LDAP Configuration

In this part, we're going to look at two of the most important configuration tasks for LDAP: indexing and security. While each LDAP Server distribution will differ in how these features are managed, understanding how to perform these tasks is universal.

Indexing

When you search any database, you want to get results back quickly. The slowest process to find an entry is to look at every record. Indexes are used to create pointers to certain data, to expedite a search. Think of it like a table of contents. If you know that people whose last name starts with a "T" begin on page 72, it will save you some page flipping. If you know everyone with the last name "Thomas' is on page 74, you can find a specific Thomas even faster.

Another way to look at indexes is that they trade disk space for speed. The more indexes you have (the more notes about where the data is located), the more storage you will need. If you load indexes into memory, this can translate directly into more required RAM, too. Most LDAP Servers support several different types of indexes—presence, equality, and substring are the most common. In terms of disk space, substring is much larger than equality and presence (because there are many more substring combinations). Use substring indexing only when necessary.

This tradeoff of disk space and memory for speed is not only worthwhile, it's essential. For IAM LDAP Servers, search speed translates directly into extra authentications per second. Indexes also make write operations faster. For an IAM infrastructure, all scoped searches (one level or subtree) must be indexed. If the LDAP Server has to look through every leaf, the performance will be terrible, and it may even crash (or seem to crash).

Note   All scoped searches MUST be indexed!

Most LDAP Servers will create a log message if there is an unindexed search. OpenLDAP will have a log message "not indexed", Fedora Directory Server "notes=U", OpenDJ uses "unindexed". It's also useful to see how many entries were returned by this search, and how much time the search took to execute. Here is a sample log from OpenDJ, which could indicate a problem:

```
[4/Jun/2015:15:47:23 +0000] SEARCH RES conn=1134564 op=4 msgID=223 result=0
nentries=1 unindexed etime=32
```

Make sure to figure out the time units for etime—seconds, milliseconds, or nanoseconds. If etime=32 were 32 seconds, that's a red flag. Any LDAP search that takes more than a few milliseconds to complete indicates a problem. The culprit for this long search is clearly visible—the keyword unindexed. There are some tools that can help you analyze large LDAP log files. For OpenDJ, look at the "slowops" and "topfilters" scripts from Chris Ridd at https://github.com/chrisridd/opendj-utils and also at "logconv7.pl", converted from the original Sun script by Ludo Poitou at https://github.com/ludomp/opendj-utils. An equivalent tool for OpenLDAP is LDAP-Stats, which can be found at http://prefetch.net/code/ldap-stats.pl.html. For FDS, there is the LDAP Access Parser at https://github.com/aidan-/ldap-access-parser.

One thing you should look out for is called the "allids threshold". The allIDs entry stands for a special index entry that stands for "every entry in the database." It saves space and never needs updating. For example, make an index for all the people with an "E" in their names, this may approach the size of every person in your LDAP Server. Many servers enable you to tune the number at which indexing is abandoned. In OpenLDAP, there is a variable called SLAPD_LDBM_MIN_MAXIDS. In FDS, there is a global database configuration attribute called allidsthreshold. In OpenDJ, this index can be set for each attribute. Tuning the allids threshold is a good idea when you see an unindexed warning in the logs, but it seems like the index for this attribute is configured. In this case, if you examine the search, it may have triggered an index that exceeds the threshold.

How to view and update indexes is always well-documented in the LDAP Server documentation. Tactically, what you need to know is that if the LDAP performance is bad, or LDAP is using too much CPU, the most common root cause is missing indexes. Look at the indexes first!

LDAP Security

LDAP is a connection-oriented protocol. A client may request operations anonymously, and at some point may authenticate to the server to gain additional privileges. In IAM deployments, anonymous access should be disabled. Simple authentication is accomplished by specifying the distinguished name of a directory entry and the entry's password (stored in the userPassword attribute). Client certificate authentication could be accomplished using StartTLS, and other types of authentication could be implemented with SASL authentication. The authentication process is called "binding" in LDAP, because the connection is made first, and then an identity is bound (or associated) to the connection.

In most LDAP Servers, there are "superuser" accounts, which may have special privileges to bypass access controls and search limitations. These entries may be stored in the configuration, not in the data itself. For example, OpenDJ stores superuser accounts are under the entry cn=Root DNs,cn=config. The default LDIF will give you an idea of the special privileges conveyed to superusers. See Listing 2-3.

Listing 2-3. OpenDJ Root DN privileges

```
dn: cn=Root DNs,cn=config
objectClass: ds-cfg-root-dn
objectClass: top
cn: Root DNs
ds-cfg-default-root-privilege-name: bypass-lockdown
ds-cfg-default-root-privilege-name: bypass-acl
ds-cfg-default-root-privilege-name: modify-acl
ds-cfg-default-root-privilege-name: config-read
-cfg-default-root-privilege-name: config-write
ds-cfg-default-root-privilege-name: ldif-import
ds-cfg-default-root-privilege-name: ldif-export
ds-cfg-default-root-privilege-name: backend-backup
ds-cfg-default-root-privilege-name: backend-restore
ds-cfg-default-root-privilege-name: server-lockdown
ds-cfg-default-root-privilege-name: server-shutdown
ds-cfg-default-root-privilege-name: server-restart
ds-cfg-default-root-privilege-name: disconnect-client
ds-cfg-default-root-privilege-name: cancel-request
ds-cfg-default-root-privilege-name: password-reset
ds-cfg-default-root-privilege-name: update-schema
ds-cfg-default-root-privilege-name: privilege-change
ds-cfg-default-root-privilege-name: unindexed-search
ds-cfg-default-root-privilege-name: subentry-write
ds-cfg-default-root-privilege-name: changelog-read
```

Like a root user in Linux, the superuser LDAP account is really powerful. It can remove the entire database! So normally, you don't want to give this credential to anyone except administrators responsible for LDAP operation.

LDAP is great as a backend persistence service for the IAM infrastructure, but it should be deprecated as an application identity interface—better to use web-based APIs. If your back is to the wall and you absolutely must give an application LDAP credentials, you will have to create a new account with access appropriate to the application's purpose.

The first decision is where to put these accounts. A good practice is to create an organizational unit in a database separate from your actual data, for example, `cn=config` could be a good place if your LDAP Server stores configuration there (see Listing 2-4).

Listing 2-4. Sample LDIF for an Organizational Unit to Store Application Accounts

```
dn: ou=application accounts,cn=config
objectClass: top
objectClass: organizationalUnit
ou: application accounts
```

And then you can create your account underneath this organizational unit. For example, something like Listing 2-5.

Listing 2-5. Sample LDIF for an Application Account

```
dn: cn=myaccount,ou=application accounts,cn=config
objectClass: top
objectClass: person
cn: myaccount
sn: myaccount
userpassword: SpamAndEggs987
```

Now that we have account credentials to send to the user, we need to give this account access to the data that is needed. This is trickier than it may sound, and it can impact performance. LDAP does not define a common access control model. Each vendor is left to implement its own security solution. Normally, you'll find it in a section about "Access Control Instructions" or ACIs. These are special operational attributes (meaning they won't show up in the schema for the respective objectclass—they are managed by the LDAP Server). ACI syntax normally allows you to specify which DNs can perform which operations on which part of the tree. If you can add ACIs in any part of the tree, normally a good place to do so are the structural parts of the tree—the root or the organizational units. You don't want to put ACIs in each leaf. The reason for this is that if an entry is returned, all ACIs need to be evaluated, which may trigger a downstream search to gather the data needed for evaluation. So it's a good idea to minimize ACIs and to move them to the most efficient part of the tree—where they will be evaluated the minimum number of times.

Some LDAP Servers can support SSL (Secure Socket Layer) and TLS (Transport Layer Security). SSL establishes a secure connection initially, prior to LDAP communication. TLS enables an existing LDAP connection on the unencrypted port (i.e., 389) to be established and then encryption to be negotiated when the client requests the startTLS extended operation. SSL (i.e., LDAPS) is better understood by most network administrators and programmers.

Managing Data

IAM administrators must be able to easily read and write LDAP data. Luckily, there are some great tools for this: command-line interfaces (CLIs), GUIs, and APIs. It is particularly essential that IAM administrators can use the CLI, which are always available if you can get an SSH session to the LDAP Server and can be used to quickly search and modify data. We can't possibly cover all the tools or even all the options for the tools that we reference here. Read the documentation for each tool to best familiarize yourself with its capabilities.

Command-Line Tools

The command-line LDAP tools are essential to master. We are going to show OpenDJ command-line tools. OpenLDAP and FDS command-line tools are very similar, but the options for SSL are a little different. At first, LDAP commands seem long—so many options to remember. By grouping the connection options in your head, you can simplify memorization. One trick is to think about the following: host | port, username | password, use SSL | trust self-signed certificate. Respectively these options are -h | -p, -D | -j, -Z | -X. Assuming you're using SSL, all LDAP commands will use these options. Note that, for password authentication, the best practice is to avoid accidentally storing the root password in the shell command history. If possible, store the password in a file and remove it when you're done.

ldapsearch

Let's start with an example shown in Listing 2-6 and Table 2-2.

Listing 2-6. Sample ldapsearch Command

```
$ /opt/opendj/bin/ldapsearch -h idp.example.com -p 1636 \
    -D "cn=directory manager" -j ~/.pw -Z -X \
    -b "o=gluu" -s one "objectclass=*" dn
```

Table 2-2. *ldapsearch Command Example*

Option	Description
-h	Hostname of the LDAP Server
-p	Port of the LDAP Server
-D	DN of the entry to bind to the connection
-j	Full path to a file containing the password for the specified DN
-Z	Use SSL
-X	Trust all certificates (handy for self-signed certificates)
-b	DN of the entry where you want to start your search, i.e. base DN
-s	Scope of the search: can be either "base", "sub" or "one"
objectclass=*	The LDAP filter
dn	Attribute list, in this case only the DN attribute will be returned

ldapsearch returns results as LDIF. Notice in this example, you can specify attributes that you want returned. If you omit attributes after the filter, the LDAP Server will return all the non-operational attributes. Consider the following, where the first grep for mail removes the dn and blank lines; the perl one-liner only prints the second column, thus removing all the mail: line prefixes. Finally, this output is directed to a local file (see Listing 2-7).

Listing 2-7. Sample ldapsearch Command to Extract Email Addresses for People in Austin

```
$ /opt/opendj/bin/ldapsearch -h idp.example.com -p 1636 \
    -D "cn=directory manager" -j ~/.pw -Z -X \
    -b "o=gluu" "(&(l=Austin)(objectclass=person))" \
    mail| grep mail | perl -nale \
    'shift@F;print"@F"'> austin_email_list.txt
```

One of the advantages of a tree structure is that you can narrow your search to the part of the tree you care about: subtree includes the base DN you specified, plus the whole tree below it; base indicates you only want the entry returned of the base DN that you specified; one indicates that you just want entries returned that are one level below the base DN. A subtree search is the default, so you only need to specify the -s option in ldapsearch if you want one or base. Consider Figure 2-3, where the top node has been specified as the root.

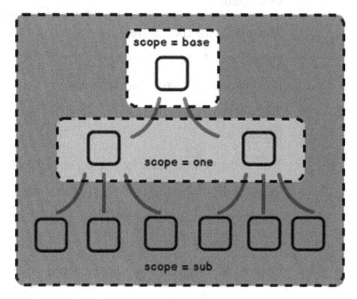

Figure 2-3. *Scopes visualization*

One thing to keep in mind when using ldapsearch is that any values that contain spaces must be quoted—double quotes are typical, although single quotes in UNIX can also be handy. For example, if your ldapsearch contains the exclamation point, Bash may interpret it as a command. In these cases, use single quotes for your parameters.

ldapmodify

Let's start with an example shown in Listing 2-8 and Table 2-3.

Listing 2-8. Sample ldapmodify Command

```
$ /opt/opendj/bin/ldapmodify -h idp.example.com -p 1636 \
  -D "cn=directory manager" -j ~/.pw -Z -X -f my.ldif
```

Table 2-3. *ldapmodify Command Example*

Option	Description
-h	Hostname of the LDAP Server
-p	Port of the LDAP Server
-D	DN of the entry to bind to the connection
-j	Full path to a file containing the password for the specified DN
-z	Use SSL
-x	Trust all certificates (handy for self-signed certificates)
-f	The path and filename that contains the LDIF

Notice that the initial options are the same as for ldapsearch. The host, port, bind dn, bind password, and SSL connection have not changed. In this simple example, we are specifying the LDIF file, which contains the instructions on what operations to perform. In an LDIF file used for modifications, the second line of the entry specifies the changetype, which can be add, modify, or delete. If the changetype is add, the second line can be omitted, and you can use the -a command-line option of ldapmodify, which will automatically insert the add changetype to each entry. In this way, LDIF output from ldapsearch can be used directly as input for ldapmodify.

If you are using changetype: modify in your LDIF, you can specify which attributes you are changing for each entry. You can string several operations for an entry by using a line with a hyphen on its own line to signal a new attribute operation. Consider this LDIF in Listing 2-9, which adds one attribute, deletes a specific attribute value, and replaces another attribute.

Listing 2-9. Sample ldapmodify to Update Specific Attributes

```
dn: uid=foo,ou=people,o=example.com
    changetype: modify
    add: description
    description: "Entry for Foo Bar"
    -
    delete: mail
    mail: foo@spam.com
    -
    replace: status
    status: active
```

Another handy trick is to use LDAP search and grep for ^dn (dn at the beginning of the line). This can be used to create a list of all the DNs you need to modify. Consider this simple Python program in Listing 2-10, which outputs LDIF that adds a counter to the description attribute.

Listing 2-10. Sample Python Script to Generate ldif for Bulk Update of Entries

```python
#!/usr/bin/python

f = open("dn_list.ldif")
lines = f.readlines()
f.close()
c = 0
for line in lines:
    if not len(line.strip()): continue
    c += 1
    print line.strip()
    print "changetype: modify"
    print "add: description"
    print "description: Entry #%i" % c
    print
```

By effectively rendering LDIF and using ldapmodify, you can automate many mundane tasks. LDIF is also great because it gives you a record of exactly which changes you made. Before you run it, you can visually inspect the changes. Learn to love LDIF!

ldapdelete

This tool is not technically needed, because you could use an LDIF with changetype: delete. It's provided as a convenience. You provide all the standard connection information and then provide the DN of the entry you want to release as the last argument.

GUI Tools

Sometimes you feel the urge to browse the data in an LDAP Server like you would browse the file system. Luckily, there are a few good free open source LDAP clients that let you do just that. We are going to cover two here, although there are other free open source alternates.

For the most part, the LDAP Servers you are trying to connect to will not have LDAP exposed on an Internet-facing network interface. SSH port tunneling is the easiest way to solve the challenge of how to use your local client to access this remote server. In some cases, multiple SSH tunnels may be required to route the traffic all the way back to your local computer. Unix SSH port forwarding is accomplished with the -L command, for example:

```
$ ssh -L localport:host:hostport user@ssh_server
```

If you are a Windows user, and you are using the popular FOSS SSH tool Putty, you configure tunneling in the SSH section of the profile, as shown in Figure 2-4.

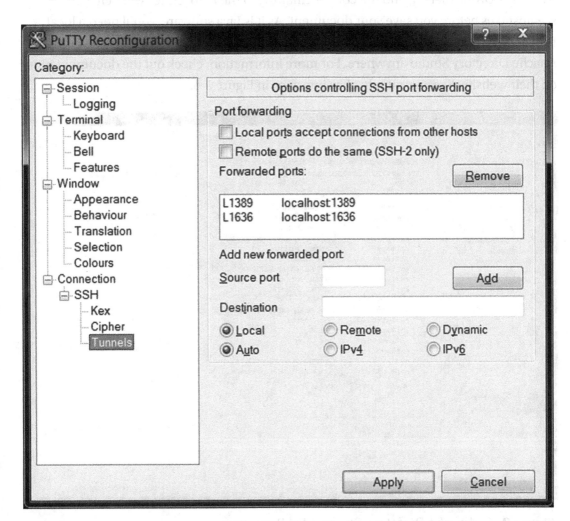

Figure 2-4. *Sample tunnel configuration in Windows Putty SSH client*

One important thing to remember when port forwarding is that you will be connecting to the LDAP Server using the hostname localhost. This may sound counterintuitive, but it's because the tunnel is doing its job and broadcasting the remote traffic on your workstation's network.

Apache Directory Studio

One of the best free open source LDAP tools available, Apache Directory Studio has a rich set of features and provides an Eclipse-based user interface. Although the schema editor and ACI editor will work only for OpenLDAP, the LDAP browser can be used with any LDAP v3 server, and the color formatting of the LDIF editor will help you see mistakes before you save your document. As it is Java software, you'll need a local JVM and to set your JAVA_HOME environment variable. Once that's done, you can unzip Apache Directory Studio anywhere. For more information, check out the documentation on their website. See an example of its interface in Figure 2-5.

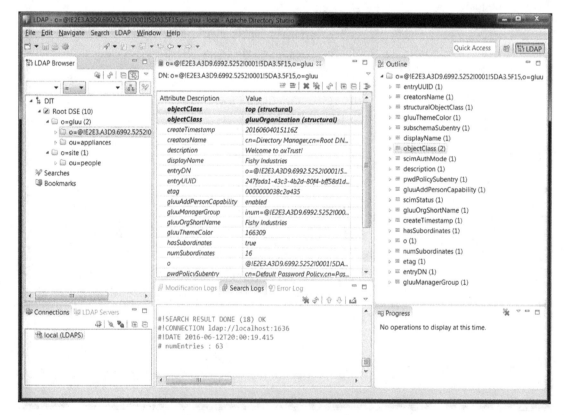

Figure 2-5. *Apache Directory Studio LDAP browser*

JXplorer

Another free open source graphical LDAP client is maintained by Christopher Betts, called JXplorer. It was originally donated to the open source community by Computer Associates, where it was first developed as part of the eTrust Directory project. It's handy for browsing, searching, and editing entries. There is also a commercial version that sells for a very nominal amount with a few more features. There are several binaries available for Windows, Mac, Linux, and other platforms. See an example of its interface in Figure 2-6.

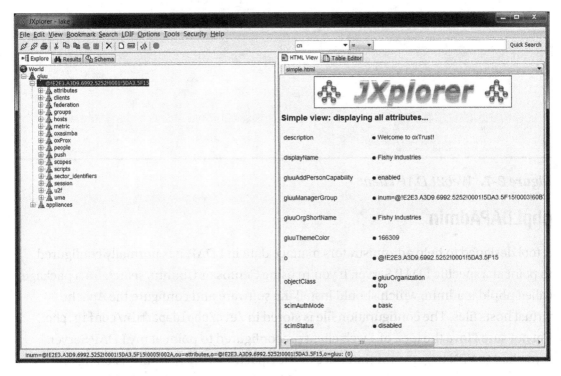

Figure 2-6. *JXplorer LDAP browser/editor*

Web2LDAP

If you'd like to have a web-based LDAP client, something like phpMyAdmin for LDAP, you're in luck. You can use the Web2LDAP, written by Michael Ströder, who is also the author of one of the most popular Python LDAP modules. It gives you a lot of information, even the operational attributes and information about the schema of the entry. See an example of its interface in Figure 2-7.

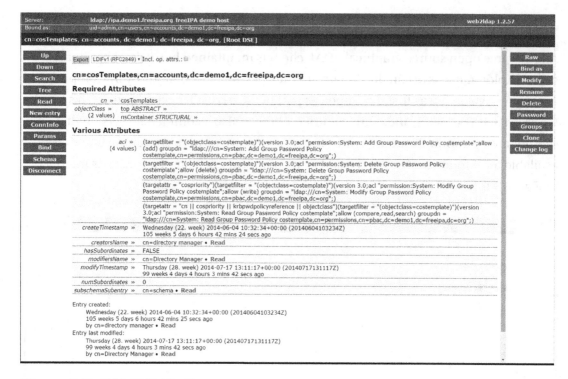

Figure 2-7. *Web2LDAP client*

phpLDAPAdmin

A tool designed to help administrators manage data in LDAP, it is normally configured to point at a specific LDAP Server. If you're using Centos or Ubuntu, search for a package called phpldapadmin, which should install the software and configure the Apache virtual hosts files. The configuration file is stored in /etc/phpldapadmin/config.php. I'm not sure I love the idea of a web client preconfigured to point at my LDAP Server. If you had to VPN to get to this interface or the Apache server was only listening on localhost (and you tunnel via SSH), you could mitigate some of the risk. See an example of its interface in Figure 2-8.

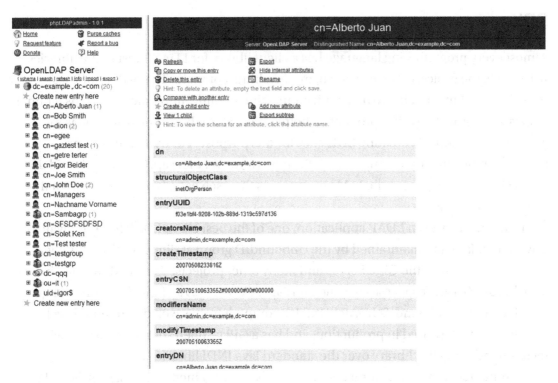

Figure 2-8. *phpLDAPadmin*

FusionDirectory

Not a directory itself, it's actually a web interface for LDAP written in PHP that provides its own access management strategy (by using a custom attribute) and several convenient plugins to manage schema for other common enterprise tools that use LDAP (like Samba, OpenSSH, and EJBCA). Packages are available for several Linux distributions. I haven't used it, but it's worth taking a look. See an example of its interface in Figure 2-9.

Figure 2-9. *FusionDirectory*

SDKs

Almost every programming language has a client library for LDAP. Most of the libraries will enable the basics: connect, search, modify, bind, compare. The better libraries provide more functionality to help with connection pooling, implementing transactional behavior, or providing other productive helper libraries. If data transformation is the goal, I recommend just creating LDIF files for this purpose. For dynamic enterprise software applications, you'll need an API. However, as very few applications should use the LDAP interface (except the IAM components themselves), it's hard to say when this use case would arise.

If you must write an LDAP application, one of the best client LDAP libraries available is written in Java and maintained by the UnboundID group at Ping Identity. This client is used extensively in the Gluu Server and many other projects. You can download it from `https://www.ldap.com/unboundid-ldap-sdk-for-java`. If that location changes, just Google for "UnboundID LDAP SDK." It's comprehensive, well documented, well maintained, widely used in production, and has a GPLv2 open source license. I highly recommend using this library over the standard Java JNDI libraries.

Another recommended library is `python-ldap`, maintained by Michael Ströder. For direct LDAP operations, it wraps the OpenLDAP C libraries. It also has a handy class for parsing and generating LDIF.

Operational Considerations

What are the key operational considerations for running a robust LDAP service? In order to achieve five nines (99.999%) availability, you need to either get lucky or build an active-active cluster. You'll also need to have a good plan in place for how to benchmark the performance of the LDAP service, to collect current performance metrics, to back up the data, and to periodically analyze the logs for long searches.

Note   Research the server Linux configuration requirements. For example, make sure you have expanded the available file descriptors to at least 65,000. This is one of the most common mistakes. The LDAP Server makes lots of connections. You don't want to be limited to the default file descriptor limit, which is around 1,000!

Replication

LDAP is known for ease of data replication. However, vendors implement very different strategies, sometimes solving replication at the database level. There was quite a bit of innovation in the area of LDAP replication. As LDAP Servers were announced, the ability to have more "master" servers expanded from two to unlimited in many LDAP Server platforms. There are many challenges with LDAP replication, including but not limited to:

- Reducing traffic on wide area network links

- Minimizing the size of the replication data stored in each entry

- Managing colliding transactions (for example, an update after a delete)

- Reporting synchronization status for each server in the topology

You'll have to read the documentation for your exact version of LDAP Server to know how to initialize new replicas, create and remove replication agreements, and monitor the health of your topology. Frequently, there is a replication service running that makes sure the data is in sync and communicates changes to the other members of the topology. The server documentation should also contain information about how to manage the replication topology and what to do when things go wrong.

Benchmark

It's really important to understand the capabilities of an LDAP Server. Lots of factors can influence performance, including hardware, software, the profile of LDAP operation traffic, the size of the data entries, the size of the entire data set, the LDAP configuration, or even the configuration of the underlying database. You don't know how fast it is unless you try it! Luckily, there are a few tools that can make that easier.

The first set of tools to consider are `searchrate`, `modrate`, and `authrate`, which can be built as part of the UnboundID LDAP SDK for Java on their GitHub site at `https://github.com/UnboundID/ldapsdk`. These command-line tools enable you to quickly test the capacity of your server; `searchrate` produces output such as shown in Table 2-4.

Table 2-4. *Sample searchrate Output*

Throughput (Ops/Second)				Response Time (Milliseconds)				
Recent	Average	Recent	Average	99.9%	99.99%	99.999%	Err/Sec	Entries/ Search
2260.7	2262.8	6.219	6.219	413.842	476.425	476.817	0.0	1.5
3857.5	3178.3	4.149	4.777	352.825	476.404	500.017	0.0	0.8
5078.2	3753.2	2.825	3.978	360.940	460.154	500.017	0.0	1.0
4557.7	3934.5	3.411	3.830	352.480	455.638	500.017	0.0	1.0

The columns are pretty self-explanatory. The entries/search value is computed by counting the number of returned entries and dividing by the number of search results. The reason the entries/search value is not initially one is due to the fact that the LDAP search was "warming up"—loading relevant data into memory. During benchmarking, it's common to include a warm-up period to make sure that the LDAP Server has been activated in memory, as would be the case in production under load.

Another tool for benchmarking is called SLAMD, by Neil Wilson, which can be found at http://dl.thezonemanager.com/slamd/. The first component is a server that collects data; the second is a client that generates load. For high-end benchmarking, these tools are really handy. You can generate lots of load by creating many clients, each of which uses many threads. In a typical deployment, you might have one SLAMD server that is dedicated to getting results, many clients that are responsible for generating load, and many LDAP Servers that are being tested as part of a replicated topology. In this way, the server generating or collecting results doesn't impart the performance of your target LDAP Server. Another advantage of SLAMD is that you can use several different "jobs," which can perform a specific combination of operations. The goal is to generate the type of traffic that would be typical in production. For example, the searchrate command-line tool might not be a good gauge of reality if a typical transaction involves a search, an authentication, and then a several write operations. You might also want to customize information collected during load testing. For example, for a given load, how is the CPU and disk usage on the LDAP Servers? Perhaps you want to map some custom variables onto your graph. SLAMD is extensible and can enable you to do this.

Backup/Restore

There are a few strategies for backing up LDAP Servers: binary backups of the database, file system backups of the folder, server image backups, and LDIF exports of the data in a standard format. My recommendation is to use LDIF for backup to supplement your speedier binary backups. The advantage of LDIF is that in a pinch, the data can be loaded relatively quickly, and if an entry gets corrupted, you can always ignore it and proceed with the rest of the backup. LDIF gives you an insurance policy.

It's really important that you test the backup/restore process from both binary and LDIF sources. You don't want to find out that your restore process doesn't work just at the time the backup is most needed. If backups can be scheduled automatically, it is nice to have daily data backups for a week or more.

Monitoring

You will need to get data back indicating the current health of the LDAP Server. One way to do this is to make a quick search to the directory. The following searches are specific for OpenDJ, but similar approaches could be utilized to monitor other LDAP Servers, which frequently publish some performance data as LDAP.

```
# /opt/opendj/bin/ldapsearch -h localhost -p 1636 \
    -D "cn=directory manager" -j ~/.pw -Z -X  \
    -s base -b "cn=monitor" "objectclass=*" currentconnection

dn: cn=monitor currentconnections: 12
```

This namespace cn=monitor is a special place where many LDAP Servers store information about performance. The results of this search told you two things: that the server is up and running and that the current number of connections to the server is 12. If this number is steadily going up and never goes down, it may indicate a connection leak somewhere in your software stack. There is some more useful information under cn=monitor that you might want to watch. See the documentation for more information on what the attributes are tracking.

You'll also want to keep an eye on the normal stuff—CPU and disk space. Make sure the logs are rotating properly. If they are not, adjust the settings in the LDAP Server configuration (and make sure you get a warning by the time the disk space is 80% full!).

Synchronization

For the foreseeable future, data about people is sprinkled across organizational systems. Identity management gurus aim to change business processes to consolidate data about people. IAM gurus don't have time to wait for business processes to change, so we try to use data about people wherever it happens to reside.

There are some data repositories that contain a lot of information about people, while others contain a small amount of high value data. If data about a person from a disparate system is needed to make an access decision, it's faster if all the required information about people is cached for quick retrieval. For this reason, what you frequently need is a "data mart"—a place to hold information about a person, aggregated in one convenient, high-performance local database.

While creating this data mart, you will need to create a mapping for how to get the information from various backend systems. When and if the business process is cleaned up by the identity management gurus, the mapping is updated. In this way, deploying the perfect IDM is not a blocker for the initial deployment of a centralized IAM.

Complexity is the enemy of security and performance. Figure 2-10 illustrates the advantage of a data mart when identity is distributed across many backend data silos. If the IAM platform in this scenario connects to each identity silo, end users may need to take a nap while waiting for an authentication response. If the IAM platform can get information about the person from a database pre-loaded in memory, it's possible to achieve much higher throughput, sometimes thousands of transactions per second.

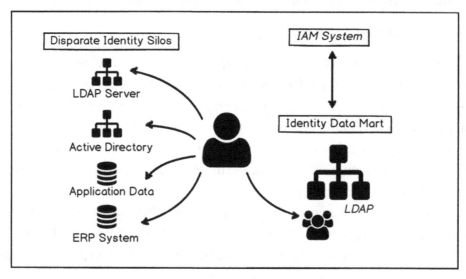

Figure 2-10. *Overview of identity data mart*

How can you aggregate the information you need and keep it up to date? How will you quickly compare data sets to make sure some changes didn't get missed, detecting any discrepancies in the data sets?

Let's assume that the data mart is an LDAP Server. The goal is to populate this LDAP Server with the latest and greatest information about people, so it's available for policy evaluation and to be shared with applications across the enterprise.

There is no way to efficiently manage a large amount of data manually. We're going to have to do some programming. The examples will use Python, but the concepts are generic and can be ported to any language.

Sets and Hashing

The first part of our recipe for synchronization is hashing. A hash algorithm is a function that converts data into a shorter unique output of fixed length. Although it's impossible to prove, good hash functions provide an assurance that no two inputs should result in the same hash value output. If anything about the data changes, the hash value will be different.

Remember *set theory*? It's the second part of our sync recipe. Perhaps you are experiencing a flashback to your school math class? Although in academic mathematics, set theory is a major area of research, for IAM, we're only going to use the basics. Set operations are magically efficient at figuring out what changed between two data sets.

Most programming languages have native support for basic Set operations. For example, let's consider the code shown in Listing 2-11, which shows Set operations in Python.

Listing 2-11. Sample Python Set Operations

```
>>> # Create set objects
>>> from sets import Set
mon_list = ["bob", "amy", "tom", "jon", "peg"]
>>> tue_list = ["bob", "amy", "tom", "sal", "jen"]
mon = Set(mon_list)
>>> tue = Set(tue_list)

>>> # Union
>>> all_items = mon | tue
```

```
>>> print list(all_items)
['amy', 'peg', 'tom', 'sal', 'bob', 'jen', 'jon']

>>> # Intersection
>>> common_items = mon & tue
>>> print list(common_items)
['amy', 'bob', 'tom']

>>> # Difference
>>> not_tue = mon - tue
>>> print list(not_tue)
['peg', 'jon']
>>> not_mon = tue - mon
>>> print list(not_mon)
['sal', 'jen']

>>> # Symmetric Difference
>>> part_timers = mon ^ tue
>>> print list(part_timers)
['sal', 'peg', 'jen', 'jon']
```

Let's say you have two big data sets. One is a list of people from today, and one is from a week ago. If you want to figure out who was added or who is missing, Set operations can instantly answer your question. The basic strategy:

1. Normalize the data.

2. Hash the data.

3. Compare the hash values—if they're different, something about this person's data has changed.

When you hash the data, the order of the information, whitespace, and capitalization must all be the same, or you will get a different hash result. You can take steps to ensure the data is formatted the same. For example, lowercase the string or trim the whitespace. Performing this task is called "normalization".

Let's look at a small example. Let's say you create a file with the primary key for several people, plus the hash value of their data. Let's call this fn1.txt (see Listing 2-12).

Listing 2-12. Sample Hash Values for fn1.txt

```
bob:b063b8e6029ba27fdb084edc2cea4572acab360adbd2ad9217ce8d71 amy:c62bde41
40cff7ec3e8d253ea709e389366caea034e68d58c76a9721 tom:0bf6cb62649c42a9ae38
76ab6f6d92ad36cb5414e495f8873292be4d jon:604383ab56fb3b6c29c7ee98a7cbfb95
3a026e3c5649de0e8d333b78 peg:d00565ed92bc556704c3b5fb75d11cd8ee843d12aced
b4be525303a0
```

And a second one that looks like this called fn2.txt (see Listing 2-13).

Listing 2-13. Sample hash values for fn2.txt

```
bob:e047c44d875407fdb49d53d8b2326fc3e20e27f08434fef1275a3981 amy:c62bde414
0cff7ec3e8d253ea709e389366caea034e68d58c76a9721 tom:0bf6cb62649c42a9ae3876
ab6f6d92ad36cb5414e495f8873292be4d jon:604383ab56fb3b6c29c7ee98a7cbfb953a
026e3c5649de0e8d333b78 pam:f9da1e2be595c9dec9dcfa77b942ca0de1c6d445788df1
8e73720712
```

Let's make a few observations about this data. First, the hash value for bob has changed. Second, peg has dropped out of the second file. Third, pam is new in the second file. A short Python script could be written like Listing 2-14 to find which users changed.

Listing 2-14. Python Set Sample Code

```python
#!/usr/bin/python

from sets import Set

def getPrimaryKey(line):
return line.split(":")[0]

f = open("fn1.txt")
file1_users = Set(f.readlines())
f.close()

f = open("fn2.txt")
file2_users = Set(f.readlines())
f.close()
```

```
# People who changed in file 2
change_list = file2_users ^ file1_users
primary_keys = map(getPrimaryKey, change_list)
print list(Set(primary_keys))
```

Running this program produces the following output:

```
['bob', 'peg', 'pam']
```

The program has identified all the records we need to update. This approach scales well. The one part of this program that might be a little confusing the creation of a Set object from a list, only to change it back to a list again? The reason is to eliminate any duplicates. For example, both of Bob's entries in the file are unique. But we only need to update Bob's record once.

Manually Synchronizing Data

This section is going to focus on LDAP as the source of data, but to synchronize data from a database, or data collected by calling web services, the basic strategy is going to be the same: get data, normalize, hash, detect changes, and update the LDAP data mart.

There are a few strategies to monitor for changes on a source LDAP Server. Some LDAP Servers have a changelog—this varies between implementations. A basic strategy that works well is to search using the LDAP protocol and detect by comparing periodic snapshots of the data (especially if hashing makes it really easy to find changes, as described previously).

You could connect to an external LDAP Server using an LDAP library. However, sometimes it's simpler to just script the ldapsearch command-line tool to do your work. Consider the following example in Listing 2-15, which creates an LDIF file based on the first letter of the person's last name.

Listing 2-15. Sample Script to Gather Data

```
#!/usr/bin/python

import os
import string

ldapsearch_cmd = "/opt/opendj/bin/ldapsearch"
```

```
network_args = "-h localhost -p 1636 -Z -X"
bind_args = '-D "cn=directory manager" -j /root/.pw'
base = "-b 'ou=people,o=@!3919.2D9C.DCCB.3133!0001!3540.15DD,o=gluu'"
scope = "-s one"
attrs = "dn objectclass"

for c in string.ascii_lowercase:
cmd = [ldapsearch_cmd,
        network_args,
        bind_args,
        base,
        scope,
        "sn=%s*" % c,
        attrs,
        "> %s.ldif" % c]
os.system(" ".join(cmd))
```

This script is a simple shell script—it could even be written in Bash. Now that you have the data, how do you read it in from LDAP and do something with it?

LDAP is particularly easy to synchronize across vendor implementations because there is a standard format for rendering data, LDIF. One handy tool is the LDIF module in Python LDAP. Many Linux distributions have packages for python-ldap. If not, you can download the source from the website at https://www.python-ldap.org. Note that ldif.py is a standalone library with no dependencies. You can just copy it into the folder in which you're working. There are many other libraries to convert ldif into native data structures. Listing 2-16 is a quick example of a python-ldap program that reads an LDIF file, performs some minimal data normalization, hashes the value, and prints the result.

Listing 2-16. Sample Python Script to Hash LDIF Data

```
#!/usr/bin/python

import hashlib
string
from ldif import LDIFParser

test_ldif = """
dn: uid=foo,ou=people,dc=example,dc=com
```

```
objectclass: top
objectclass: person
cn: Foo
sn: Foo
uid: foo

dn: uid=bar,ou=people,dc=example,dc=com
objectclass: top
objectclass: person
cn: Bar
sn: Bar
uid: bar

dn: uid=baz,ou=people,dc=example,dc=com
objectclass: top
objectclass: person
cn: Baz
sn: Baz
uid: baz
"""

# Create test file
f = open("test.ldif", "w")
f.write(test_ldif)
f.close()

class MyLDIF(LDIFParser):
def __init__(self, input, output):
    LDIFParser.__init__(self, input)

def handle(self, dn, entry):
    s = ""
    attrs = entry.keys()
    attrs.sort()
    attrs = map(string.lower, attrs)
    for attr in entry.keys():
        val = entry[attr]
```

```
      val.sort()
      s = s + "%s:%s\n" % (attr, val)
   hash = hashlib.sha224(s).hexdigest()
   print "%s:%s" % (entry['uid'][0], hash)
parser = MyLDIF(open("test.ldif", 'rb'), None)
parser.parse()
```

Excluding writing the LDIF file, this program is only 16 lines long! It's more like a haiku than a novel. Most of the action happens in the handle method of the class. That method is called once for each LDIF entry in the file. Let's say you detect an entry that needs to be changed. You can also use the LDIF module to create LDIF or even generate modify operations. Consider the following simple example in Listing 2-17 that takes an entry in Python LDAP format and outputs it to LDIF.

Listing 2-17. Sample Python Script to Print LDIF

```
#!/usr/bin/python

import ldif, sys

entry={'objectClass':['top','person'],
    'cn':['Foo Bar'],
    'sn':['Bar']}
dn='cn=Foo Bar,o=example.com'
ldif_writer=ldif.LDIFWriter(sys.stdout)
ldif_writer.unparse(dn,entry)
```

This has the output shown in Listing 2-18.

Listing 2-18. Sample Output from Listing 2-17

```
dn: cn=Foo Bar,o=example.com
cn: Foo Bar
objectClass: top
objectClass: person
sn: Bar
```

Believe it or not, with these basic ideas, you can build your own synchronization system. It's a low-tech approach, but sometimes the solutions for synchronization are just too complicated for the task at hand. At those times, it's beneficial to understand the basics and know that if you need to build rather than buy, there are options. You can simply use command-line tools like `ldapsearch`, `ldapmodify`, and `ldapdelete` and do a little hashing and text processing.

Gluu Server Cache Refresh

If you're looking for a shortcut, and the identities you need to synchronize are primarily located in LDAP data stores, the oxTrust component of the Gluu Server is a handy tool you can use to configure an internal data mart. It uses the hash and set operation strategy outlined previously by creating snapshot files in a folder. If you examine these files, you'll see a map of primary keys and hash values. oxTrust also uses an LDAP database to track the mapping between primary keys in the Gluu Server LDAP Server and in backend LDAP repositories. The oxTrust approach has some nice built-in capabilities:

- Attribute name mapping—Use this if you just need to change the name of one attribute in your source LDAP Server to another attribute in the Gluu Server LDAP Server. For example, maybe you have an attribute called `samAccountName` in Active Directory, but you want to use `uid` in the data mart.

- Attribute creation or value transformation—Using the cache refresh custom interception script, you can add new attributes or adjust the value of existing attributes. A good example of this is `eduPersonScopedAffiliation`—an attribute used in the higher education industry that rarely exists in the correct format in the source LDAP Server. However, it can be calculated algorithmically at most institutions. Another use case for value transformation is calling an API to pull in data from another data store—perhaps an API that exposes data from a relational database.

- Filtering—You can configure global LDAP filters. For example, perhaps you want to filter out all people who do not have attribute `status=active`. You can also filter easily on objectclasses.

- Scheduling—oxTrust includes a service scheduler, so you can control how often the synchronization process runs.

- Logs—There are logs for both persistence and when the scheduled process runs.

One thing to watch out for is that you only want to run oxTrust cache refresh on one server at a time. Otherwise, the source LDAP Servers will have to handle extra requests, and simultaneous updates to the same entries will probably lead to replication collisions. If you're running a cluster of oxTrust servers, you can configure the IP address of the server on which you want to run the process to avoid this situation.

Configuring oxTrust is accomplished via the web user interface. There are several forms you need to configure it—refer to the Gluu Server documentation.

LSC—LDAP Synchronization Connector

One tool you may consider for LDAP synchronization is LSC, a Java application that uses XML files to define mapping and synchronization rules. The website for this project can be found at `https://lsc-project.org`. One of the nicest features is that it supports connectors to relational database sources. There are not a lot of free open source tools in this area, so this promising tool seemed worthy of honorable mention. It could provide a head start to your synchronization project, but it may take some customization work to get it to do what you need.

LDAP Proxy

Vertically scaling means adding more memory and CPUs and increasing your storage speed. This will only get you so far. If your directory service gets large enough, you may want to horizontally scale—break up the data into smaller sets and use a cluster of smaller, cheaper servers. This has another tangible advantage—it reduces replication traffic. The only open source server that currently offers proxy capabilities is OpenLDAP. Without getting too deep into a discussion of OpenLDAP configuration, Listing 2-19 shows a sample configuration file that may help point you in the right direction, if this is something you need to do. In this example in Listing 2-19, there are three LDAP Servers, each holding one third of the entries. In addition to proxying, OpenLDAP is also caching some of the results to speed up performance. For more information on this configuration, you should read the documentation on the slapd-meta backend.

Listing 2-19. OpenLDAP Proxy Configuration

```
##################################################
moduleload   back_mdb.la
moduleload   back_meta.la
moduleload   pcache.la

...

database meta
suffix "dc=foo,dc=net"

uri "ldap://:10389/dc=foo,dc=net"
filter "(cn=[a-i]*)"
rewriteEngine on
suffixmassage "cn=Manager,dc=foo,dc=net" "dc=foo,dc=net"
rootdn cn=Manager,dc=foo,dc=net
rootpw secret
idassert-bind bindmethod=simple
credentials=secret
binddn="cn=Manager,dc=foo,dc=net"

uri "ldap://:20389/dc=foo,dc=net"
filter "(cn=[j-r]*)"
suffixmassage "cn=Manager,dc=foo,dc=net" "dc=foo,dc=net"
rootdn cn=Manager,dc=foo,dc=net
rootpw secret
idassert-bind bindmethod=simple
  credentials=secret
  binddn="cn=Manager,dc=foo,dc=net"

uri "ldap://:30389/dc=foo,dc=net"
filter "(cn=[s-z]*)"
suffixmassage "cn=Manager,dc=foo,dc=net" "dc=foo,dc=net"
rootdn cn=Manager,dc=foo,dc=net
rootpw secret
idassert-bind bindmethod=simple
credentials=secret
```

```
binddn="cn=Manager,dc=foo,dc=net"

overlay pcache
pcache mdb 150000 2 150000 500
directory /var/symas/openldap-data/pcache.foo.net
index default eq
index objectClass
index cn eq,sub

pcacheMaxQueries 999999
pcacheOffline false
pcachePersist true

pcacheAttrset 0 cn objectClass
pcacheTemplate (cn=) 0 3600
```

Conclusion

You can find many more guides on the Internet to help you complete your journey, but hopefully this overview of LDAP gave you a good idea of the "known unknowns". The only way you get good at LDAP is to get some hands-on experience moving data around and actually operating an LDAP Server. Once you get the hang of LDAP, it's fun!

CHAPTER 3

SAML

By the late 1990s, people were starting to get tired of entering the same username and password on different websites. LDAP helped organizations implement "single-password," but didn't enable web "single sign-on" (SSO). While some vendors were offering solutions for web SSO, SAML—the Security Assertion Markup Language—emerged as one of the first standards to enable a person to authenticate once and access websites both inside and outside their organization. The use case of a person accessing websites outside their home domain came to be known as *identity federation*. And the protocols that enable this are known as *federation protocols.*

Not surprisingly for technology from 2005, SAML is an XML standard. SAML was developed by a diverse group of interested parties—29 organizations and several individuals contributed to the SAML 2.0 core specification. The standard represents the confluence of several previous efforts to standardize a protocol for SSO, including SAML 1.1, Liberty Alliance ID-FF 1.2 and Shibboleth 1.3. All of these previous standards should be avoided.

Like LDAP, SAML is not defined in one document, but a number of related documents. SAML 2.0 was developed at OASIS, a nonprofit consortium that provides support for the development, convergence and adoption of open standards. At the time of this writing, OASIS has published 146 standards and 145 committee specifications. OASIS was a good home for SAML 2.0 because many organizations were already members and had agreed to its intellectual property guidelines. For more information about OASIS, you can visit their website at https://www.oasis-open.org.

The terms defined by SAML have become an important part of the IAM lexicon. For example, a "SAML assertion" is a statement written in XML and issued by an "identity provider" about a "subject" (person) for a "relying party" (the recipient of the assertion) who is normally a "service provider" (website). Identity provider is abbreviated simply as "IDP" and service provider as "SP". Assertions contain contextual information about the authentication procedure, as well as "attributes"—similar to LDAP attributes, these are little pieces of information about the person, such as first name or last name.

59

© Michael Schwartz, Maciej Machulak 2018
M. Schwartz and M. Machulak, *Securing the Perimeter*, https://doi.org/10.1007/978-1-4842-2601-8_3

SAML is a mature standard, and it's been successfully deployed to solve many business challenges. Its stability is one of its advantages—it has not been significantly updated since its 2.0 inception. Don't feel bad if you find SAML somewhat hard to understand at first. SAML was finalized before the age of developer-friendly APIs—ease of use was not a design goal. When you first start learning about SAML, it's common to get the terms IDP and SP confused. If you're new to SAML, think of the IDP as the server that holds the identity information for the person and the credentials (i.e., username and password). In most cases, you can substitute SP with "website". If SAML were LDAP, the IDP would be the LDAP server, and the SP would be the LDAP client.

Like other federation protocols, SAML uses public key cryptography to sign or encrypt messages and documents. The use of such keys enables the parties to protect and verify the integrity of information. By convention, most SAML servers use self-signed X.509 certificates, whereas browsers make use of certificates issued by Certificate Authorities (CA). For browsers, using a CA makes sense—it enables validation of a certificate by trusting the root certificate that was used to issue it, enabling vendors to ship browsers with pre-trusted keys that save most people from having to know much about certificate trust. However, in SAML, the use of self-signed certificates has the security benefit of making trust management explicit—when you trust a certain self-signed certificate, you are trusting a specific entity. Self-signed certificates are not shared between services. For example, if you have several SAML services, each would use its own certificate. And, of course, any SAML certificates would be different from the SSL certificate used by a web server (which is generally not self-signed anyway).

If you're reading this chapter, you need to learn at least the basics about SAML, so the goal is to make this as painless as possible and to discuss some of the tools at our disposal to manage SSO using SAML. We will stick to the most common SAML use cases and ignore the more esoteric SAML capabilities.

For a test IDP, you can use the Shibboleth IDP deployed in the Gluu Server. There are many other excellent free open source SAML tools—we will cover only some of the more common ones. But, hopefully, the concepts and methodologies will be transferable to other software solutions and libraries. So, without further ado, let's start with a slightly deeper dive into the standard itself, and then move onto the software!

Assertions, Bindings, Protocols, and Profiles

In this section, we talk about assertions, bindings, protocols, and profiles (see Figure 3-1).

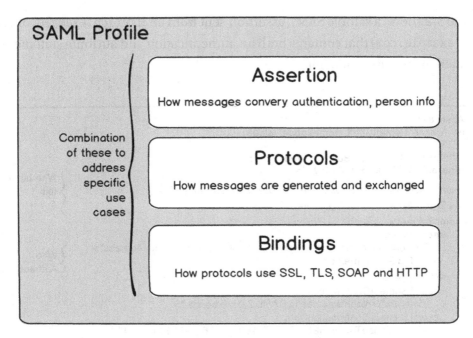

Figure 3-1. *SAML profiles, assertions, protocols, and bindings*

Assertions

Assertions contain the goods—the information that a web application needs from the Identity Provider about the person accessing the site. A SAML assertion can be composed of four different sections:

- **Subject** is an identifier for the person. This can be a one-time identifier that will change each time the person visits the site, or it can be a consistent identifier that will enable continuity with a person's previous activity.

- **Authentication statements** contain information about when and how the person was authenticated.

- **Attribute statements** contain information about the subject, like first name, last name, email address, role or group memberships.

- **Authorization statements** contain information about whether the subject should be granted access to a requested resource. This is a somewhat esoteric part of SAML, which you will probably not encounter for SSO use cases.

Figure 3-2 shows a sample SAML assertion sent from an IDP (idp.example.org) to a SP (sp.example.com) that contains both an authentication and attribute statements, abbreviated to increase readability.

Figure 3-2. *Sample SAML assertion*

Protocols

While SAML is commonly referenced as a protocol, it's actually more than that. As a matter of fact, inside the SAML specification the word "protocol" is also defined, and these protocols specify how to understand the different messages that are exchanged between the sender and receiver. The core specification defines requests sent (usually by the SP), and the responses sent (usually by the IDP) (see Figure 3-3). The core specification defines certain information that must be present in every message and then describes the details of messages that are sent for specific use cases.

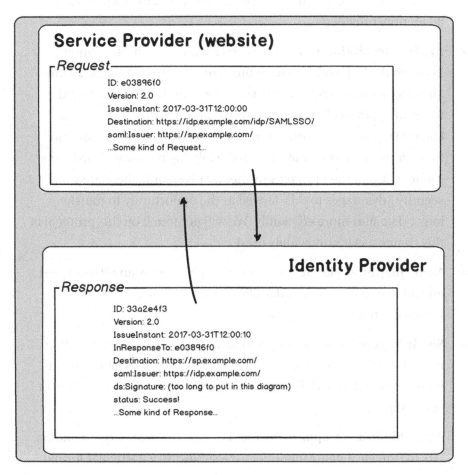

Figure 3-3. *SAML protocol visualization*

SAML defines six protocols:

- **Assertion Query and Request Protocol** defines messages and processing rules for requesting existing assertions if the requester knows the unique identifier of an assertion, or if the requester can identify the subject and statement type.

- **Authentication Request Protocol** is one of the most important protocols. It defines how an SP can find out who the subject is, as well as details about the authentication, such as when and how the authentication occurred. If a server can respond to this protocol, it is an identity provider!

- **Artifact Resolution Protocol** is used for direct communication between the IDP and SP—sometimes referred to as a "back-channel". The browser may pass along a reference identifier (artifact) used to obtain a protocol message. (Spoiler alert: It's the "code" in the OpenID Connect authorization code flow.) The IDP or SP can use that reference identifier to pick up the full payload directly from the sender without the browser's further involvement. There are some security advantages to this, as well as the opportunity to transfer larger data files more efficiently. We will not touch on this protocol in this chapter, as it's not widely used.

- **Name Identifier Management Protocol** is used by an SP to request an IDP to provide a name identifier for a subject in a particular format or context.

- **Single Logout Protocol** is a protocol that can be initiated by either the IDP or SP to affect logout. There are a lot of issues with session management due to different standards in use, so this protocol isn't very reliable.

- **Name Identifier Mapping Protocol** is used by an SP request and an IDP to provide a name identifier for a subject in a particular format.

IDP-Initiated vs SP-Initiated Authentication

What comes first, the chicken or the egg? The equivalent question in SAML is "What comes first, logging into the IDP or the SP?" Today, we know the answer to this question: log into the SP first—keep it simple and avoid all the complexity and corner cases that entertaining IDP—initiated authentication will cause by trying to figure out how to enable authentication without an authentication request! This is the reason OpenID Connect, a more modern federation protocol, did not support IDP-initiated authentication. Consider Figures 3-4 and 3-5, which represent typical (and really oversimplified) SAML flows for the purpose of highlighting the differences between these two flows.

SP Initiated Authentication

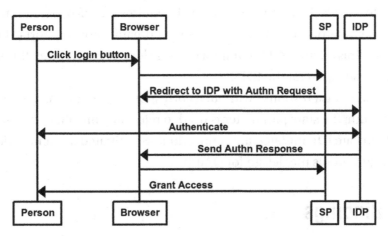

Figure 3-4. *Very simplified SP initiated authentication flow*

IDP Initiated Authentication

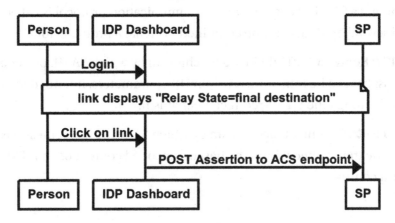

Figure 3-5. *Very simplified sample IDP-initiated authentication flow*

Some websites see advantages to IDP initiated authentication because it may seem like a simpler way to embed links. For example, consider a hypothetical banking site that uses an external service provider to handle foreign currency trades. The customer uses the bank's portal and then clicks on the link to buy some Euros. A SAML response with an assertion is created by the IDP and sent along with the customer to the third-party SP, who can validate the assertion and provide its service.

There are several reasons why IDP initiated authentication is currently discouraged. One of the main concerns is that, while this process is defined in the standard, it is not interoperable. When a website receives an unsolicited SAML response, how does it know where to send redirect the browser after consumption of the assertion, i.e., the relay state? Each website that supports IDP initiated authentication may have a different way to communicate what is the correct relay state. It requires out-of-band communication and is therefore a "one-off". The more one-offs your organization supports, the more expensive your infrastructure is to maintain over the long term. Net-net, this solution is better for the website than for the IDP.

The idea of sending a response without a corresponding request is generally troubling. In OAuth, the state parameter is used to reject any unsolicited response. You should deprecate IDP initiated authentication—SP initiated authentication is more scalable and futureproofs the design for OAuth.

Protocol Bindings

There are several technical solutions that will enable SAML messages to be passed from a sender to a receiver. For example, short messages may be carried directly in the URL query string of an HTTP GET request, while longer messages may use HTTP POST or web services. Mapping a SAML exchange onto a communication protocol is called a SAML binding, and several bindings may be combined to create a protocol flow:

- **HTTP Redirect** (GET) defines a mechanism by which SAML protocol messages can be transmitted within URL parameters, intended to be used through the HTTP-redirect mechanism.

- **HTTP POST** defines a mechanism by which SAML protocol messages may be transmitted within the base64-encoded content of an HTML form control.

- **Simple Sign** defines an HTTP POST mechanism that employs a simpler strategy to digitally sign the message. Instead of signing components of the message, the entire SAML protocol message is signed.

- **SAML SOAP** defines how to use SOAP, an XML web services standard, to send and receive SAML requests and responses.

- **Reverse SOAP** defines a mechanism in which an HTTP request is sent to a SP, which in turn returns a SAML request, normally an authentication request in a SOAP envelope. It's used in the ECP profile, which will be covered later.

- **HTTP Artifact** is a mechanism to use a reference value (or artifact), which the receiver can use to establish a direct communication channel with the sender to request the full message.

- **SAML URI** is not a request/response binding, but a mechanism to retrieve an assertion via a URI, normally via HTTPS.

SAML bindings provide some flexibility. Consider the Web Browser SSO profile: there are four SP bindings and three IDP bindings, making twelve different deployments scenarios possible. In this chapter, we focus on the two most common protocol binding: Redirect-POST and POST-POST.

HTTP Redirect Binding

One of the most important bindings, it defines a mechanism by which SAML messages can be transmitted within parameters, including the signature. One advantage of this binding is that it is easy to debug in the case of unexpected behavior. The SAML Request must be compressed (see IETF RFC 1951), base64-encoded, and then URL-encoded. If you inspect the GET URL, it will be quite long. Signatures are not included in the SAML Request; they are specified with the additional parameters. One reason to leave signatures out is to decrease the size of the parameter payload. It is inadvisable to send very long URLs, and it can cause problems with old browsers. The request may also include the RelayState parameter, which is used in SP-initiated authentication to drop unsolicited responses, or in IDP-initiated authentication to convey the final landing page. While the SAML request itself may be short, the responses may be longer. As it is inadvisable to send excessively long URLs, in practice this binding may be combined with others in a single protocol exchange. Figure 3-6 details a typical HTTP redirect binding for SP-initiated authentication.

SP Intiated: Redirect-Redirect

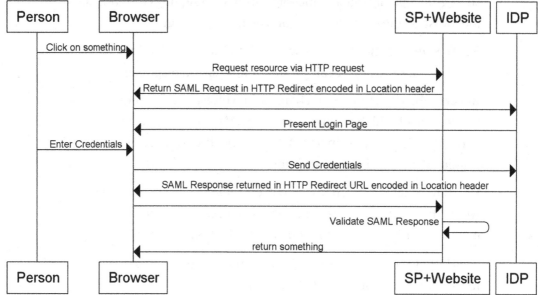

Figure 3-6. *Sample SP-initiated authentication flow using HTTP redirect bindings*

There are a few important security considerations when using this binding. Notice that the SP and IDP do not directly communicate, which means that this binding does not support confidentiality of messages from the browser. Also, if you don't want an eavesdropper seeing the SAML response and request, you must use TLS (SSL) from the browser to both the IDP and SP to hide the GET parameters. You should use a secure communication channel for all APIs and websites, but especially for authentication! It's also important for the browser not to cache the SAML response. Normally the IDP will use the HTTP Headers' Cache-Control field set to no-cache, no-store and the Pragma header set to no-cache. But, if this is missing, there is a danger of a replay attack by someone other than the subject. Another thing to keep in mind is that by using GET requests, there is a chance a web server or proxy may persist SAML messages log files, which is not desirable from a security or privacy perspective. You also need to consider that a GET URL may be retained by the browser as the referrer URL. This summary is not an exhaustive discussion, but a starting point for your research.

HTTP POST Binding

Another common binding, it uses an HTML form with the hidden fields named either SAMLRequest or SAMLResponse to send messages. The action attribute of the form is used to specify the URL to which to send the message, and JavaScript is normally used to automate submission of the form. For example, see Listing 3-1.

Listing 3-1. Sample HTML Form Used for Form POST Response

```
<form method="post"
  action="https://idp.example.com/SAML2/SSO/POST" ...>
<input type="hidden" name="SAMLRequest"
  value="(base-64 encoded xml)" />
</form>

<form method="post"
  action="https://sp.example.com/SAML2/SSO/POST" ...>
<input type="hidden" name="SAMLResponse"
  value="(base-64 encoded xml)" />
</form>

window.onload = function() {document.forms[0].submit();}
```

This strategy is handy because it can handle longer messages, and some of the security considerations around logging the GET request go away. In this scenario, the browser is also in the middle, so you won't be able to hide anything from it. As with the HTTP redirect binding, HTTP POST sends identity information embedded in SAML protocol messages across the wire (see Figure 3-7). A secure communication channel to both the SP and IDP is highly recommended. Caching the form containing SAML messages should also be discouraged.

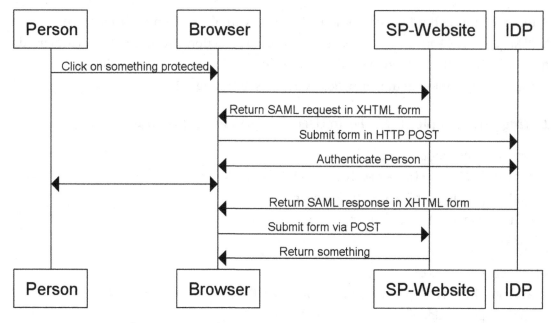

Figure 3-7. Sample SP-initiated authentication flow using HTTP POST bindings

Profiles

SAML provides a great deal of flexibility or "optionality". However, optionality is the enemy of interoperability! Profiles are used to provide more specific guidelines for how to use a combination of assertions, protocols, and bindings. By adhering to profiles that define more specifically how to use the building blocks, including the naming, syntax, and values of such elements, profiles make interoperability more likely. While the first two profiles listed here are the most important, the OASIS SAML specifications include details about five profile categories:

- **SSO Profiles** define how to use SAML for single sign-on of browsers (and hypothetically other devices, but such use cases are rather esoteric).

- **SAML Attribute Profiles** define how information about a person is conveyed in SAML.

- **Artifact Resolution Profiles** define a back-channel mechanism for the IDP and SP to communicate directly to pass SAML protocol messages by reference identifiers. Although it's potentially more secure, it's infrequently used for Enterprise IAM.

- **Assertion Query/Request Profiles** define how to request assertions by referencing an identifier or by querying based on a subject (person). It's not normally needed because the assertion included in the SSO Profiles normally contain both an authentication and attribute statement.

- **Name Identifier Mapping Profiles** define how to request an alternate name identifier for the same person in a different format. This also won't be covered due to its esoteric appeal.

Web Browser SSO Profile

This is the most important profile defined by the SAML specifications. Some people might not even realize that there is any purpose to SAML other than Web Browser SSO. In this profile, a person authenticates to the IDP, which produces an assertion that the SP uses to establish a session. This profile defines two important services, or roles, in the message exchange:

- **Single Sign-On Service,** which specifies the IDP's endpoints (URLs) to which the browser sends the message from the SP.

- **Assertion Consumer Endpoint,** which is the SP's endpoint to which the browser sends the message from the IDP.

This profile spells out more of the details about the flow of messages between the SP and IDP. We've already covered many of these details. The profile also specifies some important information about the use of "metadata," which will be covered subsequently.

Single Logout Profile (SLO)

Don't get your hopes up that the SLO profile is a logout panacea. It doesn't work in practice with many applications, even if they are all SAML—even if they support SLO! Logout requests should be signed by the SP—otherwise a malicious website could log out a person just by knowing a subject identifier. There are two mechanisms for logout— "front-channel" and "back-channel". In a front-channel logout, the browser loads a page with logout URLs for all applications to which the subject has logged in. Each of these requests are hopefully automatically sent by the browser (this can be accomplished with iframe, script or img HTML tags). With any luck, when the browser calls the logout URLs at the respective applications, the person is logged out. In back-channel logout, a notification is sent directly from the IDP to the SP to log out a specific browser session.

The likely success of front-channel logout for all the people in your domain is tenuous at best. First of all, if an error is encountered while the browser calls the logout URL (maybe the network is down?), the IDP (or the person) will usually never know something failed. To log out of an application, normally it needs to clear the application cookie it set post-authentication. A common problem with front-channel logout is that some browsers block "third-party cookies," or cookies from a domain other than that of the page. Because the IDP presents the front-channel logout page, but the iframes (or script or img tags) call logout URLs in a different domain (the application), these will be seen by the browser as third-party. Most browsers have a setting to block third-party cookies, and some even do so as the default setting. For example, Figure 3-8 shows the setting on Chrome (which is not the default setting).

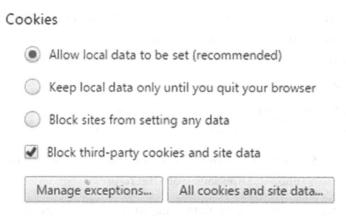

Figure 3-8. *Chrome settings interface to block third-party cookies*

So, what about back-channel logout? If the browser sends a logout request to the IDP, as the SLO profile states is preferred, the IDP would need to execute back-channel requests in parallel to all SPs to which it has sent a response. This is not a trivial undertaking, as the IDP and SP may not even have a direct connection (in the POST and redirect bindings, the browser is used as an intermediary). Also complicating the mess is that if the website relies on cookies in the browser, a back-channel notification has no way to remove the cookie in the browser.

Attribute Profile

In SAML, attributes refer to data about a person—the subject. In order to achieve interoperability, the IDP and SP must exchange attribute information in a standard manner. The SAML attribute profile provides a way to name attributes, to enable syntax validation, and to provide other attribute information using XML. The two most common attribute profile formats are generically referred to as "basic" and "LDAP".

Basic Attributes

The first thing that you might notice is that there are two elements: `Attribute` and `AttributeValue`. The `NameFormat` attribute specifies that this is a "basic" attribute (see Listing 3-2). The only other XML attribute of the SAML `Attribute` element is the `Name` attribute, which is used for comparison. Note that in this example, there are two `AttributeValue` elements—don't forget that attributes can be multi-value. The type of the attribute is also specified using XML schema types. The main types you might expect to see are `string`, `boolean`, `decimal`, `float`, `double`, `duration`, `dateTime`, `time`, and `date`. For more information about these values, and their exact syntax and values, see the "XML Schema Part 2: Datatypes" document published by the W3C: `https://www.w3.org/TR/xmlschema-2/`.

Listing 3-2. SAML Basic Attribute Element

```
<saml:Attribute Name="FirstName"
    NameFormat=
      "urn:oasis:names:tc:SAML:2.0:attrname-format:basic">
  <saml:AttributeValue xsi:type="xs:string">
    Michael
  </saml:AttributeValue>
  <saml:AttributeValue xsi:type="xs:string">
    Mike
  </saml:AttributeValue>
</saml:Attribute>
```

SAML V2.0 X.500/LDAP Attributes

The other common format you might see for attributes is based on LDAP, because organizations understandably wanted to re-use the schema they previously defined (see Listing 3-3). The name used is based on the object identifier (OID) that is commonly used in LDAP. A FriendlyName is used, because no one could possible remember these abstruse OIDs. The `AttributeValue` part is the same, but the type will always be "string" if the value can be defined as a UTF-8 string, for example, all of the following in Listing 3-4.

Listing 3-3. SAML LDAP Attribute Element

```
<saml:Attribute Name="urn:oid:2.5.4.42"
  FriendlyName="givenName" x500:Encoding="LDAP"
 xmlns:x500=
   "urn:oasis:names:tc:SAML:2.0:profiles:attribute:X500"
 NameFormat=
  "urn:oasis:names:tc:SAML:2.0:attrname-format:uri"
>
  <saml:AttributeValue xsi:type="xsd:string">
    Michael
  </saml:AttributeValue>
  <saml:AttributeValue xsi:type="xsd:string">
    Mike
  </saml:AttributeValue>
</saml:Attribute>
```

Listing 3-4. Attribute Type OIDs

```
Attribute Type Description 1.3.6.1.4.1.1466.115.121.1.3
Bit String 1.3.6.1.4.1.1466.115.121.1.6
Boolean 1.3.6.1.4.1.1466.115.121.1.7
Country String 1.3.6.1.4.1.1466.115.121.1.11
DN 1.3.6.1.4.1.1466.115.121.1.12
Directory String 1.3.6.1.4.1.1466.115.121.1.15
Facsimile Telephone Number 1.3.6.1.4.1.1466.115.121.1.22 Generalized Time
1.3.6.1.4.1.1466.115.121.1.24
```

IA5 String 1.3.6.1.4.1.1466.115.121.1.26
INTEGER 1.3.6.1.4.1.1466.115.121.1.27
LDAP Syntax Description 1.3.6.1.4.1.1466.115.121.1.54
Matching Rule Description 1.3.6.1.4.1.1466.115.121.1.30 Matching Rule
Use Description 1.3.6.1.4.1.1466.115.121.1.31 Name And Optional UID
1.3.6.1.4.1.1466.115.121.1.34
Name Form Description 1.3.6.1.4.1.1466.115.121.1.35
Numeric String 1.3.6.1.4.1.1466.115.121.1.36
Object Class Description 1.3.6.1.4.1.1466.115.121.1.37
Octet String 1.3.6.1.4.1.1466.115.121.1.40
OID 1.3.6.1.4.1.1466.115.121.1.38
Other Mailbox 1.3.6.1.4.1.1466.115.121.1.39
Postal Address 1.3.6.1.4.1.1466.115.121.1.41
Presentation Address 1.3.6.1.4.1.1466.115.121.1.43
Printable String 1.3.6.1.4.1.1466.115.121.1.44
Substring Assertion 1.3.6.1.4.1.1466.115.121.1.58
Telephone Number 1.3.6.1.4.1.1466.115.121.1.50
UTC Time 1.3.6.1.4.1.1466.115.121.1.53

If the AttributeValue can't be expressed as a UTF-8 string, the xsi:type should be base-64 encoded and the xsi:type must be set to xsd:base64Binary.

SAML Metadata

SAML metadata is an XML document that groups together all necessary SAML-related details of one party. Included are the roles the service fulfills, details on how to communicate with these services, information of the organization and its operators, as well as information on the cryptographic keys and certificates that the party uses to sign or encrypt different SAML messages.

Metadata is also used by federation operators, which are organizations that enhance trust between organizations by vetting participants. The purpose of a federation is to drive down the legal and technical costs of collaboration. Multi-party federations are covered in more detail in Chapter 10. At a technical level, the federation aggregates the metadata of many participants and publishes one large metadata document, which includes as sub-elements the metadata for all participants. This approach can lead to large files.

Figure 3-9 provides an overview of a metadata document for an IDP. The document itself contains a signature so that its integrity can be verified. One of the most important attributes is the `entityID` of the `EntityDescriptor`. Your SAML partners will need this in their configuration to identify your IDP. If this entity is an SP, it must define an `SPSSODescriptor`, which contains an `AssertionConsumerService` element, i.e., where the IDP should send the SAML response. An organization could operate an entity that fulfills both the role of SP as well as IDP. This would be reflected in the metadata defining both an `IDPSSODescriptor` element as well as an `SPSSODEscriptor` element. This is not typical, but it's not unusual either—for example a SAML proxy might have both IDP and SP endpoints. As you can see, the metadata contains a lot of descriptive information that enables SAML partners to configure their respective services without a lot of back-and-forth about what formats or data is required. Metadata saves time and enables automation.

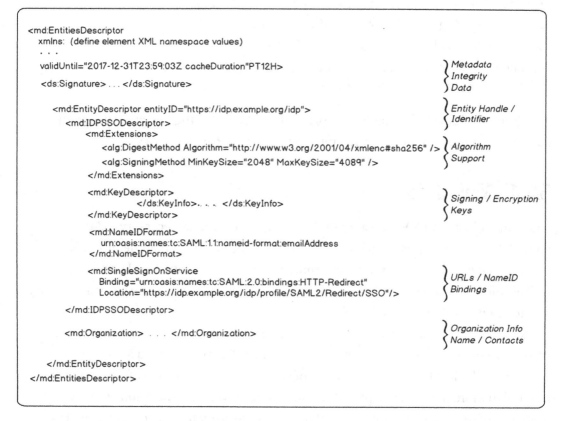

Figure 3-9. *Sample SAML IDP metadata structure*

Open Source SAML Software

Congratulations, you made it through the theoretical section of this chapter! Now it's time to roll up your sleeves and get to work. This section walks you through a number of examples that involve configuring websites for SSO with a SAML IDP. We use the Gluu Server we set up in Chapter 1 as the IDP. For the websites, we try the Shibboleth SP software, `SimpleSAMLPhp`, and a custom Python script.

Gluu Server Shibboleth Identity Provider Overview

If you installed the Gluu Server in the first chapter, then you already have a SAML IDP up and running, waiting for you to configure websites for SSO! This is because the Gluu Server bundles the Shibboleth Identity Provider in its distribution. As a test, you can view the SAML metadata for your IDP. Navigate to this URL: `https://<your-hostname>/idp/shibboleth`, replacing the `<your-hostname>`, of course, with that of your installation. If this URL returns an XML document, you're in business! The Shibboleth IDP is working.

If you're wondering why the name Shibboleth was chosen, its biblical origins tell of a word whose proper pronunciation was a way to prove membership to a tribe. It's a nice metaphor for federated identity. But why name a project after a word whose claim to fame is difficulty in pronunciation? Your guess is as good as ours. But back to the Gluu Server, to view the configuration of your IDP, you'll need to log in to the chroot container.

```
# service gluu-server-3.1.3 login
```

Note   If you are using a later version of the Gluu Server, adjust this command accordingly.

---

chroot is a file system container. It's a handy trick to simplify distribution of the Gluu Server software. Chroot containers have been around for a while. They only offer file system isolation—new Linux kernel containers also provide process and network isolation. For example, if a hacker were to get access to an application constrained to a file system container and were to run # `rm -rf /*` (normally fatal for UNIX systems), only the application folder would be deleted.

You'll notice that the chroot container contains an entire Linux distribution. The Shibboleth IDP is installed in /opt/idp. The Gluu Server creates the initial configuration during setup and you can configure the IDP through the oxTrust graphical admin interface. By default, the Gluu Server supports the redirect and POST bindings via the front-channel (browser). Back-channel protocols (like the artifact and attribute profiles) can be supported through the use of custom templates.

The Gluu Server ships with a Shibboleth IDP login handler that leverages OpenID Connect authentication. OpenID Connect is covered in more detail in Chapter 5, but for now, think of it as a modern version of SAML using JSON instead of XML. The goal of this login handler is to enable SSO across websites using either SAML or OpenID Connect, and to enable you to define authentication workflows in one place. For example, to support two-factor authentication, you would not want to configure one plugin for SAML and a different plugin for OpenID Connect.

Shibboleth Service Provider Example

The Shibboleth SP solution consists of two parts. The first is an Apache or IIS web server plugin that enables you to specify that certain web folders require an authenticated user. The second is a service called "shibd," which runs on the same server as the web server (listening on a localhost socket) and provides the SAML operations needed by the web server plugin. The advantage of this architecture is that the web server plugin is relatively "thin," as most of the heavy lifting for the SAML protocol is performed by the shibd service software.

To get you started as quickly as possible, this section will provide an end-to-end example using Ubuntu 14.04.4, and I'll explain as we go along. Prior to developing this example, install a new Ubuntu server. The only software you should select when running the Ubuntu Server installation is OpenSSH. If you want to do this with Centos, the concepts are the same but the commands and locations are a little different. Check Gluu documentation for an equivalent procedure at https://gluu.org/docs.

In this example, the hostname for the Gluu Server (IDP) is albacore.gluu.info. The hostname for the web server (SP) is squid.gluu.info.

Installing the Web Server, Certificates, and SP Metadata

Most of Listing 3-5 is standard Apache web server administration tasks. In this process we're generating self-signed certificates, which we're using for HTTPS and to generate the Shibboleth SP metadata. For a more secure deployment, each service should have a different private key. By convention, the certificates used by the SAML SP should be self-signed. The HTTPS certificate would normally be issued by a well-known certification authority, like GoDaddy, Verisign, or Let's Encrypt.

Listing 3-5. Ubuntu 14.04 Apache2 and Shibboleth SP Installation

```
# apt-get install apache2 libshibsp6 libapache2-mod-shib2
# a2enmod cgi
# a2enmod ssl
# a2enmod shib2
# a2ensite default-ssl
# mkdir /etc/certs
# cd /etc/certs
# openssl genrsa -des3 -out squid.key 2048
# openssl rsa -in squid.key -out squid.key.insecure
# mv squid.key.insecure squid.key
# openssl req -new -key squid.key -out squid.csr
# openssl x509 -req -days 365 -in squid.csr -signkey squid.key -out squid.crt
# shib-metagen -c /etc/certs/squid.crt -h squid.gluu.info >
/etc/shibboleth/squid-metadata.xml
# service apache2 start
# service shibd start
# mkdir /var/www/html/sp
# ln -s /etc/shibboleth/squid-metadata.xml /var/www/html/sp/metadata.xml
# mkdir /var/www/protected
# cd /var/www/protected
# wget
https://raw.githubusercontent.com/GluuFederation/community-edition-setup/
master/sta tic/scripts/printHeaders.py
# chmod ugo+x printHeaders.py
```

> **Note**   If you are not using DN, don't forget to update all the hosts files—this includes the hosts file on the Gluu Server VM, your test web server VM, and your laptop (or workstation). The Windows host file location is `c:\windows\system32\drivers\etc\hosts`. Run notepad.exe as Administrator!

For this sample, we are creating a public folder to publish the SP metadata. This will make it easier when we configure the IDP. There is nothing secret about SAML metadata—it contains a public certificate and information about public HTTPS endpoints. The nice thing about publishing your SP metadata is that the IDP can obtain an updated document automatically. In the last two lines of Listing 3-5, we're creating a simple `cgi-script` that prints the environment variables, which will include the HTTP headers inserted by the Shibboleth SP. The script looks like Listing 3-6.

Listing 3-6. Python Script to Print Headers

```
#!/usr/bin/python import os
d = os.environ k = d.keys() k.sort()
print "Content-type: text/html\n\n"

print  "<HTML><HEAD><TITLE>printHeaders.cgi</TITLE></Head><BODY>" print
"<h1>Environment Variables</H1>"
for item in k:
print "<p><B>%s</B>: %s </p>" % (item, d[item])
print "</BODY></HTML>"
```

To activate the Shibboleth SP, we need to update the Apache web server configuration: Edit the default site at `/etc/apache2/sites-available/default-ssl.conf`, adding what's shown in Listing 3-7 inside the `VirtualHost` directive. Then restart the apache2 service.

Listing 3-7. Sample Apache2 Folder Protected by the Shibboleth SP Apache plugin

```
ScriptAlias /protected/ /var/www/protected/
<Directory /var/www/protected>
  AddHandler cgi-script .py
  Options +ExecCGI SSLOptions +StdEnvVars
```

```
AuthType shibboleth
ShibRequestSetting requireSession true
Require valid-user
</Directory>
```

Configure the Shibboleth SP

This is probably the hardest part. We need to finish updating our Shibboleth SP to customize it for our environment. We'll want to update a few files in /etc/shibboleth:

- shibboleth2.xml specifies our entityID, which IDP we're using and some other important configuration options.

- attribute-map.xml defines which attributes we're requesting from the IDP.

- Get the metadata from your IDP.

In the attribute-map.xml file in Figure 3-10, we are mapping four user attributes: givenName (first name), sn (last name), displayName, and uid (username). The name attribute refers to the SAML name, and the id refers to the attribute name that we'll see in the HTTP headers. If you don't know the right SAML name, you can check the SAML 2 URI value in the Gluu Server, in the Configuration/Attribute section (see Figure 3-11).

```
<Attributes
  xmlns="urn:mace:shibboleth:2.0:attribute-map" xmlns:xsi="http://www.w3.org/2001/XMLSchema-instance">
  <Attribute name="urn:oid:2.5.4.42" id="givenName"/>
  <Attribute name="urn:oid:2.5.4.4" id="sn"/>
  <Attribute name="urn:oid:2.16.840.1.113730.3.1.241" id="displayName"/>
  <Attribute name="urn:oid:0.9.2342.19200300.100.1.1" id="uid"/>
</Attributes>
```

Figure 3-10. *Sample attribute-map.xml*

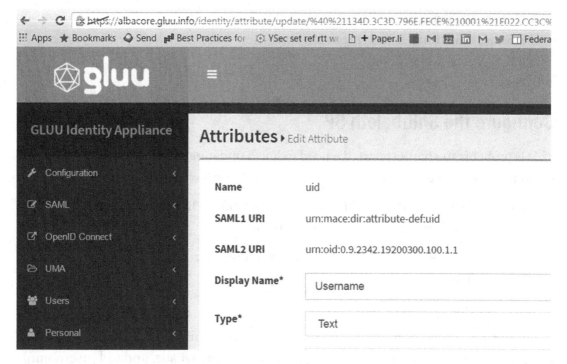

Figure 3-11. *Attribute configuration in the Gluu Server*

Most of the Shibboleth configuration that you'll need to edit is contained in the shibboleth2.xml file. Figure 3-12 is a simple example. When you first install the Shibboleth SP, the /etc/shibboleth folder will contain a file called example-shibboleth2.xml. You can copy this file, so you don't have to type in everything in everything by hand. There are a few things you'll have to change.

- entityID is the identifier for your SP, and it should match the value of entityID in your SP metadata that you generated when you ran shib-metagen.

- You should update the Errors section with an email address that makes sense for support in case something goes wrong, and also update the copy of the help HTML file.

- Note, you only specify two bindings in the sample configuration. We won't need the others in the example, so just leave them out! You can also remove the SAML 1 configuration.

- Leave the Status and Session endpoints. You can get to these by navigating to `https:///Shibboleth.sso/Session` and `https:///Shibboleth.sso/Status`. In production, you might want to remove these.

- Leave the `AttributeChecker` configuration. If `uid` is not present, the SP will display an error.

- We are just pointing at one IDP, albacore in our example. The `entityID` of the IDP is specified in the `SessionInitiator` element, and the metadata for the IDP is specified in the `MetadataProvider` element.

- The private key and public certificate (that we created) for the SP is specified in the `CredentialResolver` element.

- Change `handlerSSL` to `true`! You never want to use HTTP for any APIs. Always use HTTPS!

```
<SPConfig xmlns="urn:mace:shibboleth.2.0.native.sp.config"
  xmlns:conf="urn:mace:shibboleth:2.0:native:sp:config"
  xmlns:saml="urn:oasis:names:tc:SAML:2.0:assertion"
  xmlns:samlp="urn:oasis:names:tc:SAML:2.0:protocol"
  xmlns:md="urn:oasis:names:tc:SAML:2.0:metadata"
  logger="syslog.logger" clockSkew="180">
  <OutOfProcess logger="shibd.logger"></OutOfProcess>
  <UnixListener address="shibd.sock"/>
  <StorageService type="Memory" id="mem" cleanupInterval="900"/>
  <SessionCache type="StorageService" StorageService="mem" cacheAssertions="false"
        cacheAllowance="900" inprocTimeout="900" cleanupInterval="900"/>
  <ReplayCache StorageService="mem"/>
  <RequestMapper type="Native">
    <RequestMap>
      <Host name="squid.gluu.info">
        <Path name="protected" authType="shibboleth" requireSession="true"/>
      </Host>
    </RequestMap>
  </RequestMapper>
  <ApplicationDefaults entityID="https://squid.gluu.info/shibboleth"
                REMOTE_USER="uid"
                sessionHook="/Shibboleth.sso/AttrChecker"
                signing="false" encryption="false">

    <Sessions lifetime="28800" timeout="3600" checkAddress="true"
      handlerURL="/Shibboleth.sso" handlerSSL="true" cookieProps="https" relayState="ss:mem">
        <SessionInitiator type="Chaining" Location="/Login" isDefault="true" id="Login"
                entityID="https://albacore.gluu.info/idp/shibboleth">
          <SessionInitiator type="SAML2" template="bindingTemplate.html"/>
        </SessionInitiator>

        <md:AssertionConsumerService Location="/SAML2/POST-SimpleSign" index="2"
          Binding="urn:oasis:names:tc:SAML:2.0:bindings:HTTP-POST-SimpleSign"/>
        <md:AssertionConsumerService Location="/SAML2/POST" index="1"
          Binding="urn:oasis:names:tc:SAML:2.0:bindings:HTTP-POST"/>

        <LogoutInitiator type="Chaining" Location="/Logout">
          <LogoutInitiator type="SAML2" template="bindingTemplate.html"/>
          <LogoutInitiator type="Local"/>
        </LogoutInitiator>

        <md:SingleLogoutService Location="/SLO/Redirect" conf:template="bindingTemplate.html"
          Binding="urn:oasis:names:tc:SAML:2.0:bindings:HTTP-Redirect"/>
        <md:SingleLogoutService Location="/SLO/POST" conf:template="bindingTemplate.html"
          Binding="urn:oasis:names:tc:SAML:2.0:bindings:HTTP-POST"/>

        <Handler type="Status" Location="/Status"/>
        <Handler type="Session" Location="/Session" showAttributeValues="false"/>
        <Handler type="AttributeChecker" Location="/AttrChecker" template="attrChecker.html"
          attributes="uid" flushSession="true"/>
    </Sessions>

    <Errors supportContact="root@localhost"
      helpLocation="/about.html"
      styleSheet="/shibboleth-sp/main.css"/>
    <MetadataProvider type="XML" file="albacore.xml"/>
    <TrustEngine type="ExplicitKey"/>
    <TrustEngine type="PKIX"/>
    <AttributeExtractor type="XML" validate="true" reloadChanges="false" path="attribute-map.xml"/
    <AttributeExtractor type="Metadata" errorURL="errorURL" DisplayName="displayName"/>
    <AttributeResolver type="Query" subjectMatch="true"/>
    <AttributeFilter type="XML" validate="true" path="attribute-policy.xml"/>
    <CredentialResolver type="File" key="/etc/certs/squid.key" certificate="/etc/certs/squid.crt"/>
  </ApplicationDefaults>
  <SecurityPolicyProvider type="XML" validate="true" path="security-policy.xml"/>
  <ProtocolProvider type="XML" validate="true" reloadChanges="false" path="protocols.xml"/>

</SPConfig>
```

Figure 3-12. *Sample shibboleth2.xml*

Configure the Gluu Server Shibboleth IDP

Now we need to finish up by configuring the Shibboleth IDP in the Gluu Server to trust the SP and to release certain attributes. Since we didn't publish the metadata anywhere on a public URL—which you can do if you want, just copy it into /var/www/html— you'll need to make sure you have a copy of squid-metadata.xml sftp'd to your local workstation. Log in to the Gluu Server admin interface (oxTrust) and navigate to SAML/ Outbound/Trust Relations. Then click the Add Relationship button. You'll be presented with a form similar to the one in Figure 3-13.

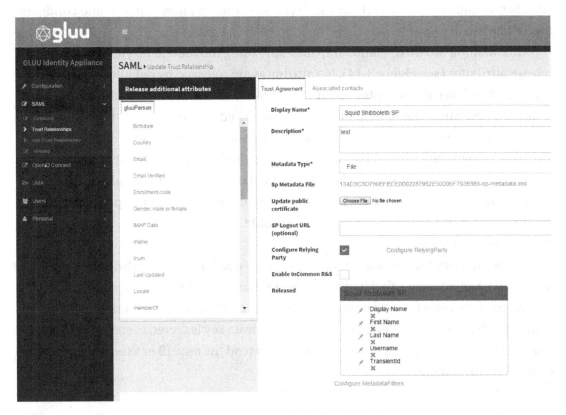

Figure 3-13. *Gluu Server SAML SP Trust Relationship Sample*

Note   Always release the TransientID attribute. It's a non-persistent session identifier that doesn't reveal any personal information about the subject. The default nameID format in the Gluu Server uses this attribute, so releasing it will save you some headaches later on.

The Gluu Server supports four workflows for uploading the SP metadata: File, URI, Federation, and Generate. In this case, we're going to use File because you have downloaded the metadata to your workstation, and you're going to upload it. URI is actually a better mechanism in practice, because if the SP updates their metadata, it will be picked up automatically. However, because this is only a test with self-signed HTTPS certificates, the Gluu Server is going to complain, so let's keep it simple.

Federation is also a good mechanism if the SP is part of a federation that you trust (more on federations later!) Generate is used when the website doesn't have a SAML SP installed yet. It enables you to generate the `shibboleth2.xml` configuration file on the Gluu Server and download a ZIP file that has instructions on how to install and configure the Shibboleth SP.

After naming the trust relationship and uploading the metadata, you need to release attributes (see Figure 3-14). No attributes are released by default—you must explicitly configure all attributes about the person that you want to release to the website. These attributes should match those required by the website—release attributes on a need-to-know basis. It's always a good idea to release the `TransientID` attribute, because the Gluu Server uses it as the default `NameID`. `TransientID` is a session identifier—it doesn't release any personal or correlatable data about the subject. Finally, you'll need to click on the Configure RP, which will display a modal window, where you'll select the SAML2SSO profile. The Shibboleth SP supports signing and encryption.

In this example, I signed the whole response (instead of signing individual assertions). Signed means that integrity is assured from the IDP. As the response is not encrypted, if the response was intercepted, anyone could read it. Encryption happens with the public key of the SP, and since the SP's private key is secret, even if an attacker intercepts the response, they would not be able to read the `nameID` or assertions that contain the meaningful data.

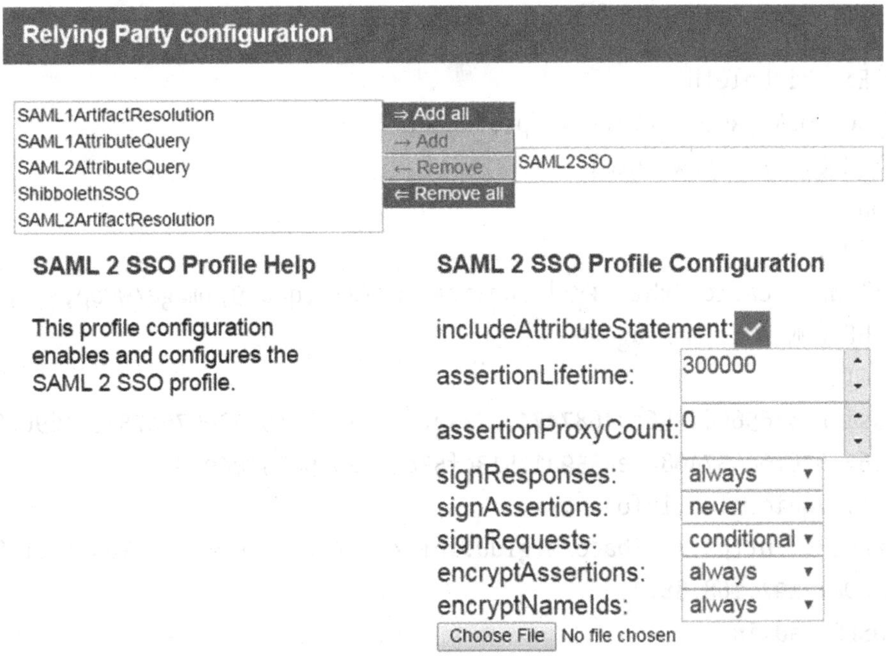

Relying Party configuration

SAML1ArtifactResolution	⇒ Add all
SAML1AttributeQuery	→ Add
SAML2AttributeQuery	← Remove SAML2SSO
ShibbolethSSO	⇐ Remove all
SAML2ArtifactResolution	

SAML 2 SSO Profile Help

This profile configuration enables and configures the SAML 2 SSO profile.

SAML 2 SSO Profile Configuration

includeAttributeStatement: ✔

assertionLifetime: 300000

assertionProxyCount: 0

signResponses: always ▾
signAssertions: never ▾
signRequests: conditional ▾
encryptAssertions: always ▾
encryptNameIds: always ▾

Choose File No file chosen

Figure 3-14. *Gluu Server SAML relying party options*

Note   If you get tired of waiting five minutes for the Shibboleth IDP to reload its configuration, you can make the polling interval shorter by editing /opt/idp/ conf/service.xml. Change it to one minute for all configurations you want to speed up: configurationResourcePollingFrequency="PT1M". You can tail -f /opt/idp/logs/idp-process.log to see when the files get reloaded.

Once you click the Update button, you'll also have to "activate" the trust relationship. This gives you an extra step to review the configuration or a way to take an SP out of service without removing its configuration. Also, you'll need to wait five minutes for the Shibboleth IDP to reload the new XML configuration that was rendered by oxTrust. So assuming everything is configured correctly, when you navigate to the url https:// squid.gluu.info/protected/printHeaders.py, you should see a page that looks like Listing 3-8, which is slightly edited for brevity. Note that you can see the user claims (uid, givenName, sn, and displayName) and also the REMOTE_USER variable has been populated with the uid. The SP sets a session cookie so it knows not to authenticate this user until its local session expires. Congratulations! You set up your first SAML protected website!

Listing 3-8. Sample Output from printHeaders.py

```
AUTH_TYPE: shibboleth
CONTEXT_DOCUMENT_ROOT: /var/www/protected/
DOCUMENT_ROOT: /var/www/html
HTTPS: on
HTTP_ACCEPT:
text/html,application/xhtml+xml,application/xml;q=0.9,image/webp,*/*;q=0.8
HTTP_CACHE_CONTROL: max-age=0
HTTP_COOKIE:
_shibsession_64656661756c7468747470733a2f2f73717569642e676c75752e696e666f
2f73686962_626f6c657468=_e4359a17513cf53c447ab26455fe4e58
HTTP_HOST: squid.gluu.info
HTTP_REFERER:  https://albacore.gluu.info/idp/profile/SAML2/Redirect/SSO
REMOTE_ADDR: 192.168.88.1
REMOTE_USER: admin
REQUEST_METHOD: GET
REQUEST_SCHEME: https
SERVER_ADDR: 192.168.88.148
SERVER_ADMIN: webmaster@localhost
SERVER_NAME: squid.gluu.info
SERVER_PORT: 443
SERVER_PROTOCOL: HTTP/1.1
Shib_Application_ID: default
Shib_Authentication_Instant:   2016-08-19T19:27:31.356Z
Shib_Authentication_Method: urn:oasis:names:tc:SAML:2.0:ac:classes:Password
ProtectedTransport
Shib_AuthnContext_Class: urn:oasis:names:tc:SAML:2.0:ac:classes:PasswordPro
tectedTransport
Shib_Identity_Provider: https://albacore.gluu.info/idp/shibboleth
Shib_Session_ID:   _e4359a17513cf53c447ab26455fe4e58 Shib_Session_
Index:   _38903d1a68e40bbeab09ff376b49e414
displayName: Default Admin User
givenName: Admin
sn: User uid: admin
```

simpleSAMLphp Service Provider Example

simpleSAMLphp is one of the most popular platforms for SAML. Although simpleSAMLphp has both IDP and SP components, in this example (see Listing 3-9), we're just going to refer to the SP example and use the Gluu Server as our IDP. These instructions will be shown using Ubuntu 14.04, but similar processes exist for most popular Linux platforms.

Listing 3-9. SimpleSAMLphp Installation

```
# apt-get install php5
# apt-get install simplesamlphp
# apt-get install php5-mcrypt
# php5enmod mcrypt
# a2enconf simplesamlphp
# service apache2 restart
# grep adminpassword /var/lib/simplesamlphp/secrets.inc.php
```

Note   This is the default password! You can use this to log in to the simpleSAMLphp web interface.

```
https://<hostname>/simplesamlphp
```

The configuration is stored in /etc/SimpleSAMLphp. The libraries are installed in /usr/share/simplesamlphp. The Apache configuration looks like Listing 3-10.

Listing 3-10. Apache2 Configuration for simpleSAMLphp

```
Alias /simplesamlphp /usr/share/simplesamlphp/www
<Directory /usr/share/simplesamlphp/www/>
    Order allow,deny
    Allow from all
</Directory>
```

The first thing you want to do is edit /etc/simplesamplephp/config.php. Update the technicalcontact_name and technicalcontact_email to something that is appropriate for your organization. While you are testing, you may want to set the logging.level to DEBUG, but don't forget to change it back to WARNING or ERR when you move into production. Then, we'll need to specify the Gluu Server IDP as the default authentication source. Edit authsources and set the idp value (see Listing 3-11).

Listing 3-11. SimpleSAMLphp Sample Configuration

```
'idp' => 'https://albacore.gluu.info/idp/shibboleth',
'default-sp' => array(
                'saml:SP',
                'privatekey' => '/etc/certs/squid.key',
                'certificate' => '/etc/certs/squid.crt')
```

Next, we're going to have to add the metadata of our IDP in the requisite PHP format. You can do this in the SimpleSAMLphp web admin https:///simplesamlphp/admin/metadata-converter.php. You can copy the XML for your Gluu Server Shibboleth IDP from the URL https://<hostname>/idp/shibboleth and paste it into the form. If the conversion is successful, you should copy the content under the heading saml20-idp-remote and create a file /etc/simplesamlphp/metadata/saml20-idp-remote.php inside a php tag, like this:

```
<?php
{paste content in here}
 ?>
```

You're done with your simpleSAMLphp configuration, but now you need to configure the Gluu Server Shibboleth IDP to trust your SP. Download the metadata to your laptop and use the File method described above. You can download the SP metadata at https://<hostname>/simplesamlphp/module.php/saml/sp/metadata.php/default-sp, or you can copy it from the SimpleSAMLphp admin web interface in the federation section. Use the same configuration as detailed above for the Shibboleth SP. To test, the SimpleSAMLphp web interface has a test application under Authentication/Test configured authentication sources/default-sp. When you click on this link, it should send you to the Gluu Server IDP. After successful authentication, you should see a page like Figure 3-15.

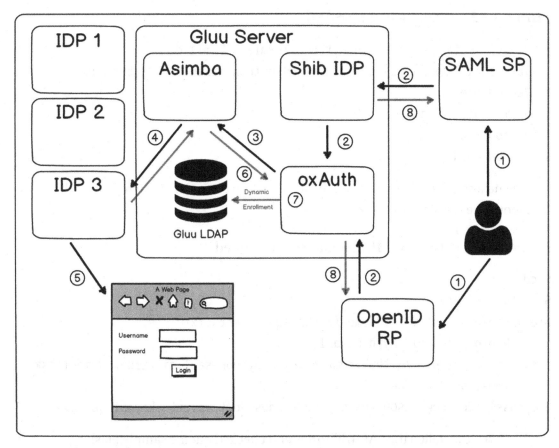

Figure 3-15. *Sample output from simpleSAMLphp test default-sp*

Python-SAML

The Python-SAML library, written by Sixto Pablo Martín García of OneLogin and others in the community. The code can be found in the Python package index at https:// pypi.python.org/pypi/python-saml. This is a really cool library, and it ships with a few sample applications.

In this example, we use the Flask application. Like many things SAML, it was a little harder to get it working than anticipated, especially compared with the Shibboleth SP and SimpleSAMLphp approaches. The first steps are to install the required packages, as shown in Listing 3-12.

Listing 3-12. Installing Python-SAML

```
# apt-get install python-pip python-libxml2 libxml2-dev \
  libxmlsec1 libxmlsec1-dev python-dev python-virtualenv subversion
# a2enmod proxy
# a2enmod proxy_http
# a2enmod rewrite
# a2enmod headers
```

The next steps involve setting up the local Python environment in my home directory (not root) (see Listing 3-13).

Listing 3-13. Python-SAML Installation Continued

```
$ cd ~
$ virtualenv env
$ env/bin/pip install -r demo-flask/requirements.txt
$ env/bin/pip install python-saml
$ svn export https://github.com/onelogin/python-saml.git/trunk/demo-flask
$ cd demo-flask/saml/certs
$ openssl req -new -x509 -days 3652 -nodes -out sp.crt -keyout sp.key
```

Now we've installed the SAML libraries and checked out the sample Flask application from GitHub. The next step is to configure the application to use our test IDP (in this sample, `albacore.gluu.info`). The first configuration file is called `settings.json`, and it's included in its entirety in Listing 3-14. The use of `strict=false`–not is something you'd want to do in production. The IDP certificate is truncated in Listing 3-14 for readability. It's worth noting that I acquired this certificate from the IDP metadata page (`https://<hostname>/idp/shibboleth`), but I removed all the spaces and line returns so that the certificate was transformed into one long string.

Listing 3-14. Python-SAML Configuration Settings

```
$ vi ~/demo-flask/saml/settings.json
{
"strict": false,
"debug": true,
"sp": {
    "entityId": "https://squid.gluu.info/python-saml-sp/metadata/",
```

```
    "assertionConsumerService": {
        "url": "https://squid.gluu.info/python-saml-sp/?acs",
        "binding": "urn:oasis:names:tc:SAML:2.0:bindings:HTTP-POST"
    },
    "singleLogoutService": {
        "url": "https://squid.gluu.info/python-saml-sp/?sls",
        "binding": "urn:oasis:names:tc:SAML:2.0:bindings:HTTP-Redirect"
    },
    "NameIDFormat": "urn:oasis:names:tc:SAML:2.0:nameid-format:transient"
},
"idp": {
    "entityId": "https://albacore.gluu.info/idp/shibboleth",
    "singleSignOnService": {
        "url": "https://albacore.gluu.info/idp/profile/SAML2/Redirect/SSO",
        "binding": "urn:oasis:names:tc:SAML:2.0:bindings:HTTP-Redirect"
    },
    "singleLogoutService": {
        "url": "https://albacore.gluu.info//idp/logout.jsp",
        "binding": "urn:oasis:names:tc:SAML:2.0:bindings:HTTP-Redirect"
    },
    "x509cert": "MIIDZjCCA....jC8Ec/aQ=="
}
}
```

Although the Flask app runs on port 8000, Apache2 is used to terminate SSL on port 443:

```
# vi /etc/apache2/sites-available/default-ssl.conf
```

Add the directives shown in Listing 3-15 and then restart Apache2.

Listing 3-15. Python-SAML Apache2 SSL Configuration

```
ProxyPreserveHost On
ProxyPass         /python-saml-sp/          http://127.0.0.1:8000/
ProxyPassReverse /python-saml-sp/          http://127.0.0.1:8000/
ProxyPass         /python-saml-sp/metadata/ http://127.0.0.1:8000/metadata/
ProxyPassReverse /python-saml-sp/metadata/ http://127.0.0.1:8000/metadata/
```

Added the directives shown in Listing 3-16, right above the final `</VirtualHost>` tag there.

Listing 3-16. Python-SAML Apache2 Default Configuration

```
# vi /etc/apache2/sites-available/000-default.conf

    ProxyPass        /attrs/ http://127.0.0.1:8000/attrs/
    ProxyPassReverse /attrs/ http://127.0.0.1:8000/attrs/

# service apache2 restart
```

Next, start the Flask server (not as root):

```
$ cd ~/demo-flask
$ ../env/bin/python index.py
```

Now, in your browser, navigate to view the metadata (note the trailing /): `https://squid.gluu.info/python-saml-sp/metadata/` and save the XML to your desktop (see Figure 3-16). Configure the Gluu Server by adding a trust relationship for the Flask website exactly as you configured for the Shibboleth SP and `SimpleSAMLphp`—sign responses and encrypt assertions. Also don't forget to release the TransientID. After waiting for the IDP to load the new configuration, click on the "Login and Access to attrs Page" link.

Figure 3-16. *python-saml Flask SAML application login page*

At this point, instead of displaying the expected login page, you should see an error page from the Shibboleth IDP. This happens a lot in SAML. In this next section, we describe our debugging procedure—being able to debug is essential to working with SAML. You need to look at the request and response, without which, you may never figure out what's wrong.

First we turned up the logging on the IDP to TRACE by editing /opt/idp/conf/logging.conf:

```
<root level="TRACE">
    <appender-ref ref="IDP_PROCESS"/>
</root>
```

Then we stared for a while at the request sent by the python-saml library, which can be viewed in the /opt/idp/idp-process.log. We compared the request to a request from the Shibboleth SP, which was working well. What we noticed was that there was this little extra piece of XML in the request from python-saml (see Listing 3-17).

Listing 3-17. Python-SAML Debug Delta

```
<samlp:RequestedAuthnContext Comparison="exact">
<saml:AuthnContextClassRef>
urn:oasis:names:tc:SAML:2.0:ac:classes:PasswordProtectedTransport
</saml:AuthnContextClassRef>
</samlp:RequestedAuthnContext>
```

We searched the Internet for AuthnContextClassRef python-saml and saw that there was an interesting line of code that looked like this in the authn_request.py module:

```
if 'requestedAuthnContext' in security.keys() and security['requestedAuthnC
ontext'] is not False:
```

We didn't see any documentation for the requestedAuthnContext property, but I added it to the advanced_settings.json file, included in Listing 3-18.

Listing 3-18. Adding a Fix for Python-SAML Settings

```
$ vi demo-flask/saml/advanced_settings.json
{
"security": {
    "requestedAuthnContext": false,
    "nameIdEncrypted": false,
    "authnRequestsSigned": false,
    "logoutRequestSigned": false,
    "logoutResponseSigned": false,
    "signMetadata": false,
    "wantMessagesSigned": false,
    "wantAssertionsSigned": true,
    "wantNameId" : false,
    "wantNameIdEncrypted": false,
    "wantAssertionsEncrypted": true,
    "signatureAlgorithm": "http://www.w3.org/2000/09/xmldsig#rsa-sha1"
},
"contactPerson": {
    "technical": {
        "givenName": "technical_name",
        "emailAddress": "technical@example.com"
    },
    "support": {
        "givenName": "support_name",
        "emailAddress": "support@example.com"
    }
},
"organization": {
    "en-US": {
        "name": "sp_test",
        "displayname": "SP test",
        "url": "http://sp.example.com"
    }
}
}
```

And voilà, it worked! At least, we got the login page of the Shibboleth IDP. After authenticating as the admin user, we were re-directed to the attrs page, as pictured in Figure 3-17.

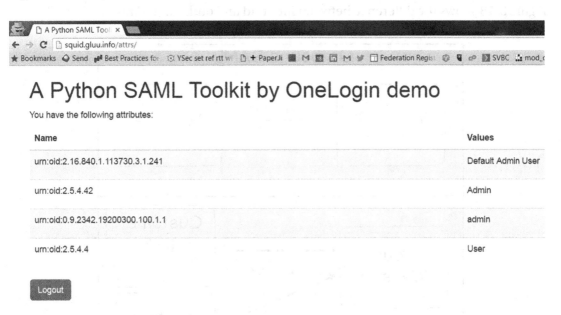

Figure 3-17. Sample output from the python-saml Flask demo app attrs page

Things don't always go as planned with SAML. Sometimes, the only way to figure out what is wrong is to be patient, read the XML requests and responses, read the log messages, use browser-based tools, tail -f logs, and to do all the other stuff that developers and system administrators do when the unexpected happens.

Inbound SAML

When you're working with SAML, it may be helpful to consider if the identity information is flowing into or out of your organization. Outbound SAML is more common. If your organization is using a SaaS service, that is outbound—your organization manages the identity data and credentials of the person, who is accessing a third-party service. If you are accepting credentials from a partner or customer's IDP—that is inbound.

If you are the SaaS provider, finding a solution for inbound SAML is critical. Some large customers will not do business with you otherwise. To drive down the cost of inbound SAML, you need to normalize the process of onboarding new customers. Figure 3-18 shows the difference between inbound and outbound SAML.

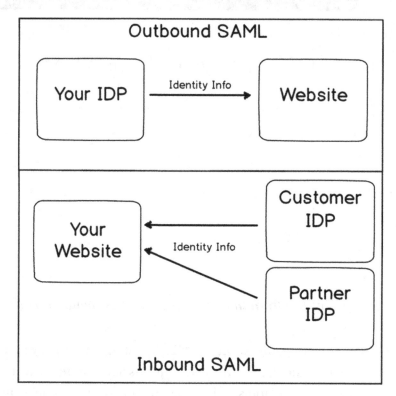

Figure 3-18. *Inbound vs. Outbound SAML*

One of the challenges with inbound SAML is that if you are a SaaS provider, your customer will say "send your metadata". They are expecting to get metadata for one SAML SP—not a whole bunch of them. But your "website" might actually consist of many websites, working together. A SAML proxy can help solve this problem. A proxy has both SP and IDP interfaces. Your customers use the one SP interface, while your internal websites use the IDP interface.

Another challenge with inbound SAML is how to provide a discovery service to solve the WAYF challenge—where are you from. In Step 1, we need to direct the person to a SAML IDP, but as the person has not been authenticated, we don't know to which IDP to send them! The easiest solution to this problem is to simply present the person with a list of available IDPs on a web page, and let the person select the right one. This solution works well if the IDPs are all public. For example, on the higher education website for Educause, this is exactly what's done—which universities are members of Educause is not a secret. However, if the list of IDPs is your company's customer list, you might not want to publish it in so public a manner, so you'll need another strategy.

There are several strategies that SaaS providers should perhaps consider. The first is to use the DNS name of the website to provide a hint to the person. For example, if we have a customer named Acme, and the landing page for this customer is `https://acme.saas.com`, we can figure out that any person visiting this site should be directed to Acme's IDP. A similar strategy is to use the URL path. For example, Acme could also use the URL `https://www.saas.com/acme`. Another strategy is to present a form and ask the person to enter some information about themselves, like their email address. Then look up this information in a database and redirect to the corresponding IDP. It would be helpful in this situation to also write a persistent cookie, so that when the person returns, you can remember the previous decision, unless they are using a new browser or erased all their cookies.

Inbound SAML is a challenging requirement. There are many SAML IDP implementations your partners may use. In a worst case scenario, your partner may enlist your help configuring a SAML IDP you have never encountered. This process can be time consuming. It's a good idea to normalize the process for onboarding IDPs, outlining all the legal and technical requirements, and implementing a standard testing process to make sure the connection is functioning properly.

Another issue you may have to consider is attribute mapping. What if the IDP releases attributes other than you are expecting, and you need to map these attributes to different internal attributes? Or another possibility is that the format of the value of the attribute doesn't meet your requirements. It may be handy to have some capability to map the attributes and transform the values.

The Gluu Server leverages a component called Passport-js to manage all kinds of inbound identity, including SAML, but also social login and OpenID Connect. Gluu's recommended solution for inbound SAML adds another level of control into the solution. oxAuth is used to just-in-time create a record in the Gluu LDAP server for a person authenticated at an external IDP, using the attributes provided by the source IDP. An overview of this process is provided in Figure 3-19.

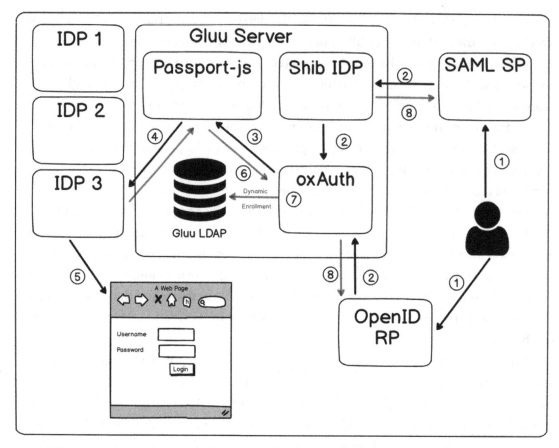

Figure 3-19. *Overview of Gluu Server inbound SAML process*

Figure 3-20 provides a more detailed sequence diagram for inbound SAML using the Gluu Server. We're jumping ahead a little here, because the flow described in this section assumes the initial client is OpenID Connect. This is perfectly feasible—an organization may use OpenID Connect internally, but still have customers who have SAML IDPs. You can read about OAuth and OpenID Connect in the following chapters. But just go with it for now! Let's go over each of the components and the authentication flow:

- The OpenID Connect client redirects the browser to the OpenID Connect Provider authorization endpoint (i.e., oxAuth), using a special base-64 encoded JSON object as the `state` parameter. This solves the discovery (WAYF) challenge, so Passport-js knows where to send the unauthenticated browser session. For example, the state would look like this:

  `{"salt":"<SALTVALUE>",provider":"<idp_name>"}(base64-encoded)`

- If a session for the user doesn't exist yet, the browser is redirected to its oxAuth component for authentication, triggering the SAML Passport Authenticator script. The script either retrieves the target IDP's ID from the `state` parameter or just presents an IDP selection page to the person.

- The script arranges a call to the Gluu Passport-js server requesting a JWT token (used to control access to the Passport APIs) .

- Passport-js generates a JWT token and returns it back to oxAuth.

- The oxAuth script constructs a URL, which Passport-js will need in order the delegate the authentication request to the selected IDP.

- The script makes a request to Passport-js, including the JWT token, and initiates the authentication flow.

- The Passport-js server redirects the person's browser to the specified external SAML IDP.

- After successful authentication, the person's browser is redirected back to Passport-js, and their personal data (i.e., attributes) are passed within the SAML response to the Passport-js callback endpoint.

- Passport-js redirects the user back to the oxAuth passport's custom interception script, submitting the user's attributes and access token to its `passportpostlogin.xhtml` page.

- The interception script verifies if an account exists in Gluu's LDAP server. If the account exists, then an oxAuth SSO session is created. If some of their attributes are changed, oxAuth updates the person's entry in LDAP.

- If an account for the person does not exist, the oxAuth interception script adds an entry in the Gluu LDAP server, and then creates the SSO session.

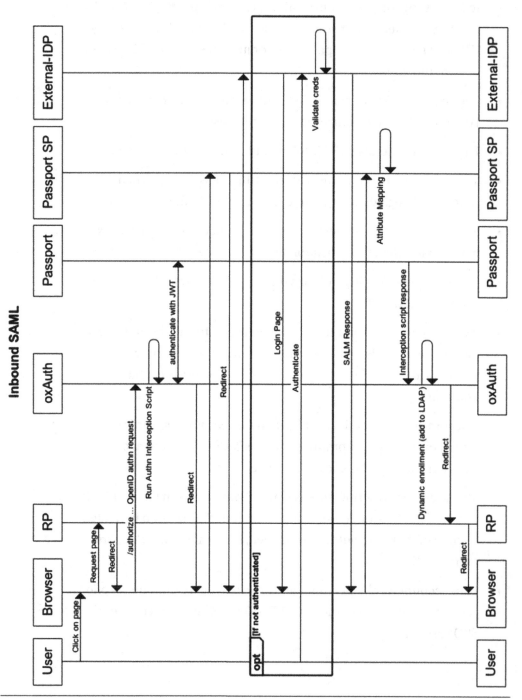

Figure 3-20. Gluu Server inbound SAML sequence diagram

This solution may seem complex, but it is also modular. If you don't need inbound identity, don't install Passport-js. Likewise, if you don't need outbound SAML, you don't install the Shibboleth IDP.

oxAuth is the place where business logic is defined for authentication, and inbound SAML is just one more possible way a person's session might be validated. One of the great aspects of this solution is that it makes it possible for developers to use OpenID Connect internally and still leverage a partner's SAML IDP.

Conclusion

Surely, much more can be said, many more examples can be presented, and many corner cases were left unexposed. But hopefully you'll be ready to at least face the world of SAML with a little more confidence than when you started this chapter! The best way to learn is by doing. Try some of the examples and just keep at it. Simplify and then incrementally add more complexity. In the end, SAML usually works!

CHAPTER 4

OAuth

OAuth 2.0 (or simply as "OAuth" because OAuth 1.0 is now irrelevant) defines a mechanism for using bearer tokens to make authorized HTTP requests. Simple possession of a bearer token enables access. For example, a long time ago in New York City, if you had a "subway token," you inserted it into the turnstile and entered the subway station. No questions asked—you have the token, you get in. Bearer tokens are also called "access tokens".

Although OAuth is known primarily as a technology for consumer applications, its popularity is expanding in enterprise IAM. A common misperception is that OAuth is a protocol. More accurately, it is a framework for authorization—a set of foundational patterns and vocabulary. OAuth is not an authentication protocol. If this were true, OAuth would need to provide specific details, like how messages are sent, the exact data structure of those messages, and how message integrity is assured. Vittorio Bertocci made an apt analogy in one of his Microsoft blogs for Microsoft[1]:

> *OAuth 2.0 as a building block for implementing a sign-in flow is not only perfectly possible, but quite handy too: a LOT of web applications take advantage of that, and it works great. But that does NOT mean that OAuth is an authentication protocol, with all the affordances you've come to expect from one, as much as using chocolate to make fudge does not make (chocolate == fudge) true.*

---

[1]https://blogs.msdn.microsoft.com/vbertocci/2013/01/02/oauth-2-0-and-sign-in/

© Michael Schwartz, Maciej Machulak 2018
M. Schwartz and M. Machulak, *Securing the Perimeter*, https://doi.org/10.1007/978-1-4842-2601-8_4

Chapter 5 focuses on a protocol that uses OAuth to define a sign in flow—OpenID Connect. Chapter 8 focuses on another OAuth protocol used for API access Management—UMA. But in this chapter, we introduce some of the common OAuth terminology and ideas that to give you some background for what's to come.

Scopes

Scopes are used to specify the extent of access for a token. Think of an airplane boarding pass. Airlines scan your boarding pass before they let you enter the plane. If the agent sees a green light, they let you pass—real-world token validation! On some airlines, not all boarding passes are the same. You might prefer a boarding pass that entitles you to sit in first class. Or your boarding pass may qualify you for a specific seat assignment. You can think of scopes as these additional constraints. For example, a resource server may offer many APIs. The authorization server may use scopes to differentiate which APIs you can access. Even within an API, certain features may not be available unless you have a token with the right scope.

Scopes may be any string value, but it's a common practice to use a URI for scopes. The advantage of this practice is that scopes will be less likely to collide. For example, many developers in an organization may want to use a scope called "write". If each developer uses a different URI namespace for their "write" scope, they will be unique. Google publishes a list of all their APIs and which scopes are required in order to call them. A small excerpt is shown in Figure 4-1.

Genomics API, v1

Scope	Description
https://www.googleapis.com/auth/bigquery	View and manage your data in Google BigQuery
https://www.googleapis.com/auth/cloud-platform	View and manage your data across Google Cloud Platform services
https://www.googleapis.com/auth/devstorage.read_write	Manage your data in Google Cloud Storage
https://www.googleapis.com/auth/genomics	View and manage Genomics data
https://www.googleapis.com/auth/genomics.readonly	View Genomics data

Genomics API, v1beta2

Scope	Description
https://www.googleapis.com/auth/bigquery	View and manage your data in Google BigQuery
https://www.googleapis.com/auth/cloud-platform	View and manage your data across Google Cloud Platform services
https://www.googleapis.com/auth/devstorage.read_write	Manage your data in Google Cloud Storage
https://www.googleapis.com/auth/genomics	View and manage Genomics data
https://www.googleapis.com/auth/genomics.readonly	View Genomics data

Gmail API, v1

Google Cloud DNS API, v1

DoubleClick Search API, v2

Drive API, v3

Firebase Rules API, v1

Fitness, v1

Fusion Tables API, v2

Google Play Game Services API, v1

Google Play Game Services Publishing API, v1configuration

Google Play Game Services Management API, v1management

Genomics API, v1

Genomics API, v1beta2

Gmail API, v1

Google Sign-In

Groups Migration API, v1

Groups Settings API, v1

Google Identity and Access Management API, v1

Google Cloud Natural Language API, v1beta1

Enterprise License Manager API, v1

Google Cloud Logging API, v2beta1

Google Mirror API, v1

Figure 4-1. *Some Google OAuth scopes*

According to Figure 4-1, if you want to call a Google API that allows you to "view and manage your data in Google BigQuery," you'll need a token with the scope `https://www.googleapis.com/auth/bigquery`. Using this approach, Google uses scopes to manage which clients can access which features of their service. Google follows the convention of using URIs for scope values. You may also notice that the APIs are versioned. If an API is updated, new features may be introduced, which may require different scopes. Client developers rely on these scopes and need to know about them before they write their code.

OAuth Roles

You'll sometimes hear OAuth referred to as "three-legged". Those legs are the "client," "resource server," and "authorization server". The client is the software (website or mobile application) that is either requesting a protected resource or connected to a person requesting a protected web resource. The resource server is the software that has web content that needs protecting, API endpoints for example. The authorization server is the software that issues tokens to a client. Another way to think about OAuth is that the resource server is the policy enforcement point (PEP), and the authorization server is the policy decision point (PDP). Figure 4-2 shows the three legs, as well as the people who interact with them.

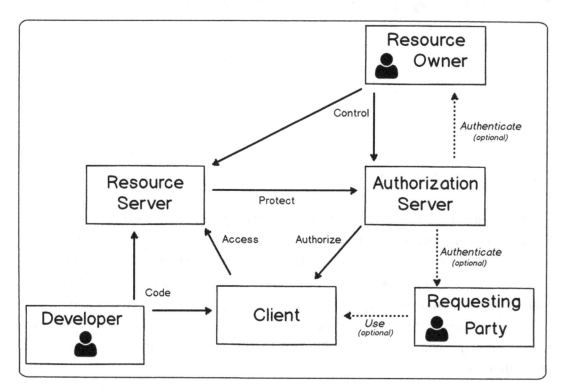

Figure 4-2. *OAuth roles*

Authorization Server

The authorization server is the most complex component of an OAuth infrastructure. For some deployments, the authorization server and the resource server may be one software process. For larger deployments, a centralized, single-purpose authorization server may issue tokens to control access to a distributed network of resource servers.

The authorization server holds client credentials—for example, an API key and secret for each client. Client credentials are important, because they enable an organization to provision specific permissions for a client. Don't confuse client credentials with a person's credentials (i.e., username and password). Person authentication is a very different requirement from client authentication. People are messy analog carbon-based things. Clients are software. There are fewer options to authenticate clients than people.

In some flows, the authorization server may also need to authenticate a person, who then directly authorizes a client. For example, if you've used Google login from a third-party website, after authenticating (unless you are already logged into Google) you are presented with a dialog asking you to authorize this client to call an API that will release information about you, as shown in Figure 4-3.

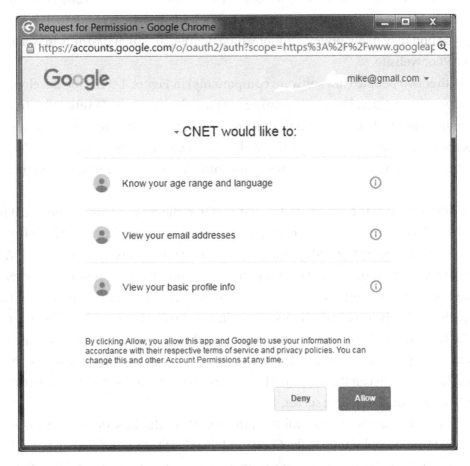

Figure 4-3. *GA sample Google authorization dialog*

A quick aside—one important thing to note is that in Figure 4-3, you can see the URL of the authorization server—https://accounts.google.com. This is especially important when you are entering your credentials. You should never share your password with a third-party website, and you should always make sure that the certificates are valid. Most modern browsers will help you out here. If the little lock icon in the address bar is not green, be concerned. Even if it is green, you may not be safe—check the hostname and make sure it's one that you trust (easier said than done, for sure...) This pattern should remind you of SAML, where you are redirected to the IDP to enter your credentials. An OAuth based flow adds an extra step for authorization.

Getting back to OAuth roles, the resource owner is the person who is responsible for making the authorization decision. When you use Google login at a third-party site, you are the resource owner—you control access to your information. In an enterprise IAM setting, the resource owner is the organization that manages the RS and AS. For example, an organization may make policies about which people, or which partners may access a certain API or website.

The other two people (not software components) in Figure 4-2 are the developer and the requesting party. Developers are active participants in the OAuth infrastructure because they obtain client credentials that are used in their software. The requesting party is the person who is using a software client to access a protected resource. The requesting party is optional. A machine-to-machine API does not require a requesting party.

The primary job of the authorization server is to evaluate policies that enable it to issue tokens. To accomplish this, clients and resource servers interact with APIs (or endpoints) published by the authorization server. Two endpoints defined by the OAuth RFC are the authorization and token endpoints. The authorization endpoint is where a client sends a person using a browser to interact with an authorization server. The token endpoint is used only by OAuth clients to obtain or refresh a bearer token. For example, using the Google sign-in flow again as an example, the first redirect to the authorization endpoint displays a dialog, such as the one shown in Figure 4-3. If you authorize the request, the client will call the token endpoint next to obtain an access token, with which it can call an API on a resource server.

The authorization server may publish other OAuth endpoints, depending on what profiles of OAuth it implements. Like LDAP and SAML, OAuth is defined by several related standards. An authorization server may implement some optional interfaces for client registration, token introspection (a way to obtain information about a particular token) or discovery information (similar to SAML metadata).

Resource Server

The resource server, acting as the policy enforcement point, plays a critical role in the security of the OAuth infrastructure. Its job is to make sure a valid token is present— that the token is not expired and that it has been authorized for the correct scopes. The resource server will also need to understand how to use the various types of tokens. In some cases, the resource server must itself call APIs of the authorization server—to validate a token, for example.

The resource server will want to minimize external calls and the processing time to decrypt tokens. For this reason, many resource server implementations cache tokens to expedite subsequent authorization for the same token value.

The developer who writes a resource server will have to coordinate with the administrators of the authorization server regarding what policies are in place to issue tokens for certain scopes. Sometimes the same group controls both the authorization server and resource servers. In other cases, the authorization server might be in control of the central access management team. This is the reason that Google publishes the scopes that are required to call its APIs, as shown in Figure 4-1.

The resource server will have to decide which policies to delegate to the authorization server. "The user has approved access" is the most common policy for consumer OAuth applications. But using UMA, a protocol that builds on OAuth (the topic of Chapter 8), you can map scopes to enterprise access policies.

Centralized policy management is a useful approach but it's not a silver bullet. In general, centralized policy management works well for coarse-grain authorization, but not for fine-grain authorization. In a web application, what to display on a certain page is normally controlled by "fine-grained" permissions. Coarse-grained policies are shared across more than one application. For example, what type of authentication is required, which internal roles can access which types of applications, which software clients to trust—implementing these policies in every application would lead to code duplication.

Client

An OAuth client is the software that calls the protected resource. It is frequently connected to a person—the requesting party. The client obtains a token from the authorization server and presents it to the resource server. In many cases, it's the job of the client developer to obtain client credentials at the authorization server and to know what scopes are needed to access the resource server. The client may need to process a redirect to enable the requesting party to interact with the authorization server. The client may also need to handle errors that are returned by either the authorization server or the resource server.

Clients may be a website or native application. In some cases, the client may even be a JavaScript application that exists entirely in the person's browser. It's important to remember that the client is not the same as the browser. The browser is software that the requesting party uses to access the Internet. SAML jargon "user agent" applies here too. The client is software that is between the browser and the protected resource.

In machine-to-machine transactions, where there is no requesting party, the policies must apply only to information about the client and the context of the transaction. For example, is this client (authenticated with a client_id and secret), calling from this network, during this time of day, authorized to obtain a token for certain scopes? A certain group of clients may be associated with a certain partner or category of applications—such information about the client is called a "client claim" and is different from user claims about the requesting party.

Tokens

A token is an abstraction that represents permission by the authorization server to do something. An access token is a short-lived token that is obtained by the client. A refresh token is a long-lived token that is presented by the client to the authorization server in exchange for a new access token. "Short-lived" means one hour or less, but actual times may vary depending on the policy of the authorization server. One to five minutes are common lengths for the lifetime of an access token.

The authorization server decides what type of token to return. Each access token type definition specifies the additional attributes (if any) sent to the client along with the access token. The client should not use a token if it does not understand the token type. Each token has a different security profile and is useful for different use cases. Long strings are frequently used as bearer tokens. OAuth provides a mechanism where additional token types can be registered as extensions. JSON Web Tokens (JWTs)—pronounced "jots"—are popular, and are sometimes used as the bearer token string. There is also an extension for something called "MAC" tokens. These are tokens that enable the client to protect the access token value and are useful for non-secure communication channels. However, due to the widespread use of TLS for OAuth, MAC tokens aren't used that much in enterprise deployments, so we'll skip discussion of these tokens.

Bearer Tokens

RFC 6570, "URI Template," describes bearer token usage in OAuth. A bearer token is any data structure that gives the possessor rights to do something—without requiring the owner of the token to verify control of a cryptographic key. A bearer token can be a string of sufficient entropy to make guessing unlikely.

It can also be an XML or JSON document encoded appropriately. OAuth relies heavily on bearer tokens, but SAML IDPs also commonly use them—i.e., signed SAML assertions. It is imperative to the security of any access management infrastructure based on bearer tokens to prevent an attacker from gaining possession of the token during transmission, in memory, or on the disk. If this happens, game over! The resource server has no way to distinguish the attacker from the authorized token owner!

Listing 4-1 is a simple example of an OAuth bearer token returned from an authorization server.

Listing 4-1. OAuth Token Endpoint Response

```
HTTP/1.1 200 OK
Content-Type: application/json;charset=UTF-8
Cache-Control: no-store
Pragma: no-cache
{
"access_token": "41902768-ae84-4a1c-8e62-566a8605b90f",
"token_type": "Bearer",
"expires_in": 3600,
"refresh_token": "d1d50489-98ac-4d21-9ddb-2358caf835c3"
}
```

The most common way for a client to send a bearer token to the resource server is to include the token in the Authorization header field, although RFC 6570 also defines mechanisms to send the access token as an HTML form encoded body parameter or in the URI (which is a bad idea). Using the header, the bearer token would look like this:

```
Authorization: Bearer 41902768-ae84-4a1c-8e62-566a8605b90f
```

In simple OAuth implementations, where the resource server and authorization server are the same, the resource server might make a query to the local database to retrieve information about a bearer token—for example, when does it expire or for what scopes was it authorized? If the authorization server is remote, RFC 7662 defines an API for "token introspection". This provides a mechanism for the resource server to retrieve a JSON object from the authorization server that describes the token. Listing 4-2 is an example from RFC 7662 of a response to the introspection API.

Listing 4-2. Sample OAuth Token Introspsection Response

```
HTTP/1.1 200 OK
Content-Type: application/json

{
 "active": true,
 "client_id": "l238j323ds-23ij4",
 "username": "jdoe",
 "scope": "read write dolphin",
 "sub": "Z5O3upPC88QrAjx00dis",
 "aud": "https://protected.example.net/resource",
 "iss": "https://server.example.com/",
 "exp": 1419356238,
 "iat": 1419350238,
 "extension_field": "twenty-seven"
}
```

JSON Web Token (JWT)

Defined in RFC 7519, the JWT token type is essentially a compact syntax to send an optionally signed and encrypted JSON object. It's surprisingly compact on the wire—you may even be able to send it as a query parameter. The token can contain user claims and can eliminate the need for token introspection. JWT tokens are also particularly advantageous in stateless web architectures. Another application for JWT is where cookies can't be used, for example, due to restrictions on writing third-party cookies.

JSON Web Tokens consist of three sections, separated by two periods:

`Header.Payload.Signature`

The header describes the cryptographic algorithms used for signing and encryption, for example: `{"alg": "RS256"}`. If you want to know the meaning of "RS256," you need to check RFC 7518, which describes JSON web algorithms. If you don't want to use any encryption or signing in your JWT, you can use {"alg":"none"}. In this case, there would be no text after the second period—you'd just have a header and payload. The header may also be used to send unencrypted claims. Note that the value of any substantive unencrypted claims should be verified against the signed JSON payload.

The JSON payload portion of the token may have three types of claims: reserved, public, and private. The reserved claims are the ones defined in the OAuth specifications, such as iss (issuer), exp (expiration time), sub (subject), and aud (audience). Public claims are registered at the IANA JSON Web Token Registry or are collision-resistant URIs. Private claims are ad hoc claims agreed upon by the organizations using them.

Validation of the signature is too complex for treatment here. The token can be encrypted, signed, signed and encrypted, or encrypted and signed. If encrypted, the client would have to previously register its public key with the authorization server. For signing, public keys of the authorization server are frequently provided on a URL for download. OAuth supports many different signing and encryption algorithms. As mentioned, check RFC 7518 for a full list. Then, check to make sure these are supported on the authorization server.

Proof-of-Possession Tokens

A proof-of-possession token, also called a holder-of-key (HoK) token, requires control of a cryptographic key to provide additional evidence that the presenter of the token is the party to whom the token was issued. This approach mitigates the risk of stolen tokens. RFC 7800 introduces how to declare in a JWT that the presenter of the JWT possesses a particular proof-of-possession private key and how the recipient can cryptographically confirm this. Thus, a JWT can be either a bearer token or a proof-of-possession token.

Token Binding

Token binding is an advanced topic that is still under development, and whose future is not 100% certain, as adoption by websites and browsers has been slow. The Google team has even discussed the possibility of dropping support for it, although hopefully they'll keep the feature. The idea is for the browser to generate a public key, private key, and an identifier (Token Binding Key) for TLS connections to a web server. These keys and identifiers are long-lived. When a connection is made between the browser and website, the identifier can be remembered at the website. When issuing a security token (e.g., an

HTTP cookie or an OAuth token) to a client, the server can include the Token Binding ID in the token, thus cryptographically binding the token to TLS connections between that client and server, as well as inoculating the token against abuse (re-use, attempted impersonation, etc.) by attackers. This would protect the token from man-in-the-middle, token export, and replay attacks.

In a typical OAuth session, there are several TLS connections: between the browser and AS, between the browser and RS, between the client and AS, and even between the RS and AS. There are several opportunities to use token binding to improve security. The initial work addresses how to protect OAuth access tokens and refresh tokens for TLS connections between the client and AS.

Token binding could be a useful tool to prevent man-in-the-middle attacks, and its use has been proposed for banking and financial services profiles. An alternative to token binding is mutual TLS, for which another OAuth draft is under development.

Registration

The authorization server needs to know information about each client before it can issue the client a token. This is similar to SAML, where the IDP needs to configure trust for each SP. What is new in OAuth is a standardized option for self-service registration. In SAML, the IDP administrator generally imports the SP's metadata or configures information about the SP. This is usually a manual process, although sometimes a website may create a proprietary process for self-provisioning. OAuth registration defines standards for client provisioning. During registration, the client is issued a client identifier. At a minimum, the client must tell the AS the URIs where it is okay to send users after the AS has finished its interaction—the redirect_uris. This is important because the AS should never redirect a person's browser to a URI that has not been previously registered. If the redirect_uri is a web address, it must always use the https scheme, and the AS must validate the TLS certificate or certificate keychain. Frequently, the authorization collects other information about the client such as a name, an icon, a URL of the home page, a link to the privacy policy, and a brief description of the application. The client may also register an asymmetric client secret. Client registration is also an appropriate time for the client to notify the AS about its preferences. What types of cryptographic algorithms are preferred? What scopes are requested? What are the default user authentication mechanisms desired? All this information may be provided during registration.

Although the API and vocabulary for registration can align to OAuth standards, the business process may still vary. The developer may need to complete a form, sign a legal agreement, or provide various pieces of information about their organization. Sometimes, the client credentials are automatically created and available for use. For example, the OpenID Connect profile of OAuth defines an API that enables a client developer to automatically register. Figure 4-4 shows Google's very minimal client registration page

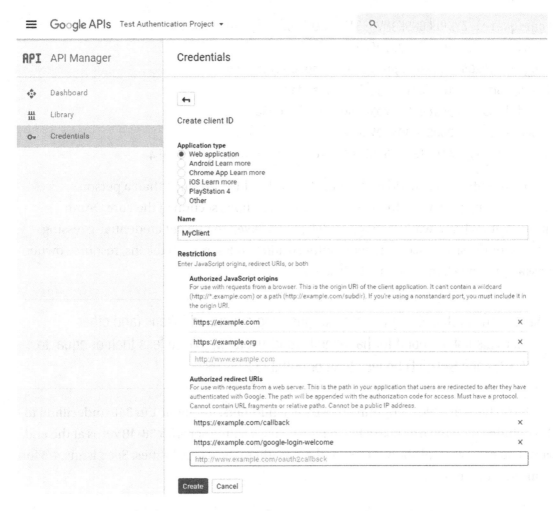

Figure 4-4. *Google client registration form*

RFC 7591 defines common conventions around dynamic client registration, including client metadata fields and details about the client registration endpoint. Also discussed is registration with software statements.

It is required that the AS return the client_id in the registration response (see Listing 4-3). A client_secret is also frequently returned. Aaron Parecki lists some common OAuth client_ids on his informative site, `http://oauth.com`.

Listing 4-3. Sample client_id Values from Popular Consumer IDPs

```
Foursquare: ZYDPLLBWSK3MVQJSIYHB1OR2JXCYOX2C5UJ2QAR2MAAIT5Q
Github: 6779ef20e75817b79602
Google: 292085223830.apps.googleusercontent.com
Instagram: f2a1ed52710d4533bde25be6da03b6e3
SoundCloud: 269d98e4922fb3895e9ae2108cbb5064
Windows Live: 00000000400ECB04
Gluu: @!AA77.E41E.1889.6F5E!0001!09FB.4FBB!0008!3CDC.3AF4
```

The combined client_id and client_secret should be stronger than a person's username and password. In the security considerations section of the core OAuth authorization framework section, guidelines are given to prevent credential-guessing attacks for the size of access tokens, authorization codes, refresh tokens, resource owner passwords, and client credentials. It states:

Note   The probability of an attacker guessing generated tokens (and other credentials not intended for handling by end-users) MUST be less than or equal to 2^{-128} and SHOULD be less than or equal to 2^{-160}.

If you have trouble computing those huge numbers, it's about 1 in 340 undecillion to 1.5 quindecillion (give or take a few billion). That's a number with 38-48 zeros at the end. How you can accomplish this is beyond my mathematical capabilities. See Listing 4-3 for some good examples.

Grants

The process or method by which a client obtains an access token is called an authorization grant. The grant represents a permission for the client to access an API endpoint. Each type of authorization grant has a different flow with its own security characteristics. Following is a description of the different grants, and when their use is appropriate. Figure 4-5 presents a flowchart to help explain when you use each grant type.

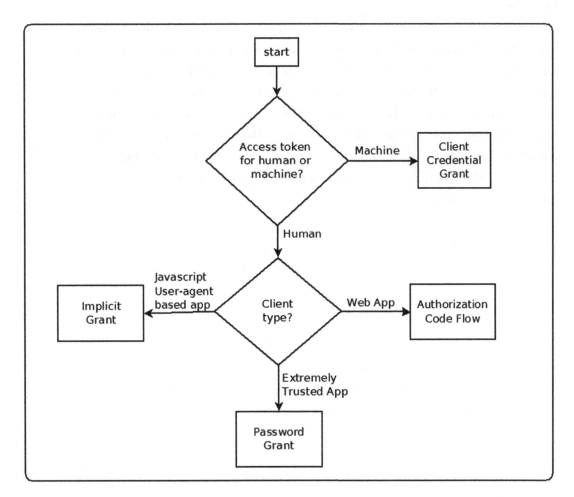

Figure 4-5. *Grant type flowchart*

Authorization Code Grant

This flow, for web-based client applications, uses a "code" (a guess resistant string) to represent a person's delegation to the client. The code is returned to the person's browser and is forwarded to the client, who exchanges it (with client credentials) for a token or tokens. The code can only be used once, which reduces the risk of it leaking. Figure 4-6 provides a sequence diagram for a common use case for the authorization code grant—how it can be used as the basis for a login flow.

Like SAML, this grant uses browser redirects to enable a person to interact with a central security server. In Figure 4-6, the login form and the authorization form might confuse you—what's the difference? The login form is where the person enters their username and password or uses another authentication technology (e.g., token or biometric). The person uses the authorization form to approve some action. Figure 4-3 shows an authorization where the person authorizes the release of information to a third party. Before enabling you to authorize, the AS may need to authenticate who you are, then it can enable you to authorize something.

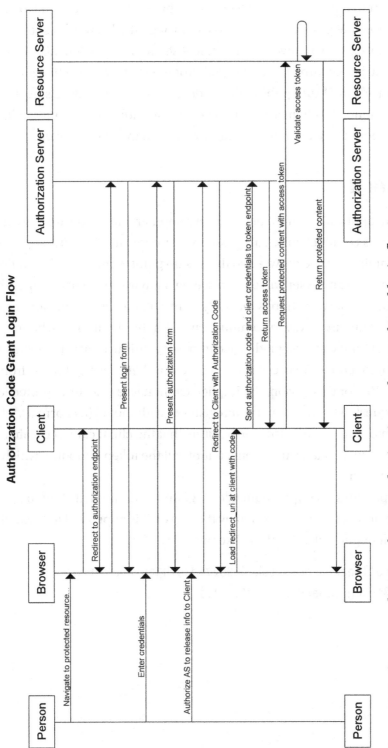

Figure 4-6. *Sequence diagram for an authorization code grant based login flow*

It's important that the code be protected and that it's sufficiently long to prevent guessing. However, because the code is passed through the browser, it's still susceptible to interception by existing malware. If additional security is needed, there is an extra security step that can be implemented called Proof Key for Code Exchange (PKCE, pronounced "pixy") by OAuth public clients, described in RFC 7636. Using this mitigation technique, the client adds a nonce to the authorization request. If the code is intercepted, without this extra nonce, it cannot be exchanged for a token.

Implicit Grant

JavaScript client applications have become very popular and powerful. Sometimes these applications act as OAuth clients. This presents an interesting security challenge because the client is contained in the browser, so there is no point using an authorization code to hide the token—the browser will end up seeing it anyway when it executes the JavaScript! Another consideration is that only front-channel communication can be used—the AS has no direct way to communicate with the client (back-channel).

The Implicit Grant was designed to accommodate this use case. It enables a JavaScript client to request an access token without a client secret, directly from the authorization URI. For this reason, the Implicit Grant has less security protection. The redirect_uri requested by the client is preregistered with the AS (as normal), which is the main security mechanism. It's also worth noting that the client cannot obtain a refresh token using this flow (because the client cannot call the token endpoint, which requires client authentication).

Figure 4-7 provides a sample sequence diagram for an Implicit Grant based login flow. When the access token is returned by the server, it is appended to the redirect_uri as a fragment. It might look something like this:

```
GET /client-callback#access_token=8027ad39-9316-49d5-9b3b-
10cce3e9b02d&token_type=Bearer HTTP/1.1
```

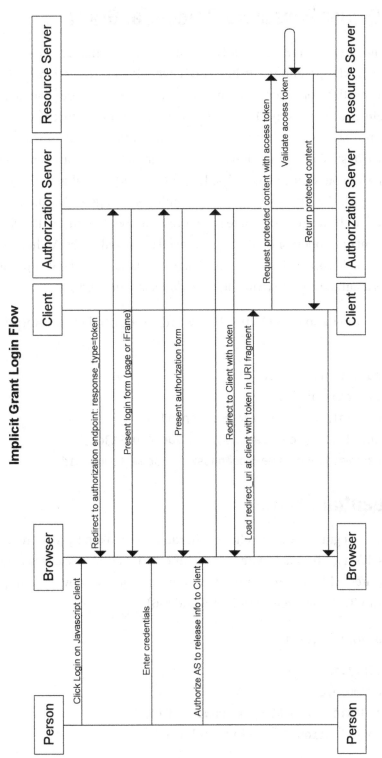

Figure 4-7. Sequence diagram for an implicit grant-based login flow

Resource Owner Password Credential Grant

Can't you just validate username/password credentials at the authorization server, like you can with an LDAP BIND operation? The Resource Owner Password Credential Grant lets a client do just that, posting both client credentials and the person's credentials at the token endpoint to obtain an access token. One disadvantage of this grant is that all communication is performed on the back channel by the client, so the authorization server will not be able to write any cookie or session information in the browser (defeating many single sign-on implementations). Of course, the biggest disadvantage of this flow is that the client sees the person's password. This flow should be vehemently discouraged—it is the OAuth anti-pattern. It should only be used where there is a supreme amount of trust in the client. And even then, the client developers should be encouraged to use either the Authorization Code Flow (for web or mobile applications) or implicit flow (for JavaScript client applications). Listing 4-4 shows a sample request (with client credentials sent as Basic).

Listing 4-4. Sample Resource Owner Password Credential Grant Request

```
POST /token
  Host: trusted_client.example.local
  Accept: application/json
  Content-type: application/x-www-form-encoded
  Authorization: Basic 32c0992ae4194701a12dc7440d513d45
  grant_type=password&username=foo&password=spam&scope=uid
```

Client Credential Grant

Probably the simplest grant type, the client gains an access token by just providing its own credentials. It's a useful grant type for machine-to-machine use cases where there is no person associated with an API request. It's so simple, I'll just show the sample request and response from RFC 6749 (see Listings 4-5 and 4-6).

Listing 4-5. Sample Request

```
POST /token HTTP/1.1
Host: server.example.com
Authorization: Basic czZCaGRSa3FOMzpnWDFmQmF0M2JW
Content-Type: application/x-www-form-urlencoded

grant_type=client_credentials
```

Listing 4-6. Sample Response

```
HTTP/1.1 200 OK
  Content-Type: application/json;charset=UTF-8
  Cache-Control: no-store
  Pragma: no-cache

  {
  "access_token":"2YotnFZFEjr1zCsicMWpAA",
  "token_type":"example",
  "expires_in":3600,
  "example_parameter":"example_value"
  }
```

Token Introspection

If a resource server receives an access token issued by an external authorization server, it needs some way to understand what the access token means. Is it still valid? When was it issued? For what scopes was it authorized? Sometimes this information is available in a shared database. Encoded JWT tokens are sometimes used as access tokens. But if the bearer token value is only a reference identifier, RFC 7662 describes a mechanism where a resource server can request information about it. This process is called "token introspection". It's a simple flow. Listings 4-7 and 4-8 show the sample introspection request and response from the RFC.

Listing 4-7. Sample Request

```
POST /introspect HTTP/1.1
Host: server.example.com
Accept: application/json
Content-Type: application/x-www-form-urlencoded
Authorization: Bearer 23410913-abewfq.123483

token=2YotnFZFEjr1zCsicMWpAA
```

Listing 4-8. Sample Response

```
HTTP/1.1 200 OK
  Content-Type: application/json

  {
    "active": true,
          "client_id": "l238j323ds-23ij4",
    "username": "jdoe",
    "scope": "read write dolphin",
    "sub": "Z5O3upPC88QrAjx00dis",
    "aud": "https://protected.example.net/resource",
    "iss": "https://server.example.com/",
    "exp": 1419356238,
    "iat": 1419350238,
    "extension_field": "twenty-seven"
  }
```

RFC 7662 says the RS must authenticate to introspect a token to prevent a token scanning attack. This normally happens by presenting an OAuth token or by including basic client credentials. Given the entropy and short lifetime of access tokens, you could allow unauthenticated responses if you understand the risks.

If the token is valid, the active response claim is true. If the token is not valid, it should be false, and no other information should be returned. RFC 7662 defines some standard claims, but a domain may use any claims. If the intention is to use token claims across domains, they should be registered with IANA.

OAuth Client Example: Calling a Google API

Enough theory, let's work on an example of using Google's free open source Python client library to call an OAuth protected API—in this case Google's URL shortening service. In subsequent chapters, we cover in more detail how to use OAuth to protect enterprise resources—how to configure a resource server and authorization server for your organization. Google has a lot of APIs, and their policies and procedures are typical of a well-run application service.

This chapter uses a sample project called "urlias" (like alias for a URL). It will submit a long URL and get back from Google a shorter URL that can be used for tracking. For example, if you post a blog and want to know how many people click on your blog, it is convenient to use a tracking URL. The sample code will be in Python, but the process will be the same across any platform. The code is available in the GitHub repository for this book.

Obtaining Client Credentials

Remember that each authorization server will have its own policies and procedures for obtaining client credentials. Google has a website that enables you to enroll (agree to the terms of services) and to automatically register your application, and in the process, obtain client credentials. Start this process by opening `https://console.developers.google.com` in your browser.

In the Library tab, search for URL, as shown in Figure 4-8.

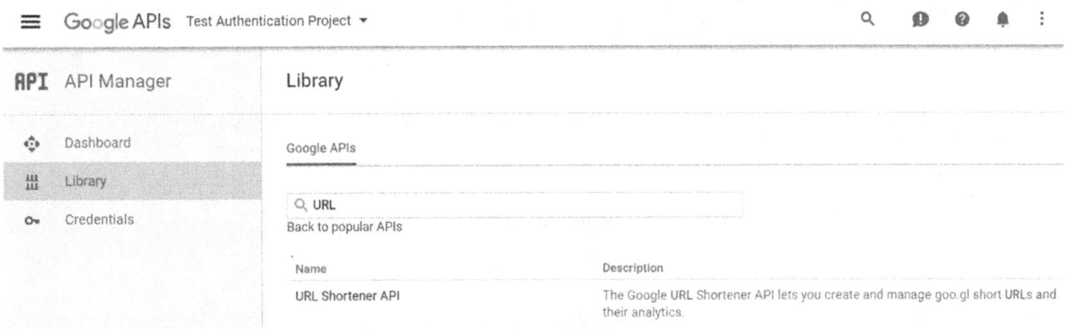

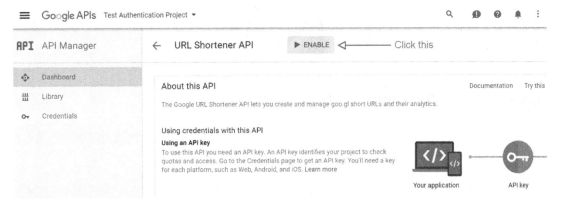

Figure 4-8. *Searching Google libraries for URL shortener*

After clicking on the URL Shortener API, you'll need to enable it, as shown in Figure 4-9.

Figure 4-9. *Enabling Google URL shortener*

Google does not offer a dynamic client registration API, so you'll need to manually register your client in the dashboard. First, you'll need to set up some general properties, like the name, contact information, and logo of your application, which Google will use to render the OAuth consent notification. Note that the values shown in Figure 4-10 are just an example. You would use information appropriate to your application.

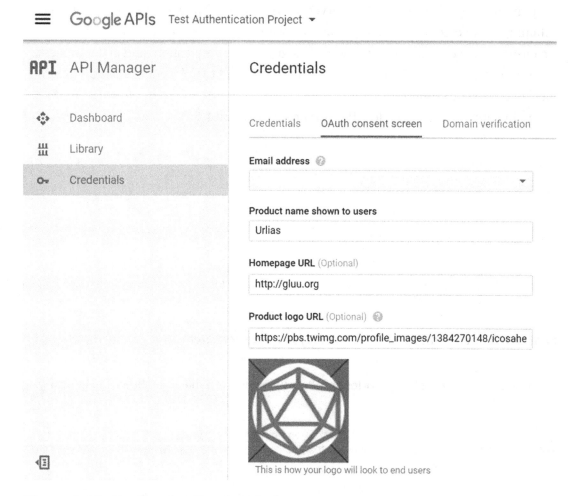

Figure 4-10. *Configuring Google OAuth consent screen*

Click on the Credentials tab, then on Create Credentials. Then choose OAuth Client ID, as shown in Figure 4-11.

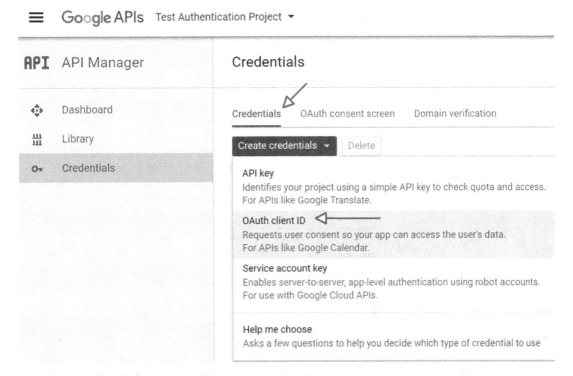

Figure 4-11. *Creating a Google OAuth client ID*

The form to create client credentials is actually rather short. To create a web client, there are only three pieces of information you need to supply: the application type, name, and redirect_uris, as shown in Figure 4-12.

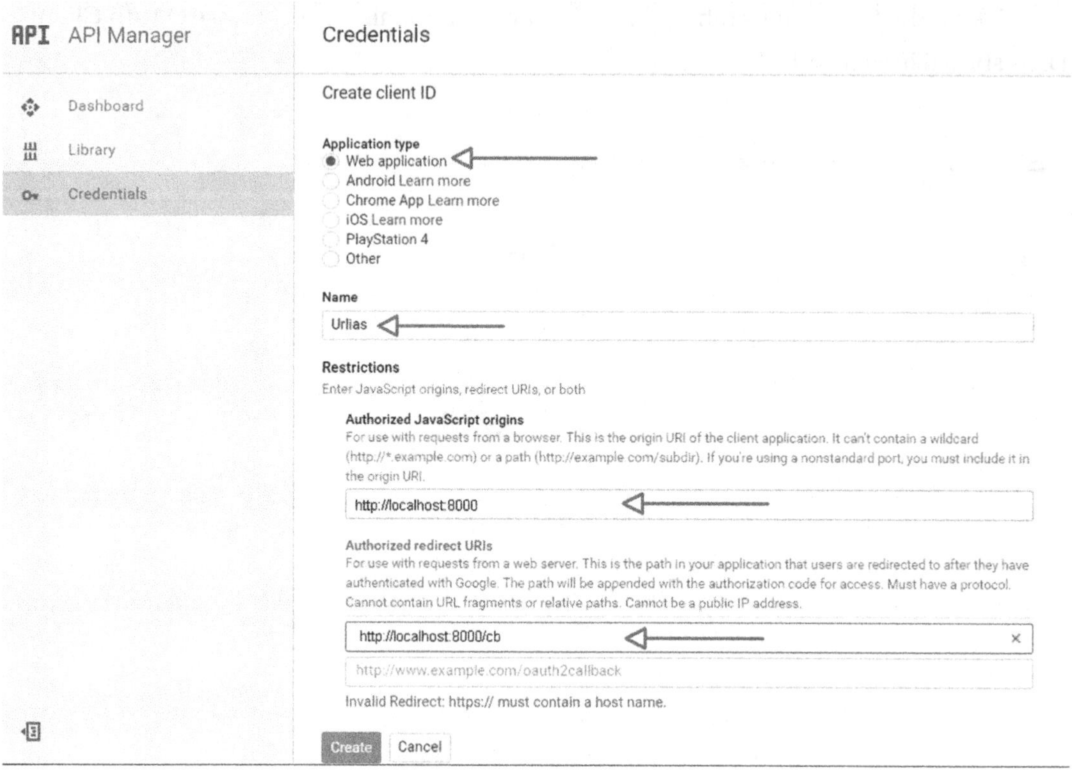

Figure 4-12. *Google client ID request form*

If successful, you should see a modal window with your client credentials—record these in a secure place. You should never share your client credentials. Hypothetical examples are shown in Figure 4-13.

Figure 4-13. *Final client credentials*

Calling the Google API

Now that you have client credentials, it's time to call the API. To show this I'd like to reference a sample node project called google-oauth-implicit-example in my GitHub project for this book at https://github.com/GluuFederation/iam-book. This is a two-page application: page one displays a login button that enables the user to authorize the use of their Google account; page two is a JavaScript application that uses the returned access token to call the API. Figure 4-14 shows the sequence diagram for this application.

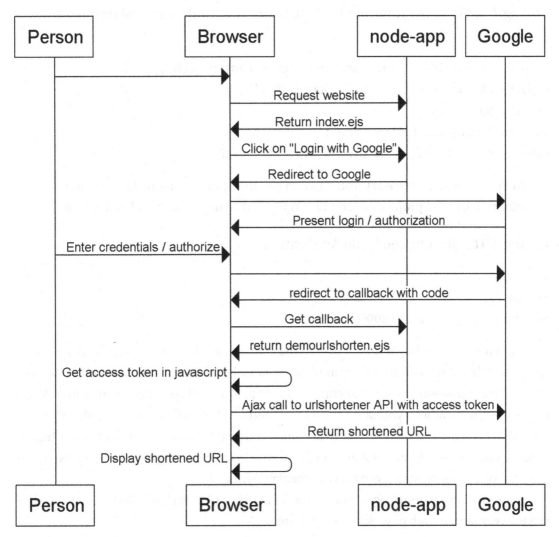

Figure 4-14. *Sequence diagram for URL shortener application*

To run this application, you'll need node.js installed on your workstation or server. Follow the relevant instructions on http://nodejs.org for your operating system. After cloning the project from GitHub, the first thing you'll need to do is to set the properties files, called settings.js, to enter the client credentials retrieved in the preceding steps (see Listing 4-9). Don't forget to quote the strings and to use a semicolon at the end of each line. Just as an example, settings.js should look something like Listing 4-9 (again, those are not real Google API creds.). Note that the callback must match the one you registered for this client with Google. For this demo, I was running the server on port 8000, but you can choose any free port on your system.

Listing 4-9. Sample Properties for URL Shortener Application (Shortened for Display)

```
exports.client_id = '6fb8.apps.googleusercontent.com';
exports.client_secret = ' ghoeg&qecyic8_1';
exports.port = 8000;
exports.redirectURIPath = '/cb';
exports.redirectURI = 'http://localhost:8000/cb';
```

To download the necessary libraries and run the application, navigate via the command line to the project folder and run the commands shown in Listing 4-10.

Listing 4-10. Starting the Node Application

```
$ npm install
$ node app
Server Started on port 8000
```

It might be confusing at first as to why the callback works using localhost. How can Google call back to localhost? The simple answer is that Google gets your browser to call the callback. So as long as you can connect to http://localhost:8000, you're fine. Also, if you're using localhost, you don't need to use https—the traffic is not traversing the network. If you are redirecting over to anywhere other than localhost, then https is highly recommended. The client must protect the access token, so using a non-encrypted protocol would be unwise, even on your local network.

To test the application, point your browser at http://localhost:8000. You should see the very simple web page shown in Figure 4-15.

Figure 4-15. *Page one of the URL shortener application*

When you click on the button, you may be prompted to log in to Google if you don't already have a session in your browser. Once Google knows who you are, you will be asked to authorize the client and then will be redirected to page two, shown in Figure 4-16.

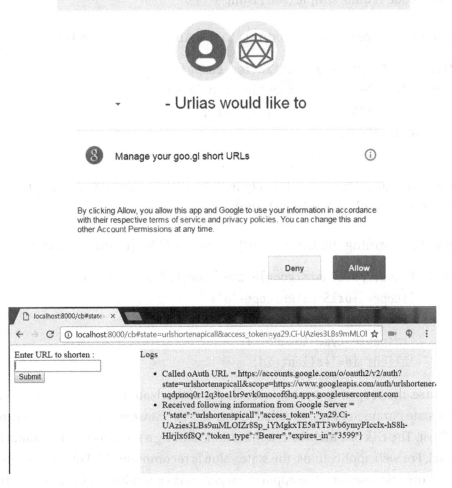

Figure 4-16. *Authorization and page two of the URL shortener application**

The app is simple: enter a URL and it will obtain a Google-shortened version for you. The action of calling the API actually happens in the JavaScript in the browser, which uses the access token returned in the URL fragment (a fragment is content returned in a URL after the #). The callback URL and fragment in Figure 4-16 is:

```
http://localhost:8000/cb#state=urlshortenapicall&access_token=ya29.Ci-
UAzies3LBs9mMLOIZr8Sp_iYMgkxTE5aTT3wb6ymyPIccIx-hS8h-
Hlrjlx6f8Q&token_type=Bearer&expires_in=3599
```

You can see the parameters access_token, token_type, and expires_in, which are listed after the hash mark (#) of the callback URI. You shouldn't share an access token, but this one will be long expired by the time you read this! Let's take a quick look at some of the more interesting parts of the code. The interesting part starts after you click the button. This code is quite simple (see Listing 4-11).

Listing 4-11. Sample Code to Redirect to the Authorization Endpoint

```
// Redirect to Google's authorization endpoint
   app.post('/authRequest', function(req, res) {
      console.log('Redirect to : ', url);
      res.redirect(url);
  });
```

The authorization URL sends the required parameters scope, redirect_uri, response_type, and client_id (see Listing 4-12).

Listing 4-12. Forming the Correct URL Value for OAuth Authorization

```
var url = 'https://accounts.google.com/o/OAuth/v2/auth?' +
            'scope='+urlShortenScope+'&'+
            'redirect_uri='+redirectURI+'&'+
            'response_type=token&' +
            'client_id='+client_id;
```

Of course, the response_type token tells the authorization server that this is implicit flow. The state parameter is not needed in this case, because the application is running on localhost. The risk of a malicious application sending a response to the callback URI is minimal. For web applications, the state value is recommended. The state is returned by the authorization server—the application generates a random, hard-to-guess state value and caches it. When a response is received on the callback, the state should be looked up. If it doesn't exist, the response should be discarded—it was unsolicited. If the state exists in the cache, it should be removed, and the response should be processed.

When the callback is called, it renders the `demourlshorten.ejs` page. When the Submit button is clicked, a JavaScript script is called: `$('#submit').click(function())`, which gathers the URL from the text field and submits it with the access token to the `urlshortener` API. The results are just printed to a log message on the page itself, along with a log of the exact request that was sent, so you can understand what is going on in the background.

Client Credential Grant Example with the Gluu Server

If you are wondering how to put OAuth to work in your environment, it's not that hard! Let's look at a simple "machine-to-machine" example of a script that calls a protected API. The example is written in Python, using the easy-to-read "requests" module.

Configuring the Gluu Server

In this example, the Gluu Server acts as the authorization server. The easiest way to run this demo is to add both a scope (`myScope`) and a client using the oxTrust administrative interface. Figure 4-17 shows a sample of the scope. OAuth scopes are managed under the "OpenID Connect" section. That might be a little confusing, but OpenID Connect does a really good job of defining how to manage OAuth clients. When you add the client, select Scope Type OAuth. In this example, we made the scope available for dynamically registered clients. It wasn't necessary, because we're going to add the scope to the client manually. In general, if you make scopes available by default, make sure they are not protecting any resources that require user explicit user approval. When adding the client, make sure to add Client Credential Grant and two scopes: `myScope` and `uma_protection` (see Figure 4-18). The latter will enable you to reuse these credentials for both the client and resource server. The `uma_protection` scope is needed to call the OAuth token introspection endpoint. You can disable protection of the introspection endpoint, but by default, it's protected. The thought is you may not want any client to be able to convert a bearer token into its JSON equivalent.

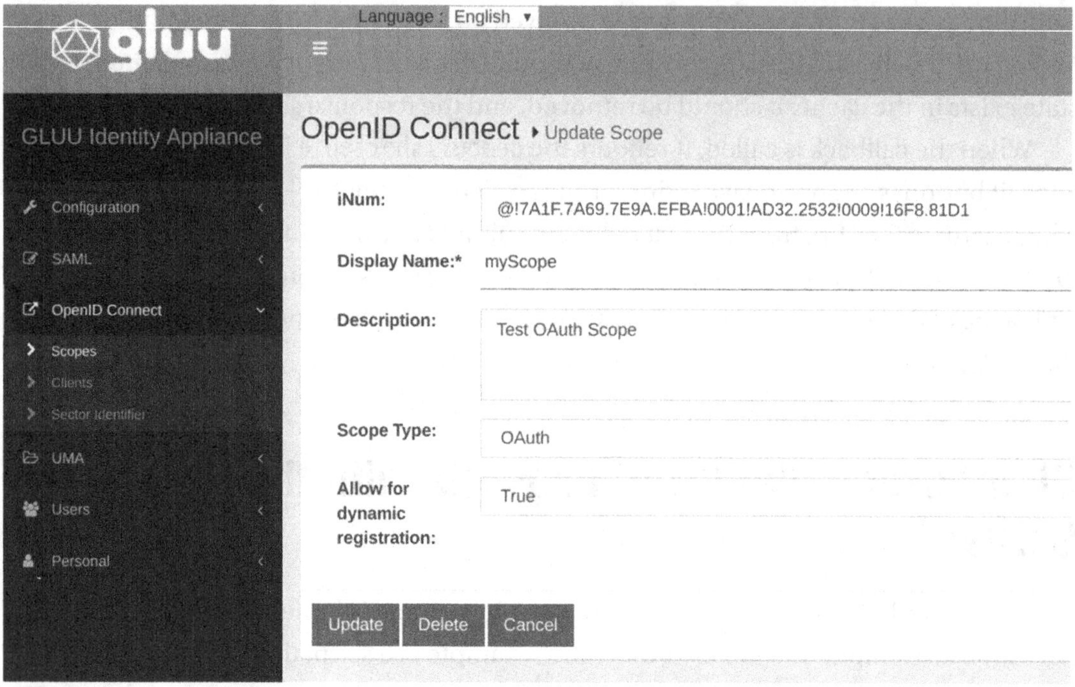

Figure 4-17. *Gluu Server OAuth scope configuration*

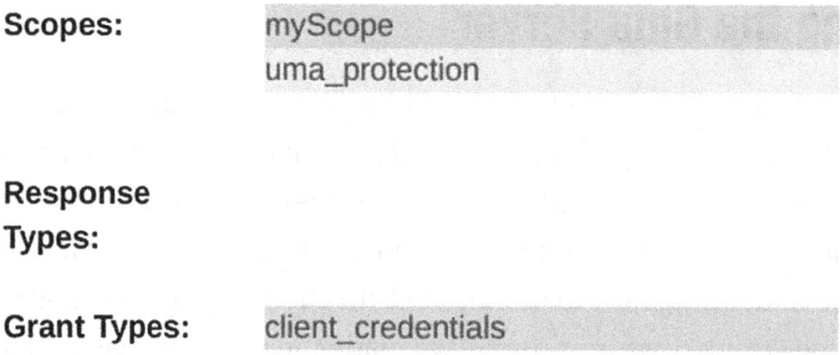

Figure 4-18. *Gluu Server client configuration detail on scopes and grant type*

The sample client in Listing 4-13 is pretty simple: it gets a token and calls the API. The sample RS is almost as simple: it looks at the token sent by the client, introspects it, checks to see if it has the required scopes, and if so, returns the content. Of course you'll have to insert your own client credentials and fix the URLs. Note: we aren't using SSL for the sample API. If you want to use SSL, just add `verify=False` or read more about the Python requests module to properly validate the SSL certificate (a requirement for any production system).

Listing 4-13. Simple Python OAuth Client

```python
#!/usr/bin/python

import requests, json

# Get access token
client_id = '12345676890abcdefg'
client_secret = "secret"
token_endpoint = "https://idp.example.com/token"
scope = "myScope"
payload = {"grant_type":"client_credentials", "scope":scope}
response = requests.post(token_endpoint, data=payload, verify=False,
auth=(client_id, client_secret))
j = json.loads(response.text)
access_token = j['access_token']
# Call API
api_endpoint = "http://api.example.com/cgi-bin/oauth-rs.cgi"
h = {'Authorization': 'Bearer %s' % access_token}
response = requests.post(api_endpoint, headers=h)
print response.text
```

The sample RS in Listing 4-14 is almost as simple: it looks at the token sent by the client, introspects it, checks to see if it has the required scopes, and if so, returns the content. Of course, you'll have to insert your own client credentials and fix the URLs. Note: we aren't using SSL for the sample API. If you want to use SSL, just add verify=False or read more about the Python requests module to properly validate the SSL certificate (a requirement for any production system).

Listing 4-14. Simple OAuth Protected Python API

```python
#!/usr/bin/python

import requests, json, os
from sets import Set

result = None
client_token = None
required_scopes = Set(['myScope'])
```

```
try:
    client_token = os.environ['HTTP_AUTHORIZATION'].split('Bearer')[-1].
strip()
except:
    print "HTTP/1.0 200 OK"
    print "Content-type: text/html\n\n"
    print 'Access token not found'
# First get access token to call introspection endpoint
client_id = '1234567890abcdefg'
client_secret = 'secret'
token_endpoint = 'https://idp.example.com/token'
payload = {'grant_type':'client_credentials', 'scope':'uma_protection'}
response = requests.post(token_endpoint,
                         data=payload,
                         verify=False,
                         auth=(client_id, client_secret))
j = json.loads(response.text)
introspection_token = j['access_token']

# Introspect token
introspection_endpoint = 'https://idp.example.com/introspection'
h = {'Authorization': 'Bearer %s' % introspection_token}
token = {'token': client_token}
response = requests.post(introspection_endpoint,
                         verify=False,
                         headers=h,
                         data=token)
result = response.text
j = response.json()
try:
    scopes = Set(j['scopes'][0].strip().split(' '))
except:
    print "HTTP/1.0 200 OK"
    print "Content-type: text/html\n\n"
    print "No scopes found"
    print "Result:\n" + result
```

```
missing_scopes = required_scopes - scopes
if len(missing_scopes):
    print "HTTP/1.0 200 OK"
    print "Content-type: text/html\n\n"
    print "Missing scopes: %s" % `list(missing_scopes)`
elif len(missing_scopes)==0:
    print "HTTP/1.0 200 OK"
    print "Content-type: text/html\n\n"
    print "Scopes %s all found" % `list(required_scopes)`
```

Make sure the web server is sending the request headers—if it's not, the RS script will complain that it can't find the access token. You can use the print headers example from Chapter 3. Look for the Authorization header: you should see the bearer token. Also, see the print headers example from Chapter 3 if you're not sure how to deploy a CGI script.

This RS script was tested with nginx. For Apache you may need to remove the print "HTTP/1.0 200 OK" lines. The client script can be run from anywhere, even from your laptop. If you are not sure where the token and introspection endpoint are located on your Gluu Server, use the OpenID Connect discovery endpoint. This is a simple JSON object with the location of all the endpoints (and a bunch of other stuff you'll learn more about in the next chapter), and you can view it by pointing your browser to https://gluu.server.hostname/.well-known/openid-configuration.

OAuth Glossary and IANA Registry Terms

OAuth has a large vocabulary of terms, some of which are registered at the Internet Assigned Numbers Authority (IANA). This is a department of ICANN, a nonprofit organization that oversees domain names, IP addresses, and protocol parameters. IANA publishes many standard names, which are essential for the Internet to work. Port numbers, media types, and language tags are some examples.

The Internet Engineering Task Force (IETF) community writes drafts, which become Requests for Comments (RFCs) when they are final. Many RFCs contain guidance to the IANA department for the creation of unique registry for protocol parameters, the registration policy, and initial registrations of reserved values. There are almost 3,000 protocol registries published on http://www.iana.org. The two of interest to us are the OAuth Parameters Registry and the JSON Web Token Registry. Familiarizing yourself with these parameters shown in Tables 4-1 through 4-9 will help you understand which part of a profile is OAuth and which part is custom.

Table 4-1. *OAuth Access Token Types*

Parameter	Reference	Description
bearer	RFC 6750	Any party in possession of this type of token can use it to access a protected resource.

Table 4-2. *OAuth Authorization Endpoint Response Types*

Parameter	Reference	Description
code	RFC 6749	Authorization Code Flow
token	RFC 6749	Implicit Flow

Table 4-3. *OAuth Extensions Errors*

Parameter	Reference	Description
invalid_request	RFC 6750	The request is missing a required parameter, includes an unsupported parameter or parameter value, repeats the same parameter, uses more than one method for including an access token, or is otherwise malformed. The resource server SHOULD respond with the HTTP 400 (Bad Request) status code.
invalid_token	RFC 6750	The access token provided is expired, revoked, malformed, or invalid for other reasons. The resource SHOULD respond with the HTTP 401 (Unauthorized) status code. The client MAY request a new access token and retry the protected resource request.
insufficient_ scope	RFC 6750	The request requires higher privileges than provided by the access token. The resource server SHOULD respond with the HTTP 403 (Forbidden) status code and MAY include the "scope" attribute with the scope necessary to access the protected resource.

(continued)

Table 4-3. (*continued*)

Parameter	Reference	Description
unsupported_ token_type	RFC 7009	The authorization server does not support the revocation of the presented token type. That is, the client tried to revoke an access token on a server not supporting this feature. If the server responds with HTTP status code 503, the client must assume the token still exists and may retry after a reasonable delay.
unauthorized_ client	RFC 6749	The client is not authorized to request an authorization code using this method.
access_denied	RFC 6749	The resource owner or authorization server denied the request.
unsupported_ response_type	RFC 6749	The authorization server does not support obtaining an authorization code using this method.
invalid_scope	RFC 6749	The requested scope is invalid, unknown, or malformed.
server_error	RFC 6749	The authorization server encountered an unexpected condition that prevented it from fulfilling the request. (This error code is needed because a 500 Internal Server Error HTTP status code cannot be returned to the client via an HTTP redirect.)
temporarily_ unavailable	RFC 6749	The authorization server is currently unable to handle the request due to a temporary overloading or maintenance of the server. (This error code is needed because a 503 Service Unavailable HTTP status code cannot be returned to the client via an HTTP redirect.)
invalid_client	RFC 6749	Client authentication failed.
invalid_grant	RFC 6749	The provided authorization grant or refresh token is invalid, expired, revoked, does not match the redirection URI used in the authorization request, or was issued to another client.
invalid_scope	RFC 6749	The requested scope is invalid, unknown, malformed, or exceeds the scope granted by the resource owner.

Table 4-4. *OAuth Parameters*

Parameter	Parameter Usage Location	Reference	Description
client_id	authorization request, token request	RFC 6749	The client identifier issued to the client during the registration process.
client_secret	token request	RFC 6749	A string with sufficient entropy to prevent a credential guessing attack.
response_type	authorization request	RFC 6749	The expected response from the authorization endpoint, can be 'code', 'token', or other registered extension values.
redirect_uri	authorization request, token request	RFC 6749	After completing its interaction with the resource owner, the authorization server redirects the user-agent to this URI.
scope	authorization request, authorization response, token request, token response	RFC 6749	The permissions associated with the access token.
state	authorization request, authorization response	RFC 6749	An opaque value used by the client to maintain state between the request and callback. The authorization server includes this value when redirecting the user-agent back to the client. The parameter SHOULD be used for preventing cross-site request forgery.

(*continued*)

Table 4-4. (*continued*)

Parameter	Parameter Usage Location	Reference	Description
code	authorization response, token request	RFC 6749	A string generated by the authorization server that's used by the client to obtain tokens. It should be short-lived (less than 10 minutes), one-time use, and bound to a client-id.
error	authorization response, token response	RFC 6749	A single ASCII error code specified in the OAuth Extensions Error Registry.
error_ description	authorization response, token response	RFC 6749	Human-readable ASCII [USASCII] text providing additional information, used to assist the client developer in understanding the error that occurred.
error_uri	authorization response, token response	RFC 6749	A URI identifying a human-readable web page with information about the error, used to provide the client.
grant_type	token request	RFC 6749	Credential representing the resource owner's authorization (to access its protected resources) used by the client to obtain an access token.
access_token	authorization response, token response	RFC 6749	A string denoting a specific scope, lifetime, and other access attributes.
token_type	authorization response, token response	RFC 6749	Information the client needs to successfully utilize the access token.

(*continued*)

Table 4-4. (*continued*)

Parameter	Parameter Usage Location	Reference	Description
expires_in	authorization response, token response	RFC 6749	The lifetime in seconds of the access token. For example, the value "3600" denotes that the access token will expire in one hour from the time the response was generated.
username	token request	RFC 6749	The identifier for the resource owner.
password	token request	RFC 6749	The resource owner's ASCII secret.
refresh_token	token request, token response	RFC 6749	A token that can be used to obtain a new access token from the authorization server.
assertion	token request	RFC 7521	A package of information that facilitates the sharing of identity and security information across security domains.
client_ assertion	token request	RFC 7521	An assertion about the client.
client_ assertion_type	token request	RFC 7521	The format of the assertion.
code_verifier	token request	RFC 7636	A cryptographically random string that is used to correlate the authorization request to the token request.
code_challenge	authorization request	RFC 7636	A challenge derived from the code verifier that is sent in the authorization request, to be verified against later.
code_challenge_ method	authorization request	RFC 7636	A mechanism that was used to derive code challenge.

Table 4-5. *OAuth Dynamic Client Registration Metadata*

Parameter	Reference	Description
redirect_uris	RFC 7591	Array of redirection URIs for use in redirect-based flows.
token_endpoint_auth_method	RFC 7591	Requested authentication method for the token endpoint.
grant_types	RFC 7591	Array of OAuth 2.0 grant types that the client may use.
response_types	RFC 7591	Array of the OAuth 2.0 response types that the client may use.
client_name	RFC 7591	Human-readable name of the client to be presented to the user.
client_uri	RFC 7591	URL of a web page providing information about the client.
logo_uri	RFC 7591	URL that references a logo for the client.
scope	RFC 7591	Space-separated list of OAuth 2.0 scope values.
contacts	RFC 7591	Array of strings representing ways to contact people responsible for this client, typically email addresses.
tos_uri	RFC 7591	URL that points to a human-readable terms of service document for the client.
policy_uri	RFC 7591	URL that points to a human-readable policy document for the client.
jwks_uri	RFC 7591	URL referencing the client's JSON Web Key Set [RFC7517] document representing the client's public keys.
jwks	RFC 7591	Client's JSON Web Key Set [RFC7517] document representing the client's public keys.
software_id	RFC 7591	Identifier for the software that comprises a client.

(*continued*)

Table 4-5. (*continued*)

Parameter	Reference	Description
software_version	RFC 7591	Version identifier for the software that comprises a client.
client_id	RFC 7591	Client identifier.
client_secret	RFC 7591	Client secret.
client_id_issued_at	RFC 7591	Time at which the client identifier was issued.
client_secret_expires_at	RFC 7591	Time at which the client secret will expire.
registration_access_token	RFC 7591	OAuth 2.0 Bearer Token used to access the client configuration endpoint.
registration_client_uri	RFC 7591	Fully qualified URI of the client registration endpoint.

Table 4-6. *OAuth Token Endpoint Authentication Methods*

Parameter	Reference	Description
none	RFC 7591	No authentication.
client_secret_post	RFC 7591	The client uses the HTTP POST parameters as defined in OAuth 2.0, Section 2.3.1.
client_secret_basic	RFC 7591	HTTP Basic authentication.

Table 4-7. *OAuth Token Introspection Responses*

Parameter	Reference	Description
active	RFC 7662	Token active status.
username	RFC 7662	User identifier of the resource owner.
client_id	RFC 7662	Client identifier of the client.
scope	RFC 7662	Authorized scopes of the token.
token_type	RFC 7662	Type of the token.
exp	RFC 7662	Expiration timestamp of the token.
iat	RFC 7662	Issuance timestamp of the token.
nbf	RFC 7662	Timestamp before which the token is not valid.
sub	RFC 7662	Subject of the token.
aud	RFC 7662	Audience of the token.
iss	RFC 7662	Issuer of the token.
jti	RFC 7662	Unique identifier of the token.

Table 4-8. *JSON Web Token Claims*

Parameter	Reference	Description
iss	RFC 7519	Issuer
sub	RFC 7519	Subject
aud	RFC 7519	Audience
exp	RFC 7519	Expiration Time
nbf	RFC 7519	Not Before
iat	RFC 7519	Issued At
jti	RFC 7519	JWT ID
cnf	RFC 7800	Confirmation

Table 4-9. *JWT Confirmation Methods*

Parameter	Reference	Description
jwk	RFC 7800	JSON Web Key Representing Public Key
jwe	RFC 7800	Encrypted JSON Web Key
kid	RFC 7800	Key Identifier
jku	RFC 7800	JWK Set URL

Conclusion

Didn't get enough OAuth? Now that you know the OAuth basics, it's time to move on. The preceding examples showed how to write a client to call an OAuth protected API. Chapter 5 deep dives on using OAuth for authentication, using the OpenID Connect profile. Chapter 6 details using a web proxy and OAuth to protect APIs. Chapter 8 discusses using the User Managed Access protocol (UMA), a profile of OAuth for API access management.

References

1. "OAuth 2.0 and Sign-In," 1/2/2013, `http://www.cloudidentity.com/blog/2013/01/02/oauth-2-0-and-sign-in-4/`

2. Google Scopes page: `https://developers.google.com/identity/protocols/googlescopes?linkId=17886206`

3. "JSON Web Token (JWT)," Jones, Bradley, Sakimura, May 2015, `https://tools.ietf.org/html/rfc7519#section-10.2.1`

4. "OAuth 2.0 Message Authentication Code (MAC) Tokens," Richer, Mills, Tschofenig, January 2014, `https://tools.ietf.org/html/draft-ietf-oauth-v2-http-mac-05`

5. "The OAuth 2.0 Authorization Framework: Bearer Token Usage," Jones, Hardt, October 2012, `https://tools.ietf.org/html/rfc6750`

6. OAuth 2.0 Token Introspection, J. Richer, October 2015, `https://tools.ietf.org/html/rfc7662`

7. "JSON Web Algorithms (JWA)," Jones, M., May 2015, `http://www.rfc-editor.org/info/rfc7518`

8. "Proof-of-Possession Key Semantics for JSON Web Tokens (JWTs)," Jones, Bradley, Tschofenig, April 2016, `https://tools.ietf.org/html/rfc7800`

9. "OAuth 2.0 Dynamic Client Registration Protocol," Jone, Bradley, Machalak, Hunt, July 2015, `https://tools.ietf.org/html/rfc7591`

10. `https://tools.ietf.org/html/rfc6749#section-10.10`

11. "Proof Key for Code Exchange by OAuth Public Clients," Sakimura, Bradley, Agarwal, September 2015, `https://tools.ietf.org/html/rfc7636`

CHAPTER 5

OpenID Connect

Despite OAuth's close association with authentication, if you want to use it for web or mobile login, you'll should use OpenID Connect. Both a profile and extension of OAuth, OpenID Connect defines some of the features necessary to use OAuth for federated identity.

Note   To save space, sometimes "OpenID Connect" is shortened to simply "Connect". "OpenID" would not be specific enough, because there are several OpenID working groups with product standards.

OpenID Connect was formulated at a time when Google, Microsoft, Facebook, and other large consumer identity providers had already introduced their own OAuth based identity APIs. These services were already processing millions of transactions per day, and the design of Connect benefited from the experience collected on security, developer usability, and end user behavior. It was confusing for developers to keep track of the little differences between the OAuth login services of the various consumer services. For example, the identity service of Google was almost the same as that of Facebook. But these little differences were annoying, and resulted in one-off code.

OpenID Connect has many parallels to SAML. The OpenID Provider (OP) is analogous to the SAML IDP—the software component that authenticates the person and returns an assertion to the relying party (or RP), roughly equivalent to the SAML SP. While in SAML we might call pieces of information about a person "attributes," in Connect, we call these things "user claims". The equivalent of the SAML assertion (signed XML document that contains information about the authentication event, and optionally attributes of the person), is an id_token, a signed JSON Web Token, or JWT (pronounced "jot") that contains very similar information.

© Michael Schwartz, Maciej Machulak 2018
M. Schwartz and M. Machulak, *Securing the Perimeter*, https://doi.org/10.1007/978-1-4842-2601-8_5

The overriding design goal of Connect was to keep simple things simple, but also make complex things possible. As opposed to SAML, which was developed before the release of the iPhone in 2007, the initial Connect functional specifications released in 2011 incorporated new requirements brought about by mobile use cases. Connect also embraced JSON data structures and RESTful web services. This architecture is more efficient on the wire than XML data structures, and it requires less compute power on small devices. Also, the complexity of parsing XML has resulted in many security problems, as different implementations may mess it up. Also, while SAML was primarily focused on enterprise use cases, Connect was designed to address both enterprise and consumer requirements, which included a wider range of security levels, from non-sensitive information to highly secure transactions.

Figure 5-1, which is based on a slide from one of Nat Sakimura's presentations, shows how Connect layers security. Depending on the Connect features you use, you can mitigate additional risk. In the implicit flow, tokens are retrieved from the authorization endpoint without client credentials. This results in less security than for the hybrid flow, where the client is authenticated and signing and encryption are used for the request and responses.

Security Level	Flow	Remarks	Client Options
	Hybrid Flow	Authorization request protected	request_object_encryption_alg request_object_signing_alg
	Hybrid Flow	Authorization response protected	id_token_encrypted_response_alg id_token_signed_response_alg
	Code Flow	Client authentication	token_endpoint_auth_method=private_key_jwt token_endpoint_auth_method=client_secret_basic
	Implicit Flow	No client authentication	none
	OAuth2 Implicit / Code	No integrity	Without id_token, missing nonce and at_hash

Figure 5-1. *OpenID Connect security levels*

Connect is an architecture that leverages several related standards developed by the OpenID Connect working group and standards from the IETF. This chapter provides a deep dive into those components and provides some examples for how you can put Connect to use in your organization for access management.

OpenID Connect Overview

If you think back to Figure 4-2 about OAuth, it showed three software roles (the client, resource server, and authorization server) and three human roles (resource owner, requesting party, and developer). All six are present in Connect, although there are two conflations, illustrated in Figure 5-2:

- The OpenID Provider (hereafter referred to as the OP) is a combination of the authorization and resource server.

- The subject is both the resource owner and the requesting party.

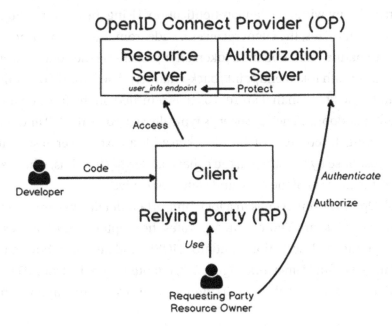

Figure 5-2. *Conflated OAuth2 roles in OpenID Connect*

In OAuth terms, the OP is the authorization server—it issues access token and publishes the authorization and token endpoints. It is also the resource server, because it hosts the protected endpoint—the "Userinfo endpoint" that returns a JSON object containing the user claims of the subject. When you log in, you are both the requesting party (the person asking to get access) and the resource owner. It's information about you that you are authorizing the client to access. Note that in Connect, unlike in most OAuth scenarios, a developer does not code the protected API—only the client.

OpenID Connect introduces a new token, called the id_token, which is like a SAML assertion. The id_token contains a subject identifier (for example, a username) and other information about the authentication event, such as who issued the token, to whom it was issued, when the authentication occurred, or what type of authentication happened. Like SAML, id_token may contain attributes (user claims). We'll go into more detail on the id_token later in this chapter. The key thing to keep in mind is that it's not really a token—something that grants access. It's an identity assertion.

OpenID Connect also introduces a new flow—the hybrid flow. As you might remember from Chapter 4, the implicit flow allows the client to request a token from the authorization endpoint without client authentication. Using the authorization code flow, after the subject authorizes, the client receives a code from the OAuth authorization endpoint (front-channel) and obtains a token after presenting the code plus client credentials at the OAuth token endpoint (back-channel). The hybrid flow combines the implicit and code flows, in that an id_token is returned on the front-channel from the authorization endpoint. The id_token is typically signed by the OP and may be encrypted. Verifying the contents of the id_token adds an extra layer of security to the front-channel response by introducing the c_hash and s_hash claims, which enable the client to verify the integrity of the code and state, respectively.

In general, OpenID Connect fills in a lot of important details that are necessary to use OAuth for a secure sign-in flow. It incorporates the cryptographic features of the the JSON Object Signing and Encryption standards (JOSE) and describes how to use them together within an OAuth framework. Figure 5-3, adapted from the OpenID Connect website, provides an overview of OpenID Connect features and the underpinnings in OAuth.

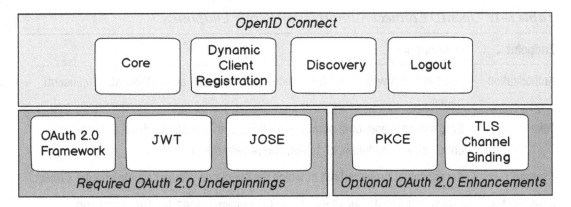

Figure 5-3. *OpenID Connect overview with OAuth underpinnings*

While new OpenID Connect specifications are under development, there are four key specifications:

- **Core**—How a person is authenticated and authorizes the release of claims.

- **Dynamic Client Registration**—How a client obtains a client_id and a secret (or registers a public key).

- **Discovery**—How a client figures out how to bootstrap authentication with an OP (many similarities to the publication of SAML IDP metadata).

- **Logout**—How clients can attempt to implement single-logout (SLO).

OpenID Connect Authorization Server Endpoints

The OpenID Connect authorization server endpoints are described in Table 5-1.

Table 5-1. *OpenID Connect Authorization Server Endpoints*

Endpoint	Description
Authorization	Front-channel web pages that render the login page and authorization (consent) pages.
Token	Back-channel endpoint, normally requiring authentication, where a client can obtain an access token, id_token, and refresh token.
Userinfo	Access token protected API at which the client can request claims about a subject.
Configuration	Provider metadata published at `.well-known/openid-configuration`, including the location of endpoints, supported cryptographic algorithms, and other information needed by the client to interact with the OP.
JWKS	The current public keys of the OP used for signing and encryption.
Client registration	Endpoint for an application to create or update an OAuth client.
Session management	Used by all three OpenID logout specs (none working that well) .
WebFinger	Used to bootstrap OP discovery working backwards from an email address (or other identifier), i.e. how do you figure out the configuration endpoint for a domain.

If the OP supports the OpenID Federation specification (an implementer's draft at the time of this book's publication), it would also optionally publish these endpoints in Table 5-2.

Table 5-2. *OpenID Federation Endpoints*

Endpoint	Description
Signing keys	Stable keys used for signing and encryption, published to a federation.
Signed JWKS	Signed version of the JWKS endpoint.
Metadata Statements	JWTs issued to an OP by federations to indicate membership.

id_token

The id_token is a JWT that binds the subject identifier (and potentially other claims) with the authentication event. As previously mentioned, it is analogous to the SAML assertion. The id_token must be signed by the OP and may be encrypted if the client so requests. Figure 5-4 shows a summary of the id_token claims. For a full list, see the OpenID Connect Core specification.

Claim	Description
iss	URL of OP that issued token
sub	Subject identifier
aud	Audience – client_id of the client to which the token was issued
exp	Expiration time of the token
iat	Time at which the token was issued
auth_time	Time at which the subject authenticated
nonce	Correlates the token to a specific authentication request
acr	String that indicates the authentication
amr	Array of strings with additional details about authentication event

Figure 5-4. *id_token claims*

An example of the JSON representation of an id_token is shown in Listing 5-1.

Listing 5-1. Sample id_token JSON Object

```
{
  "iss"        : "https://login.example.com",
  "sub"        : "foo@example.com",
  "aud"        : "b250c4a7-5551",
  "nonce"      : "5zTdd3302Rf9",
  "auth_time"  : 1530986231,
  "acr"        : "otp",
  "iat"        : 1530986231,
  "exp"        : 1311288231,
  "orgClaim"   : "spam"
}
```

If you're wondering if orgClaim is valid, good eye! The Core spec says the id_token MAY contain other claims. Similarly, a SAML IDP may include user attributes in a SAML identity assertion. Sending user claims in the id_token impacts security. It may lack interoperability—RPs may not expect it. But it's not contrary to the specification.

When sent over the wire, the id_token is base-64 encoded. Remember, according to RFC 7619, JWTs have three parts: the header, payload, and signature. For example, with a header of {"alg": "HS512","typ": "JWT"} and using a shared secret of spam, the example id_token looks like this:

```
eyJhbGciOiJIUzUxMiIsInR5cCI6IkpXVCJ9.eyJpc3MiOiJodHRwczovL2xvZ2luLmV4YW1wbG
UuY29tIiwic3ViIjoiZm9vQGV4YW1wbGUuY29tIiwiYXVkIjoiYjI1MGM0YTctNT
U1MSIsIm5vbmNlIjoiNXpiUZGQzMzAyUmY5IiwiYXV0aF90aW1lIjoxNTMwOTg2MjM
xLCJhY3IiOiJvdHAiLCJpYXQiOjE1MzA5ODYyMzEsImV4cCI6MTMxMTI4ODIzMSwib3JnQ
2xhaW0iOiJzcGFtIn0.OLG72c2GstOGaBhrSHaksCkpld7uU9qpPb32CdisIes
XsUhQifoWHrAj_PBe7MzviVOw_yB23SSYXu9W2zxREA
```

OpenID Authentication on the Fly

An interesting feature of Connect is that it describes how a client could bootstrap authentication against an external Internet domain without knowing anything more than a person's email address. Although rarely used in practice, and keeping in mind that there are some potential security vulnerabilities associated with dynamic discovery and client registration, it offers a glimpse into a future in which cross-domain security is possible without prior out-of-band configuration. Figure 5-5 summarizes this discovery process for a hypothetical person foo@bar.com. In this very simple sequence diagram, the Person and User Agent are combined into one unit.

OpenID Connect Dynamic Security

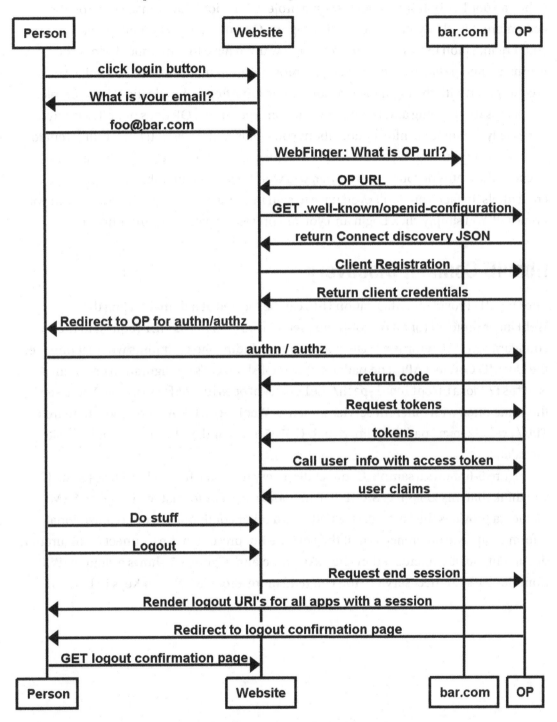

Figure 5-5. *OpenID Connect Dynamic cross-domain authentication*

Here is the scenario: imagine you are browsing around, and you decide you need to buy a cool T-shirt from an open source project. You don't have an account on the ecommerce site, but you notice that it supports OpenID Connect. That's great, because your organization uses an OP, and you don't want to have to remember yet another username and password. You click login, provide your email address, and voilà, you are presented with the login page of your home OP. After authentication, you complete the necessary shipping and billing information. Your home OP does not release any personally identifiable information about you—only a "pairwise" ID that is different for every website you visit. If you ever need to return to this ecommerce site, for example to check the status of your T-shirt order, you won't need to remember site-specific credentials. In fact, you don't even have to sign in if you already have a session with your home OP. You simply click Login and you are presented with your order history.

OpenID Connect Discovery

The OpenID Provider configuration URL can be located at a domain using the WebFinger protocol (or an out-of-band mechanism). An `https` GET request to the configuration URL returns a JSON document, including the endpoints where it provides the OpenID Connect API. The path used to publish an OP's configuration endpoint is `https://domain/optional-path/.well-known/openid-configuration`. You'll see this quite often with different services, such as WebFinger, UMA, and other standards. The `/.well-known/` path is defined in RFC 5785 as a standard location to publish site metadata.

Figure 5-6 shows a sample Connect discovery response from a local test server. If you think that this looks like SAML IDP metadata in JSON format, you're right. SAML metadata provides the keys, service URLs, and other configuration or organizational information. One difference is that the keys are not present in the Connect configuration document, but are referenced by the `jwks_uri` claim. Figure 5-7 shows a sample JWKS from Google's Connect service. You can read more about JSON Web Keys in RFC 7517.

```
{
    "issuer": "https://albacore.gluu.info",
    "authorization_endpoint": "https://albacore.gluu.info/oxauth/seam/resource/restv1/oxauth/authorize",
    "token_endpoint": "https://albacore.gluu.info/oxauth/seam/resource/restv1/oxauth/token",
    "userinfo_endpoint": "https://albacore.gluu.info/oxauth/seam/resource/restv1/oxauth/userinfo",
    "clientinfo_endpoint": "https://albacore.gluu.info/oxauth/seam/resource/restv1/oxauth/clientinfo",
    "check_session_iframe": "https://albacore.gluu.info/oxauth/opiframe",
    "end_session_endpoint": "https://albacore.gluu.info/oxauth/seam/resource/restv1/oxauth/end_session",
    "jwks_uri": "https://albacore.gluu.info/oxauth/seam/resource/restv1/oxauth/jwks",
    "registration_endpoint": "https://albacore.gluu.info/oxauth/seam/resource/restv1/oxauth/register",
    "validate_token_endpoint": "https://albacore.gluu.info/oxauth/seam/resource/restv1/oxauth/validate",
    "id_generation_endpoint": "https://albacore.gluu.info/oxauth/seam/resource/restv1/id",
    "introspection_endpoint": "https://albacore.gluu.info/oxauth/seam/resource/restv1/introspection",
    "scopes_supported": [
        "clientinfo",
        "address",
        "profile",
        "mobile_phone",
        "email",
        "phone",
        "user_name",
        "openid"
    ],
    "response_types_supported": [
        "code",
        "code id_token",
        "token",
        "token id_token",
        "code token",
        "code token id_token",
        "id_token"
    ],
    "grant_types_supported": [
        "authorization_code",
        "implicit",
        "urn:ietf:params:oauth:grant-type:jwt-bearer"
    ],
    "acr_values_supported": [
        "internal",
        "u2f",
        "saml"
    ],
    "subject_types_supported": [
        "public",
        "pairwise"
    ],
    "userinfo_signing_alg_values_supported": [
        "HS256",
        "HS384",
        "HS512",
        "RS256",
        "RS384",
        "RS512",
        "ES256",
        "ES384",
        "ES512"
    ],
    "userinfo_encryption_alg_values_supported": [
        "RSA1_5",
        "RSA-OAEP",
        "A128KW",
        "A256KW"
    ],
    "userinfo_encryption_enc_values_supported": [
        "RSA1_5",
        "RSA-OAEP",
        "A128KW",
        "A256KW"
    ],
    "id_token_signing_alg_values_supported": [
        "HS256",
        "HS384",
        "HS512",
        "RS256",
        "RS384",
        "RS512",
        "ES256",
        "ES384",
        "ES512"
    ],
    "id_token_encryption_alg_values_supported": [
        "RSA1_5",
        "RSA-OAEP",
        "A128KW",
        "A256KW"
    ],
    "id_token_encryption_enc_values_supported": [
        "A128CBC+HS256",
        "A256CBC+HS512",
        "A128GCM",
        "A256GCM"
    ],
    "request_object_signing_alg_values_supported": [
        "none",
        "HS256",
        "HS384",
        "HS512",
        "RS256",
        "RS384",
        "RS512",
        "ES256",
        "ES384",
        "ES512"
    ],
    "request_object_encryption_alg_values_supported": [
        "RSA1_5",
        "RSA-OAEP",
        "A128KW",
        "A256KW"
    ],
    "request_object_encryption_enc_values_supported": [
        "A128CBC+HS256",
        "A256CBC+HS512",
        "A128GCM",
        "A256GCM"
    ],
    "token_endpoint_auth_methods_supported": [
        "client_secret_basic",
        "client_secret_post",
        "client_secret_jwt",
        "private_key_jwt"
    ],
    "token_endpoint_auth_signing_alg_values_supported": [
        "HS256",
        "HS384",
        "HS512",
        "RS256",
        "RS384",
        "RS512",
        "ES256",
        "ES384",
        "ES512"
    ],
    "display_values_supported": [
        "page",
        "popup"
    ],
    "claim_types_supported": "normal",
    "claims_supported": [
        "birthdate",
        "country",
        "name",
        "email",
        "email_verified",
        "given_name",
        "gender",
        "family_name",
        "updated_at",
        "locale",
        "middle_name",
        "nickname",
        "phone_number_verified",
        "picture",
        "preferred_username",
        "profile",
        "zoneinfo",
        "user_name",
        "website"
    ],
    "service_documentation": "http://gluu.org/docs",
    "claims_locales_supported": "en",
    "ui_locales_supported": [
        "en",
        "es"
    ],
    "claims_parameter_supported": true,
    "request_parameter_supported": true,
    "request_uri_parameter_supported": true,
    "require_request_uri_registration": false,
    "op_policy_uri": "http://ox.gluu.org/doku.php?id=oxauth:policy",
    "op_tos_uri": "http://ox.gluu.org/doku.php?id=oxauth:tos",
    "http_logout_supported": "true",
    "logout_session_supported": "true"
}
```

Figure 5-6. *Sample OpenID Connect configuration response*

```
{
 "keys": [
  {
   "kty": "RSA",
   "alg": "RS256",
   "use": "sig",
   "kid": "e571445873d190dd1c3d88e6972115932 1a5931c",
   "n": "yL6kzV9p4o4QkKxLT3haLBTAb0yguebw2vKhGxm7uyuhrezwdCdJhIYoJ10_fl2jyXZoB2jdtHr3knCuIL6asmDQULh0yJIYKIR1oZxWIFqUEtEOvtlHwWEPEwTKyQw6GuN-Kmtq146vGg0L6j1-a5usxZjGK51e8e0bqrab5R7bqTm9uduyLmbr5S6t0OemxiDSJDjKP4-nHnKkt9tQo3qqL7mG9M41Fq6oeNx2mrwqcJ3PQNK-EG7Cs2mH65fDHbMhwrPhrdc-bgQUksV3kVmWeaCWKU60oJN2Nxijd7xN-mcsaifvBpGoBImSdDdjiNcgqnx96ppnrkAMbh2jpw",
   "e": "AQAB"
  },
  {
   "kty": "RSA",
   "alg": "RS256",
   "use": "sig",
   "kid": "7042f54d6bc9410a692e8973029105a0c026c7db",
   "n": "x2FbGqCVNy4shioQrqBHy-QBU2riuWKBV18KiDX0YcLi7bcwvGSrxIYDLHsfXogzXkMf5_4vuTUMc7L8uhRePK-Sx-4HUazZwW_5kbo36gxfykxJarhaIV6X52T-IVnlroWaSwK44ATbd7UIwqjfKPYGV7cnT_H1880ovfQADw-RPeAaeO6yTMPkbMJ1oHoHWm1cV5JCpIFokpMYTR0aDdfw9AdYR1rCVuXISFw90ezZN7p35t1Nz-FKpYLV4f6aycswDBImPUhUxi_yhhQ7C1G12iQIxYu07VEPO7Lxdy9AIVH_nbpUAGFwCuBBDZPgGo08Dv5d5VZs7m7guuN1Zw",
   "e": "AQAB"
  },
  {
   "kty": "RSA",
   "alg": "RS256",
   "use": "sig",
   "kid": "53610fd61ea263e124f16b328e327bc89a342f70",
   "n": "sF0dOIKKniMxeIVD_XP7cic0NNfv5r4uQ5reb0cNhepXmV6h9TJ_z2JiskPyHVrWgjwiEGC2IXKKiXpFZduOU0rToDBimL-TAHzwEkvLChzLtLIgYQjEcBcuXilFNtZ_R7UKBPm8JscGnxVRgUndhGovDOsEqUQSMMFrv3ty03vb83Kg8B5S9CvfiTTo2sT2S4ZfTXibZI2cZGbKjpFVMyaEDexId_SgJ-9e8-9F1VoM8Rfdg1cKuzK8ADTDjfGJUaeO3CtSwjIJNAHdE158_Vp3_hBy8I2Rnqo1jhlH0C4EdzeD6Zcvx7Zn2jhmR3Sd1MipLazLq-b4raW7wto9ww",
   "e": "AQAB"
  }
 ]
}
```

Figure 5-7. *Sample JWKS from Google's OpenID Connect service*

From the client perspective, after receiving and processing the Connect discovery configuration response, a request can be made to obtain client credentials. In addition to knowing the URLs where the service is hosted, the client can also discover which cryptographic algorithms, scopes, user claims, and features are supported. The OpenID Connect Discovery specification defines what each of these values means, and conventions for some of the values. Some of the values are out of scope of the specification and are addressed in other standards.

Because the OP's public key is required to validate the signatures of the id_token and Userinfo JWTs, publishing OpenID Connect discovery information is a requirement for most OPs. It is a best practice to rotate keys every two days. Many SAML IDPs rotate keys much less frequently—once a year is not uncommon. The design goal behind such quick key rotation is to quickly identify problems. If key rotation is broken on the RP, and you find out a year later, the developers may have moved onto another project and lost familiarity with the client.

As with all security APIs, it is essential that https is used and that the certificate is properly validated. If an attacker can return incorrect discovery information, bad things can happen. For example, what if the hacker leaves the authorization_endpoint the same as the target OP, so the client obtains a valid code, but changes the `token_endpoint` so the client presents its client credentials and code to the hacker! Or if your client redirects the subject to the OP of an attacker, and it presents a reasonable looking login page, the person may leak their username and password!

This is also one of the risks that multi-party federations seek to mitigate—providing a trusted source for clients to obtain OP configuration metadata.

Client Registration

As OpenID Connect is a profile of OAuth, the client must tell the AS its `redirect_uri`—where to send the browser and authorization response after user interaction at the AS is complete. After processing a registration request, the OP will issue the client an identifier (`client_id`). Depending on the implementation, the client either registers or is issued a client secret. Client authentication is used to increase the security of obtaining a token on the back-channel. After successful registration, the OP may also return a registration access token, which can be used for subsequent update operations.

Client registration enables a client to register a JWKS document (containing its public key) or to specify a `jwks_uri`. This improves security because it avoids authentication based on a shared secret with the authorization server.

In SAML, the IDP normally either imports the SP metadata or manually configures the endpoints and imports its public certificates. The SP itself chooses its identifier—the `entityID`. In OAuth, this process is reversed: the OP issues the client identifier and sometimes even a shared secret used for client authentication.

In the interest of making this process more streamlined, the OpenID Connect Dynamic Client Registration API was introduced. In parallel, at around the same time, work began on OAuth client registration, which became RFC 7592. Other protocols, like the User Managed Access protocol, also take advantage of OpenID client registration. OpenID Connect client registration is simple: you can register and obtain information about your registration. In OAuth, there is also a client configuration API that can be used to update or delete client configuration. In practice, it is beneficial for OPs to also support the OAuth client configuration API. Figure 5-8 shows the registration flow from RFC 7592.

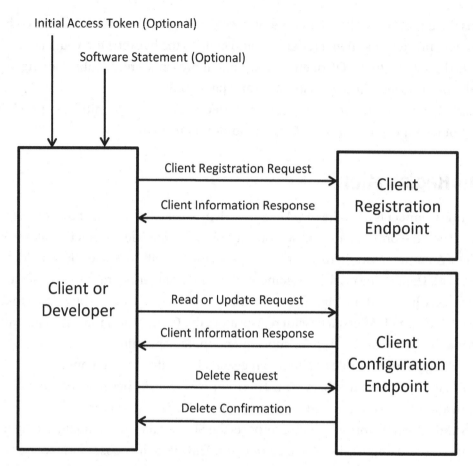

Figure 5-8. *RFC 7592 dynamic client registration flow diagram*

One of the most important parts of the Connect client registration specification is the section entitled "Client Metadata". In addition to specifying the redirect_uri, the client can tell the OP how it wants to interact—what algorithms to use for signing and encryption, what grant types it needs, what responses types it expects, and so on. While most OPs implement default values to keep client registration simple, to use advanced features, you'll need to understand the more esoteric parameters.

The Connect client registration API by itself is not always enough information to handle the requirements of enterprise IAM services. There is policy to consider. For example, in some cases, a client may request a certain configuration preference, but the OP may not allow it. The OP may also have client configuration requirements to handle enterprise requirements. For example, the Gluu Server has a client configuration parameter to signal to the OP to suppress the authorization approval message. In a corporate portal, which may be comprised on several client applications, it would be confusing to present the subject with multiple approval requests. Also, authorization is not needed if the websites in the portal are controlled by the same organization that operates the OP. Another example from the Gluu Server regarding authorization is a setting to enable the OP to only ask the subject to authorize a client once—remembering the person's past decision for subsequent requests.

Although there is a client registration API, there may be a manual workflow to approve registration requests—trust may require manual intervention. If unknown clients can register with an OP, what personal information about the subject should be released by default? In most situations, the OP should not release any PII in that situation. Connect requires the OP to release the openid scope to the client, which includes the subject identifier (which could be pairwise, thus not leaking any PII). An administrator at the OP may approve the release of additional information about the subject post-registration.

Another way to authorize clients to dynamically register, but request PII is to issue it a "software statement," which is like a registration access token. The software statement could be a signed JWT that the client presents to the OP to automate trust management. If the software statement is issued from a trusted source, like a federation operator, it can enable an OP to release claims without requiring a manual approval workflow. However, the mechanism for acquiring registration access tokens and software statements, presenting them during registration, or validating them is currently unspecified in the Connect and OAuth client registration specifications.

Authentication/Authorization

Like SAML, Connect is a federation protocol, not an authentication protocol. And like SAML, it is based on redirecting the person's web browser to an identity provider. Whether the person is authenticated by matching a password or validating possession of a hardware token, it doesn't matter—the authentication mechanism is outside the scope of Connect. However, Connect does care that the person was authenticated—that the physical person was present at some point to provide the necessary input. After the subject has been authenticated, Connect defines a flow to enable the person to authorize the release of user claims. The authentication and authorization processes are both defined in the Connect Core specification.

As discussed, after the client is registered, it can use the three endpoints that will enable it to authenticate a subject: the authorization endpoint, token endpoint, and Userinfo endpoint. Depending on the flow used, one, two, or three of these endpoints may be utilized. Different flows have different security profiles. Even the same flow used with different parameters can have a different security profile. The next few sections provide more details about how to use these different flows.

Response Types

OAuth 2.0 RFC 6749 defines response_type as a space-delimited list of values used by the client to signal to the authorization server the desired grant type. An OpenID Connect specification describes the use of multiple response types. The most common response type is code—which specifies the authorization code flow. Figure 5-9 summarizes the response_type values you might use. The none response_type is used to signal to the client a successful authorization without granting access to any API. Like the token response, it is not used for authentication, which would require an id_token.

response_type	Flow
code	Authorization code
token	Implicit – OAuth2 only
id_token	Implicit – OpenID Connect
id_token token	Implicit – OpenID Connect
code id_token	Hybrid
code token	Hybrid
code id_token token	Hybrid
none	See "OAuth 2.0 Multiple Response Type Encoding Practices"

Figure 5-9. *OpenID Connect response types*

Scopes

In OAuth scopes communicate the extent of access. In OpenID Connect, the extent of access maps to the release of user claims—the granting of a client access to certain information about the subject. Using scopes, an OP can group the release of user claims and present a person with one human understandable description for approval. For example, let's say we have a scope called `address` that includes information about a person's street, city, state, ZIP code, and country. Instead of prompting the person to approve each claim individually, the OP can simply ask, "Is it okay to release to this client information about your physical mailing address?" Connect requires that the `openid` scope is always present. This scope maps the subject identifier. If the `openid` scope is not present, you're not using OpenID Connect! How clients are assigned additional scopes can vary between OP implementations and trust models.

Authorization Code Flow

The code flow is the most common OpenID Connect authentication flow. Server-side applications should use it or the hybrid flow—not the implicit flow. Over-simplifying, it's a three step process:

1. Redirect the subject to the authorization endpoint.

2. Use the code and client credentials at the token endpoint to get the access token, `id_token`, and refresh token.

3. Use the access token at the Userinfo endpoint to get user claims.

Code Flow Step 1: Redirect to Authorization Endpoint

An example authentication request to an imaginary OP `login.example.com` is shown in Listing 5-2.

Listing 5-2. Sample Redirect to the Authorization Endpoint, an OpenID Authentication Request

```
HTTP/1.1 302 Found
Location: https://login.example.com/authorize?
          response_type=code
          &scope=openid
```

```
&client_id=b250c4a7-5551
&redirect_uri=https%3A%2F%2Fclient.example.com%2Fcb
&state=6d19327
&nonce=b722ff419a24
&acr_values=otp
```

The OP will render the login and authorization pages, as necessary. If everything goes well (i.e., the subject successfully authenticates and authorizes the request), the OP will respond with the code and state (see Listing 5-3).

Listing 5-3. Sample Successful Authentication Response

```
HTTP/1.1 302 Found
Location: https://client.example.com/cb?
          code=00e33be00c97
          &state=6d19327
```

The client must validate that the code returned is the one sent. This prevents cross-site request forgery (CSRF), which tries to execute unwanted actions on the client web application.

Code Flow Step 2: Get Tokens

Using the code and `redirect_uri` from Step 1, and base-64 encoded client credentials (or other supported client authentication methods), the client calls the token endpoint (see Listing 5-4).

Listing 5-4. Sample Token Request

```
POST /token HTTP/1.1
Host: login.example.com
Content-Type: application/x-www-form-urlencoded
Authorization: Basic YjI1MGM0YTctNTU1MTpzZWNyZXQ=

grant_type=authorization_code
 &code=00e33be00c97
 &redirect_uri=https%3A%2F%2Fclient.example.com%2Fcb
```

If the code and the client credentials are valid, the OP should return tokens (see Listing 5-5).

Listing 5-5. Sample Token Response

```
HTTP/1.1 200 OK
Content-Type: application/json
Cache-Control: no-store
Pragma: no-cache

{
  "access_token": "3b32043dbc5d",
  "refresh_token": "8984e43005c4",
  "token_type": "Bearer",
  "expires_in": 300,
  "id_token": "{header}.{payload}.{signature} )"
}
```

Note that this response is identical to an OAuth2 token response, as described in section 5.1 of RFC 6749, with the exception of the id_token, which is defined by OpenID Connect.

Step 3: Call Userinfo

In Step 3, you call the Userinfo endpoint with the access token you got in Step 2 (see Listing 5-6).

Listing 5-6. Sample Userinfo Request

```
GET /userinfo HTTP/1.1
  Host: login.example.com
  Authorization: Bearer 3b32043dbc5d
```

A sample Userinfo response from the OpenID Connect Core specification is shown in Listing 5-7 (the request we showed above would have been pretty boring because it only requested the openid scope). A more complete discussion of the Userinfo endpoint follows. This sample in Listing 5-7 will give you an idea of what it looks like.

Listing 5-7. Sample Userinfo Response

```
HTTP/1.1 200 OK
  Content-Type: application/json

  {
   "sub": "248289761001",
   "name": "Jane Doe",
   "given_name": "Jane",
   "family_name": "Doe",
   "preferred_username": "j.doe",
   "email": "janedoe@example.com",
   "picture": "http://example.com/janedoe/me.jpg"
  }
```

Connect defines several parameters that can be used during the call to the authorization_endpoint, which are summarized in Figure 5-10.

Param	Description
response_mode	How to return the response parameters: query, fragment, or form
nonce	Guess resistant string, returned in id_token, used to mitigate replay attacks
display	How the OP should display the authn / authz consent interface: page, popup, touch, or wap
prompt	Whether the OP should prompt for reauthentication and consent: none, login, consent, and select_account
max_age	Allowable elapsed time in seconds since the last time the end-user was actively authenticated
ui_locales	Subject's preferred languages and scripts for the user interface
id_token_hint	Used when prompt=none to acquire a new access token
login_hint	A mechanism to enable the OP to know the username of the subject
acr_values	Space delimited string specifying authentication preference of subject or client

Figure 5-10. *Authentication request parameters*

170

A few of these parameters need some more explaining. First of all, the `response_mode` parameter can use `query`, `fragment`, or `form`. `query` uses parameters in the URL to send back response data (key/value pairs after the ? in the URL); `fragment` puts information after the # in a URL; `fragment` includes some security advantages. On a redirect, the query is sent to the host, whereas the fragment is evaluated locally by the browser. The form `response_mode` is a Connect extension—it is not in defined in the OAuth specifications. There is an OpenID specification called OAuth 2.0 Form Post Response Mode that defines a mechanism to return a response to the client, which is similar to SAML's `POST` binding—response parameters are included in an HTML form, which uses JavaScript to automatically post back to the client `redirect_uri`.

Another interesting parameter is `prompt`. If you want to re-authenticate the subject, you can use `prompt=login`. If you want to receive a new access token without prompting the subject, you can use `prompt=none` with the `id_token_hint` parameter. Using `prompt=none` may trigger error responses if interaction with the end user is required, so if you use this feature, make sure you check for errors. Requesting `prompt=consent` should force re-authorization. If you wanted to achieve stepped-up authentication, you could use the `prompt=login` and `acr_`values parameters together.

On success, after the authorization endpoint returns a code, the client will make a request to the token endpoint. While this request is largely similar to the token request outlined in OAuth, Connect provides some extra considerations, the first of which is client authentication. During registration, the client can specify the `token_endpoint_auth_method` parameter. The options are `client_secret_post`, `client_secret_basic`, `client_secret_jwt`, `private_key_jwt`, and none. The default value is `client_secret_basic`. Of particular interest for enterprise IAM is `private_key_jwt`. Web SSO agents have been using asymmetric client credential secrets for some time, so using a shared client secret seems like a downgrade. One challenge with this is that it's harder for clients to generate a JWKS credentials.

If you are wondering how to create a JWKS, you can use a free utility published at
`https://mkjwk.org/`. Or you can download the command-line tool from GitHub at
`https://github.com/mitreid-connect/json-web-key-generator/`. You'll have to
follow the instructions on the README to compile the package and generate your keys,
but it's pretty easy.

The token response from the OP will include an access token and an `id_token`, and
usually a refresh token. The `id_token` will be a signed JWT, and as previously mentioned,
will be encrypted if the client provided a JWKS and requested encryption during client
registration. The `id_token` should be validated in a similar manner as the implicit flow.

Implicit Flow

The main difference between the OAuth and OpenID Connect implicit flows lies in the
use of the `id_token`, which must be returned in Connect. The `id_token` adds some extra
security. When the client calls the authorization endpoint, it includes a `nonce` value.
This value is returned unmodified in the signed `id_token`. The client must validate that
the `nonce` has not changed, which mitigates a replay attack. The `nonce` may be stored in
HTML5 local storage, or a hash of the `nonce` can be stored in a browser session cookie.
The OAuth2 state parameter should still be used—it serves a different purpose
(to quickly discard bad requests).

There is one more step to ensure the integrity of the transaction. Connect defines an
`id_token` claim called `at_hash`, which can be used to verify that the value of the access
token has not changed from when it was issued. If the `id_token` and `token` are both
returned from the authorization endpoint, as shown in Figure 5-11, then the client must
verify the `at_hash`.

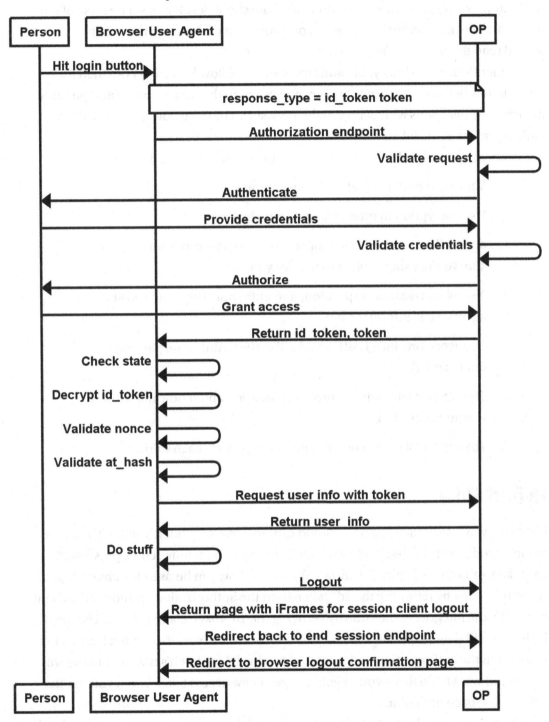

Figure 5-11. OpenID Connect implicit flow sequence diagram

You can see that Connect adds quite a bit of security over the generic flow described in OAuth. Also, other features are available to the client developer, such as use of the login parameter. For more information, or if you are a developer writing a client, you should read the *Implicit Client Implementer's Guide.*

As mentioned previously, the authorization code flow is more secure than the implicit flow because the tokens are never exposed to the web browser (and possibly malicious applications with access to the browser). The code flow also adds client authentication at the token endpoint.

Validating the id_token improves the security of the implicit flow:

1. Validate the JWT signature to ensure integrity.

2. Use encryption to protect against data leaking.

3. aud verification protects against token re-use—you want to make sure you're using a token issued for you.

4. The token issuance, expiration, and authentication times protect against stale information

5. The nonce prevents CSRF attacks, like the OAuth state parameter, but is signed.

6. The acr and amr claims convey information about how the subject was authenticated.

7. The access token can be validated using the at_hash value.

Hybrid Flow

Hybrid flow is one of the least understood Connect features, but it's actually not that complicated. The response_type for hybrid flow always includes code, plus token, id_token, or both. As Figure 5-1 shows, the hybrid flow can be used to achieve higher security levels—by returning the id_token from the authorization endpoint, the client can verify the integrity of the code by verifying the id_token claim c_hash. The most logical hybrid flow response_type is code id_token. You can also get back an access token from the authorization endpoint in the hybrid flow, but it's not clear to me why you would want to do this—you're going to get a new access token when you use the code at the token endpoint.

Figure 5-12 provides an overview of the hybrid flow for response type code id_token.

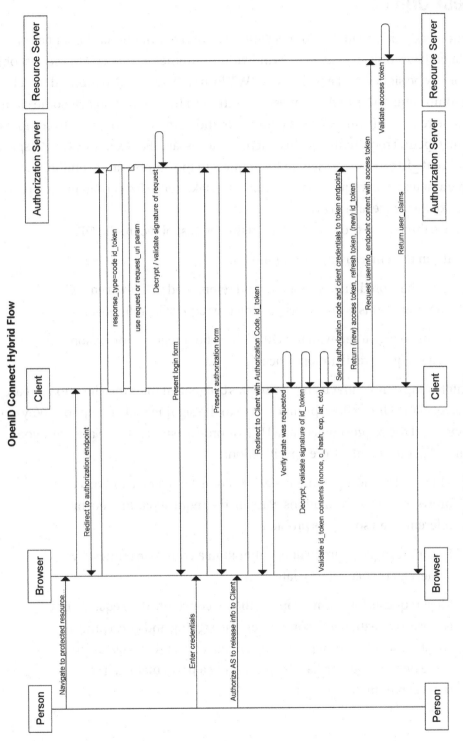

Figure 5-12. OpenID Connect hybrid flow sequence diagram

Request Object

The parameters used to call the Connect authorization endpoint may be sent as one consolidated JSON object, instead of as individual parameters. This JSON request object can optionally be signed and encrypted in JWT format. You can also mix and match—sending some parameters in the request and others in the request object. Some claims may even be repeated (sent as both a parameter and in the JSON object). To comply with OAuth and OpenID requirements, this might be necessary. For example, OAuth specifies that the client_id must be present in the request to the authorization endpoint. Mixing parameters with request objects can also make sense for certain parameters that change—like the nonce and state.

There are three ways the client can send the request object to the OP.

- It can be sent as a request parameter.

- It can be stored on a web server and referenced with the request_uri parameter. This is known as passing the request by reference.

- It can be registered with the OP during client registration or some other request registration process.

It's interesting to note that using the request object enables the client to increase the security level of the OAuth flow, primarily due to the signing and encryption. Why would you want to send the request object as a URI, or pre-register it? There are a few good reasons listed in the OpenID Core Specification:

- The set of request parameters can become large and can exceed browser URI size limitations. Passing the request parameters by reference can solve this problem.

- Passing a request_uri value, rather than a complete request by value, can reduce request latency.

- Most requests for claims from an RP are constant. The request_uri is a way of creating and sometimes also signing and encrypting a constant set of request parameters in advance. (The request_uri value becomes an "artifact" representing a particular fixed set of request parameters.)

- Pre-registering a fixed set of request parameters at registration time enables OPs to cache and pre-validate the request parameters at registration time, meaning they need not be retrieved at request time.

- Pre-registering a fixed set of request parameters at registration time also enables OPs to vet the contents of the request from consumer protection and other points of views, either itself or by utilizing a third party.

Userinfo Endpoint

The subject identifier is intrinsically interesting. It allows you to correlate a person's visits to your website. But very often, you want to know more information about the person that was identified at the OpenID Provider. While some of this information may be passed in the id_token itself, the Userinfo endpoint can provide additional claims about the subject (attributes in SAML or LDAP jargon).

In order to access the Userinfo endpoint, the client needs to obtain an access token from the token endpoint. One interesting characteristic of an OpenID Provider is that the Userinfo endpoint is that only protected API, as shown in Figure 5-2. Thus the OAuth resource server and authorization server are conflated into one logical unit.

Connect defines standard user claims. For dynamic configuration, the standardization of claims and scopes reduces one of the barriers to interoperability—agreement on user claim schema. Although standards people are famous for not agreeing on schema, there are a few issues with this part of the OpenID Connect standard. The first thing that could use improvement is that as the standard claims are defined in Section 5.1 of the Connect Core specification are difficult to reference. LDAP and SAML both provide a better mechanism for the identification of user attributes.

For example, no identifier is used other than the claim name—LDAP uses OIDs, SAML uses URIs. Another questionable decision is the use of the underscore character in the attribute names, which is not valid for an LDAP attribute name. The only explanation I've heard about why there are underscores in these attribute names is that an engineer at Facebook said that developers like them. If you want to do a direct mapping to LDAP, you'll have to do some kind of claims mapping.

Connect also defines four standard scopes, which enable a person to authorize the release of personal information in bulk: profile, email, address, and phone. Profile is interesting because it contains many commonly released attributes, including first name, last name, and username. It's handy to use OAuth scopes to enable a person to authorize the release of a group of claims. SAML never provided such a mechanism, so it's not clear how to handle this requirement—although people have tried (for example, search the Internet for Shibboleth uApprove).

But what if you have your own custom attributes? You could define your own scope and map your custom claims to this scope. The Connect Discovery specification enables an OP to publish `scopes_supported` and `claims_supported`. Unfortunately, there is no way for an OP to specify which claims are associated with which scopes. For this reason, the Gluu Server OP publishes a non-standard attribute called `scope_to_claims_mapping`. But even without this OP discovery claim, the correct scope could be communicated out-of-band. Figure 5-13 shows a custom OpenID scope being configured in the Gluu Server.

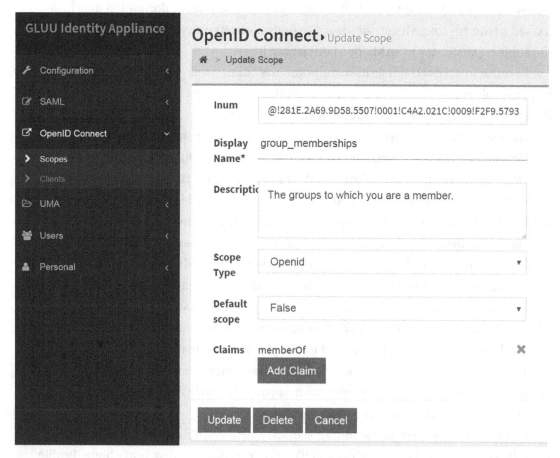

Figure 5-13. *Custom scope configuration in the Gluu Server*

It is also possible to request individual claims from the Userinfo endpoint. The OP signals to the client that this is possible by publishing the `claims_parameter_supported` discovery claim. The claims parameter value is a JSON object that provides details about the desired data. It may be advantageous to obtain specific combinations of claims that cannot be specified using scope values.

Logout

The bane of IAM professionals is currently logout—especially "single logout" or SLO. One of the challenges is that expectations vary. Consider this example: let's say you are logged into Google, and you have used Google login to authenticate to several websites, each open in a browser tab. After a while, you close some of these tabs (without indicated that you want to log out). And after some more time, you click the logout button on a website. What is your expectation? Would you expect to be logged out of Google? What about the other applications? What if, instead of Google as the OP, we change the scenario to websites that are hosted by your organization and connected to your corporate OP. Your expectation might be different?

The other challenge is that SLO is an inherently asynchronous process, and it's hard to solve with synchronous protocols that define requests and responses. In this example, to achieve SLO, we need to send messages to each of the applications, and to the OP. Some of those messages may be lost on the network and require retransmission. But how long does a person who just clicked a logout button want to wait to see a confirmation that they've been logged out?

OpenID Connect has defined three different imperfect mechanisms to affect SLO. The first is called Session Management, and involves using a JavaScript component in each tab that listens for a logout event, and sends a notification to the respective backend web server to end the application session. This is rarely implemented because it's so unreliable—if the browser tab is closed at the time logout is needed, it will never be executed, and the backend application will never be notified. It's also been logistically difficult to get applications to update their content to support this mechanism.

The other two mechanisms were introduced after OpenID Connect 1.0 was released, as it became apparent that the JavaScript logout approach was flawed. The two new specifications define front-channel and back-channel logout mechanisms, and overload the same `end_session` endpoint that was previously defined in the Session Management specification. Back-channel logout requires the OP to notify the application that a logout event happened. Front-channel logout requires the OP to return an HTML page, with an iFrame for each application that requires logout. The iFrame should cause the browser to call the logout page for each application. When it works, front-channel logout is a good option because it offloads the network traffic and processing to the browser. Also, the web applications can clean up cookies in the browser. The disadvantage of front-channel logout is that a person may disable third-party cookies, breaking logout. The other problem is that the OP has no idea what happened. Its best efforts—it returned the logout URLs to the browser and never receives any confirmation if each logout was successful. Consequently, it's possible that failed logouts won't be retried, and application sessions may persist.

Keep in mind that sessions are always in the context of a browser. If you have two different browsers open, and you log out of one browser, you would not expect to be logged out of the other browser. You would probably be even more surprised if you logged out on your laptop, and your sessions on your mobile device ended! It's up to the OP to track which clients are associated with each session and to attempt logout appropriately.

The elusive nature of logout may frustrate management at your organization. The best way to handle this is to make sure you understand the expectations for logout and try your best to achieve them. Things may get even more complicated if you have to consider logout across multiple protocols—for example if you are using both SAML and OpenID Connect in your organization.

Pairwise Identifiers

In our new world of big data analysis tools, the more websites you visit, the more digital breadcrumbs you leave across the Internet. It's important for some websites to know who we are—for example, your bank or the government. But other websites, you'd rather they not know your true identity. In the Shibboleth SAML IDP, there is a feature called "persistent non-correlatable identifiers". In Connect, the same idea exists, called "pairwise identifiers". The goal is to release a different subject identifier to each website, but to always release the same identifier for that person, each time the website is visited. This prevents several websites from colluding to correlate your identity, thereby protecting your privacy.

There are a few strategies for generating pairwise identifiers. The OP could store the information in a database and lookup the identifier when the subject returns. The other option is to use an algorithm to generate the identifier. You could for example use a hash of the subject's username, the `client_id`, and a salt value. Every time the person visits the site, the value for this function would be the same—so it avoids the need to write this information to the database.

A complication arises: what if there are a group of related websites that need a consistent identifier for the subject across the domain? Think of a portal application that is comprised of several related web components. If we issue each client a different identifier, it could break the portal. Connect defines a client claim called `sector_identifier_uri`. This URI is hosted by the RP and should return a JSON document with an array of related `redirect_uri` values. By specifying the `sector_identifier_uri` at registration, the client signals to the OP to use it instead of the client identifier to generate pairwise identifiers. Aspects of the algorithm for pairwise identifiers are defined in the Connect Core specification, but the exact algorithm is up to the OP implementation.

ACR/AMR Parameters

Since 1983, when the *WarGames* protagonist David Lightman (played by Matthew Broderick) snatched the password for his school district's mainframe ("pencil"), it's been well known that passwords are vulnerable to compromise. Connect defines two parameters to facilitate the use of strong authentication technologies: "acr" (Authentication Context Class Reference), and "amr" (Authentication Methods Reference).

The acr concept has existed since SAML, which defines a `AuthnContextClassRef` element as part of a `RequestedAuthnContext`. The values used for acr vary based on the administrative domain. The acr can carry meaning about trust, not just authentication strength. For example, the acr value is sometimes used to specify a NIST 800-63 level of assurance (1-4). The Connect Core specification indicates that an acr value of 0 signals to the RP that the authentication should not be used to secure a transaction of any monetary value. A common convention is to use a URI for the value of the acr, to enable the policies and procedures around to be externally defined. URIs are a good choice because they are in a collision-resistant namespace.

The amr authentication claim is new in Connect. This value is returned in the id_token, and it provides the OP with an opportunity to provide additional context around the authentication event. An OAuth draft proposes standard values for the amr claim, including `face`, `pwd`, `iris`, and `mfa`. The OP and client would have to know from some out-of-band mechanism what these values mean.

Let's consider an end-to-end example. Let's say a person uses a password to authenticate at the Gluu Server, and then navigates to a website. The Gluu Server returns an integer value as the first value of the amr array. This value corresponds to a "level," which can be associated with different types of authentication. Integers are convenient for automated policy evaluation. If the level is not sufficient, the client can direct the person back to the authorization endpoint, with an extra parameter `prompt=login`. This signals to the OP to re-authenticate the person. At that time, the client can also use the `acr_values` parameter to request a specific type of authentication.

The Gluu Server OpenID Connect Provider

While there are several open source OpenID Connect provider implementations, the Gluu Server was one of the first, and it is used in a wide array of consumer facing industries such as banking, telco, healthcare, government, education, and retail.

If you have been reading this book sequentially, you may already have installed it in Chapter 1. OpenID Connect is a required component. You may want to tweak some of the OpenID Connect settings. For example, perhaps you want to disable dynamic client registration. In general, the default settings ardently protect privacy. In a trusted enterprise setting, you may want to loosen some of the defaults, like token and session timeouts. You may want to extend client expiration time beyond one day.

The OpenID Connect features are derived from the oxAuth component. oxTrust is the administrative web interface for oxAuth to configure system settings, manually add or configure clients, define scopes, and associate user claims with scopes. You can script configuration using oxTrust administrative APIs.

The Gluu Server uses "interception scripts" to enable you to customize the behavior of the OpenID Provider. There are four in particular that apply to OpenID Connect, as outlined in Table 5-3.

Table 5-3. *Gluu Server Login Related Interception Scripts*

Script	Description
Person Authentication	Allows the definition of multi-step authentication workflows, including adaptive authentication, where the number of steps varies depending on the context.
Consent Gathering	Allows exact customization of the authorization (or consent) process. By default, the OP will request authorization for each scope, and display the respective scope description.
Dynamic Scopes	Enables admin to generate scopes on the fly, for example by calling external APIs.
Application Session	Called at the end of a web browser session to clean up third-party sessions or implement other business logic.

The Gluu Server was designed for high performance. You can use Redis to store short-lived objects, like the authorization code and access tokens. Long-lived data is written to the database—version 3.x uses LDAP and version 4.x introduces a database option for Couchbase, which allows for sharded deployments for very large data sets with requirements for high concurrency. For elasticity and automation, Docker and Kubernetes versions are also available, in addition to the virtual machine distribution you installed in Chapter 1. Following are some highlights of Gluu OpenID Connect features.

Gluu has some OpenID Connect client configuration options that you may find handy. One is called "Pre-Authorization". You can enable this if you trust a client and don't want to present the authorization (consent) screen when a person is accessing an application. For example, when you use a third-party application, Google asks for your permission. But when you use a Google application, they do not.

The Gluu Server supports pairwise identifiers and gives you two options to generate them: algorithmic and persistent. The former are generated dynamically as needed based on a hash of the `client_id` and subject identifier. If multiple clients are grouped using a `sector_identifier_uri`, it is used instead of the `client_id`. The advantage of algorithmically generated subject identifiers is that they reduce storage requirements. However, it's hard to search for a person with a specific algorithmic pairwise identifier. So the other approach is to generate a pairwise identifier for each client (or `sector_identifier_uri`) and store it in the database. This data is stored with the person's entry in LDAP or Couchbase.

The Gluu Server supports all authentication types at the token endpoint, including private key. Client_id and secret is a shared secret. If the client registers a public key for token authentication during registration, it improves security by avoiding shared secrets.

The Gluu Server provides a way to publish `sector_identifier` URIs. You could use a flat file for this, but the oxTrust provides an interface to search for clients, or to manually add redirect URIs.

For more information on the Gluu Server, see the documentation at `https://gluu.org/docs`.

Developing OpenID Connect Client Code

Now for the fun part! The next four sections will provide just an overview of client software, and a few examples of how to use OpenID Connect. All of these examples can be tested against the Gluu Server you setup in Chapter 1, although they should work against any OpenID Provider.

Easy JavaScript Client

This JavaScript client is one of the easiest ways to test OpenID Connect, although it's not the most secure (remember Figure 5-1). The client we will use was forked from a sample application written to demonstrate how easy it is to use Connect. Gluu forked the code and has enhanced it since that time. The project can be found at `https://github.com/GluuFederation/openid-implicit-client`.

It's not a fancy app—it sends the person to the authorization endpoint to be authenticated and then prints the claims that are returned in the `id_token`. Figures 5-12 and 5-13 are the two pages of the demo from that project. This client doesn't support dynamic client registration, so you'll have to add the client manually to the Gluu Server via the oxTrust Admin UI (or use the oxAuth RP web application, described later). When adding the client in oxTrust, the fields you should configure for the client are shown in Listing 5-8.

Listing 5-8. oxTrust Client Configuration for the OpenID Implicit Client Sample

```
Client Name: Implicit Test Client
response_type: token id_token
Application Type: Web
Pre-Authorization: Enabled
Subject Type: public
Scopes:openid, profile, email
Response Types: token id_token
Grant Types: implicit
```

Once you have registered the client, all you need to do is to update the client_id, redirect_uri, and providerInfo values in the login page HTML. Assuming you've checked out the project into a web accessible folder, then navigate to the page and test (see Figures 5-14 and 5-15)! Check the latest documentation for other features, like logout or calling the Userinfo endpoint. In this demo, you should configure the Gluu Server to return user claims in the id_token. Unfortunately, this client does not support logout.

Implicit Flow Test Login Page

Click button to login!   [Authenticate]

Figure 5-14. *Login page for OpenID Connect implicit client (implicit-test.html)*

Implicit Flow Test Callback

id_token

iss	https://albacore.gluu.info
aud	@!281E.2A69.9D58.5507!0001!C4A2.021C!0008!CEA9.AC75
exp	1481605690
iat	1481602090
nonce	rzhh37
auth_time	1481602090
at_hash	hY5bELWY_hK8g4JZbtV4ZA
oxValidationURI	https://albacore.gluu.info/oxauth/opiframe
oxOpenIDConnectVersion	openidconnect-1.0
inum	@!281E.2A69.9D58.5507!0001!C4A2.021C!0000!A8F2.DE1E.D7FB
name	Default Admin User
family_name	User
given_name	Admin
sub	@!281E.2A69.9D58.5507!0001!C4A2.021C!0000!A8F2.DE1E.D7FB

Figure 5-15. *Callback page for the OpenID Connect implicit client (login-callback.html)*

Apache httpd Module

One of the common approaches to protect a web application is to use a web server filter to intercept the request and make sure the person using that connection is authenticated and authorized (see Figure 5-16). The web server with the filter may directly serve the application, or may proxy to a backend service. Leveraging the web server is a well-established pattern, used by older access management platforms as old as CA Siteminder and SAML platforms like the Shibboleth SP.

Option 1: Application calls APIs directly

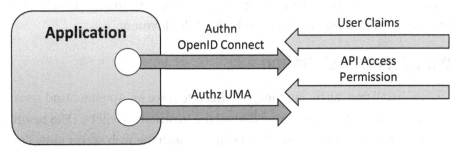

Option 2: Application is behind web server

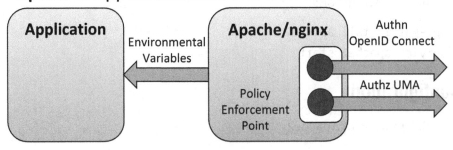

Figure 5-16. *Two approaches to web access management*

One of the advantages of the web server filter approach is that the application developer does not need to know that much about the security protocols—if the request makes it through to the application, the person has been authenticated, and the request is authorized. Another advantage is that application security is administered by the system administrators, not by developers. It may be easier to manage and audit Apache configuration files than to read a bunch of code.

One of the best OpenID Connect relying party implementations was written by Hans Zandbelt, called mod_auth_openidc. It is an authentication/authorization module for the Apache 2.x HTTP server that authenticates users against an OpenID Connect Provider. Currently, the software can be found at https://github.com/zmartzone/ mod_auth_openidc and is included in the package management system for several Linux distributions. There are binary packages available, and if you are good at compiling C code, you can build it yourself from the source. Note, if you are an Nginx fan, you can also take a look at a similar extension, also by Zandbelt, at https://github.com/ zmartzone/lua-resty-openidc.

Following are instructions for setting up an Apache HTTPD server on Ubuntu 14 (trusty). If you're using a Red Hat based system, you may have to adjust some of these commands to align with its style of Apache HTTPD deployment.

Basic Web Server Installation

Before you can install mod_auth_openidc, you need to have an Apache httpd server running with SSL enabled. It is assumed that all the hostnames will be DNS resolvable. If not, then add the entries in the /etc/hosts file on both the web server and Gluu Server. If you don't have the Apache HTTPD server installed, use apt-get to install the Ubuntu standard distribution:

```
#  apt-get install apache2
#  service apache2 start
```

SSL Configuration

Enable the SSL module in Apache2.

```
#  a2enmod ssl
```

Create a self-signed certificate. Answer the certificate signing request questions, using the server hostname for the "Common Name". If this is a production deployment, you should replace this with a certificate with one issued by a certification authority whose public key is in most browsers, like LetsEncrypt, https://letsencrypt.org

```
# openssl req -x509 -nodes -days 365 -newkey rsa:2048 -keyout/etc/ssl/
private/server.key -out /etc/ssl/certs/server.crt
```

Configure Apache to Use SSL

Open the default-ssl.conf file and update the certificate locations with the newly created private key and certificate:

```
# vi /etc/apache2/sites-available/default-ssl.conf
```

Activate the SSL virtual host and CGI:

```
# a2ensite default-ssl.conf
# a2enmod cgid
# service apache2 restart
```

Configuration of mod_auth_openid

The mod_auth_openidc module depends on the Ubuntu package libjansson4:

```
# apt-get install libjansson
```

You'll also need the mod_auth_openidc and libjose packages, which can be downloaded from the Releases page at https://github.com/zmartzone/lua-resty-openidc/releases. If there is no binary package for your distribution, you can build from source. Follow the instructions on the GitHub project page README.

For example, at this time the current release is 2.3.7, which depends on libjose 2.3 (see Listing 5-9).

Listing 5-9. Installing mod_auth_openidc

```
# wget https://github.com/zmartzone/mod_auth_openidc/releases/download/
  v2.3.0/libcjose0_0.5.1-1.trusty.1_amd64.deb
# wget https://github.com/zmartzone/mod_auth_openidc/releases/download/
  v2.3.7/libapache2-mod-auth-openidc_2.3.7-1.trusty.1_amd64.deb
# dpkg -i libcjose0_0.5.1-1.trusty.1_amd64.deb
# dpkg -i libapache2-mod-auth-openidc_2.3.7-1.trusty.1_amd64.deb
```

Now you can enable the module:

```
 # sudo a2enmod auth_openidc
 # sudo service apache2 restart
```

Client Registration

You could use either dynamic or manual client registration with mod_auth_openidc. For this example, let's create the client manually in the Gluu Server. When you add the client, use the parameters in Listing 5-10.

Listing 5-10. oxTrust configuration the OpenID Connect Client for mod_auth_openidc

```
Name: mod_auth_openidc
Client Secret: something-sufficiently-unguessable
Application Type: Web
```

```
Pre-Authorization: Enabled
login uri: https://www.mydomain.com/callback
Subject Type: Public
copes: openid, profile, email
Response Types: code
```

Make a note of the client secret (you won't get to see it again)! You'll also need the `client_id` for the next step.

Configuring the Apache VirtualHost

You are almost done! You'll need to configure `mod_auth_openidc` to protect your server.

```
# vi /etc/apache2/sites-available/default-ssl.conf
```

Add the code from Listing 5-11 right under `<VirtualHost _default_:443>`.

Listing 5-11. mod_auth_openidc Apache Web Server Directives

```
OIDCProviderMetadataURL https://idp.mydomain.com/.well-known/openid-
configuration
OIDCClientID (client-id-you-got-back-when-you-added-the-client)
OIDCClientSecret (your-client-secret)
OIDCRedirectURI https://www.mydomain.com/callback
OIDCResponseType code
OIDCScope "openid profile email"
OIDCSSLValidateServer Off
OIDCCryptoPassphrase (a-random-seed-value)
OIDCPassClaimsAs environment
OIDCClaimPrefix Userinfo_
OIDCPassIDTokenAs payload
<Location "/">
Require valid-user
AuthType openid-connect
</Location>
```

Then restart Apache to affect the changes.

```
# service apache2 restart
```

The most confusing part here is the OIDCRedirectURI—don't set this to a path used by your server. The Apache filter uses the redirect_uri to process the response from the OP.

Install CGI script

We're going to use the same sample script that we used in Chapter 3. If you don't have a copy somewhere, edit the printHeaders.cgi file and add the content from Listing 5-12.

Listing 5-12. Sample Python cgi-script to Print the HTTP Headers

```
#!/usr/bin/python

# Install in /usr/lib/cgi-bin/printHeaders.cgi

import os

d = os.environ
k = d.keys()
k.sort()

print "Content-type: text/html\n\n"

print "<HTML><HEAD><TITLE>printHeaders.cgi</TITLE></Head><BODY>"
print "<h1>Environment Variables</H1>"
for item in k:
    print "<p><B>%s</B>: %s </p>" % (item, d[item])
print "</BODY></HTML>"
```

Then you'll need to make the script executable by the Apache.

```
# chown www-data:www-data /usr/lib/cgi-bin/printHeaders.cgi
# chmod ug+x /usr/lib/cgi-bin/printHeaders.cgi
```

Now you're ready to test. Open your web browser and point it at https://www.mydomain.com/cgi-bin/printHeaders.py.

If you're not logged in already, you should be redirected to the authentication page. If you are logged in, you should just see an HTML page with the REMOTE_USER variable populated. Also check out OIDC_id_token_payload and all the claims for Userinfo.

oxAuth RP

The Gluu Server ships with an optional OpenID Connect relying party web application, called oxauth-rp, which is handy for testing because it prints the full request and response. During setup, you'll be asked if you want to install it, which you should on a development environment. It will be deployed on https://<hostname>/oxauth-rp. Using this tool, you can exercise all of the basic OpenID Connect APIs, including discovery, client registration, authorization, token, Userinfo, and end_session. Figure 5-17 shows a screenshot of the form you should see if oxauth-rp was installed successfully.

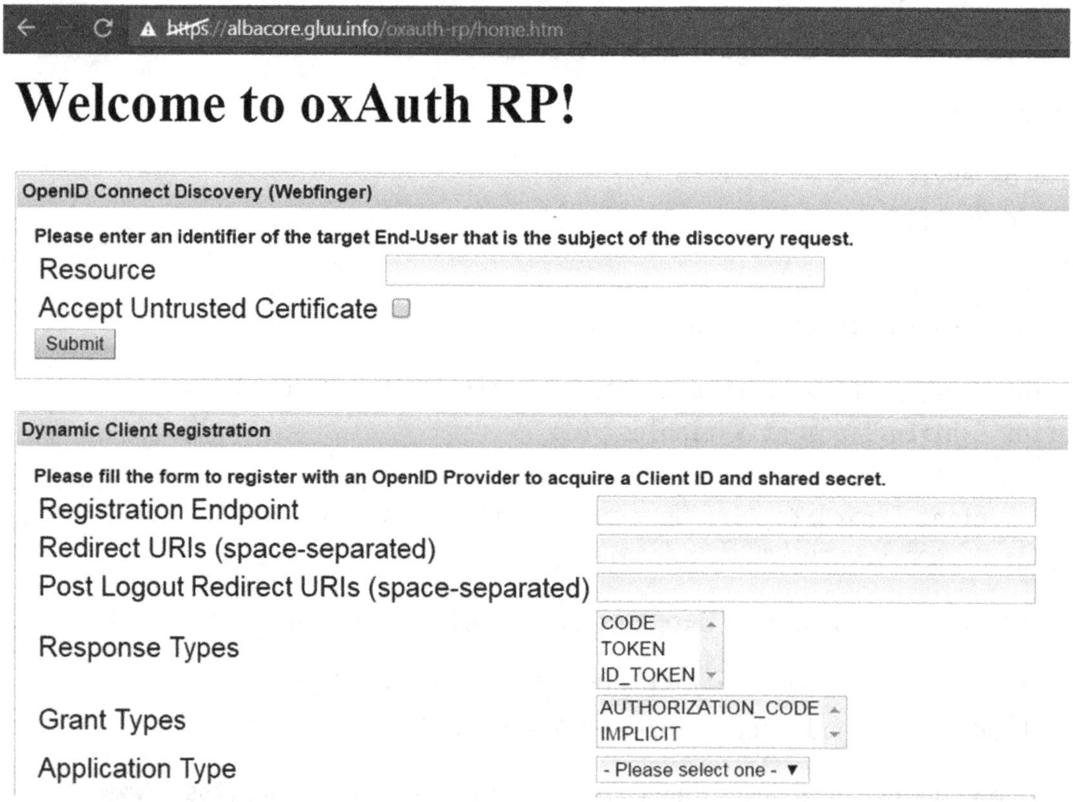

Figure 5-17. *oxauth-rp screenshot*

If you want to test an OP like the Gluu Server, you can follow this procedure. First, in the Discovery section, enter the hostname or email address of the OP. This will trigger a WebFinger request, which will return the configuration URL at which the OP's endpoints and configuration can be detected. The `oxauth-rp` web application parses the configuration JSON and populates the form accordingly. One handy feature of `oxauth-rp` is that it will show you the corresponding requests and responses.

Second, you'll want to register a client. Use the URL of `oxauth-rp` as the Redirect URI, for example, `https://<hostname>/oxauth-rp/home.htm`. You should also specify Response Type as `CODE`, Grant Type as `AUTHORIZATION_CODE`, the Application Type as `WEB`, Client Name as `oxauth-rp`, Subject Type as `PUBLIC`. Make sure the response returns a `client_id` and `client_secret`.

Third, you can move to the Authorization Endpoint form. If you registered as specified, use the Response Type as `CODE`, Scope as `openid`, `redirect_uri` should be populated for you already, State set to `12345`, `nonce` set to `abcd12345`, Display set to `Page`, and Claims set to `{}`. After clicking Submit, you should be redirected the OP login page (if you don't already have a session). After authentication and authorization, you should be redirected back to `oxauth-rp`.

Fourth, you should be able to submit your request to the token endpoint. You'll need to add Grant Type as `AUTHORIZATION CODE`, Redirect URI to `https://<hostname>/oxauth-rp/home.htm`, and Scope to `openid`. This response should include a JSON object that includes the `access_token`, refresh token, and `id_token` as keys in a JSON object. Finally, you'll just click Submit on the Userinfo form. The access token should already be populated.

AppAuth Mobile Applications

One of the most compelling reasons to use OpenID Connect is to authenticate people from a mobile application (see Figure 5-18). RFC 8252 "OAuth2 for Native Apps" provides an overview of an improved design for mobile security. In addition to the security features of OpenID Connect, this draft suggests the use of PKCE (briefly discussed in the previous chapter on OAuth) and custom URI schemes (i.e., an application can register a URI such as `myapp://` instead of `https://`). You can test AppAuth against the Gluu Server, as it supports PKCE and custom URI schemes.

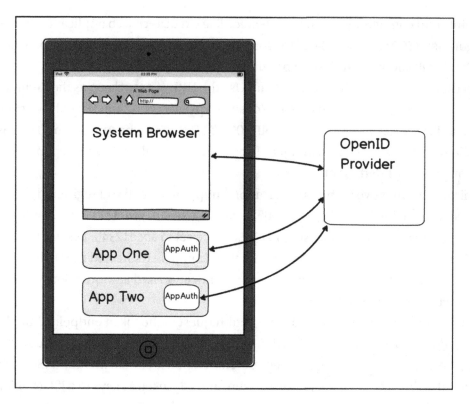

Figure 5-18. *AppAuth mobile SSO overview*

In 2016, Google released and then donated code to the OpenID Foundation called AppAuth for Android and IOS. Simultaneously, Google announced that it was deprecating the use of WebView—a strategy used by mobile application developers that is vulnerable to malicious application code. Not only does AppAuth provide secure authentication, it also enables SSO across the system browser and mobile applications. It uses operating system hooks so that the system browser does not enable an application developer to steal a person's credentials, codes, or tokens. Using this approach, mobile application developers can use the authorization code or hybrid flow. You can find the AppAuth code on GitHub:

```
https://github.com/openid/AppAuth-Android
https://github.com/openid/AppAuth-iOS https://github.com/openid/AppAuth-JS
```

oxd Client Middleware Service

Many applications are "server-side," meaning the web page displays content, but most of the dynamic business logic resides on the web server. Many server-side libraries, some of which are free open source, are listed on the OpenID Foundation website at `http://openid.net/developers/libraries`. The features of these libraries vary. At a high level, the OpenID Foundation RP certification program sheds light on which libraries support which flows (see Figure 5-19). However, the certification tests don't tell you anything about optional features (like private key authentication at the token endpoint) or usability. Unfortunately, some libraries are hard to use, not well documented, or lack examples.

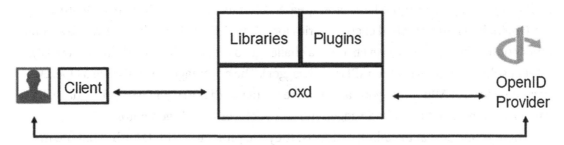

Figure 5-19. *oxd overview*

Even if a client library makes it possible to use certain Connect features, developers may not bother. After login works, developers have a tendency to ignore extras, like checking signatures and state values. For this reason, Gluu releases the `oxd-server` client middleware service. It provides an easy RESTful interface that helps Connect client developers quickly use an OP, while letting the `oxd-server` do some of the heavy lifting, like checking the state and signature.

Another good reason to use the `oxd-server` is to facilitate updates. If your organization uses several client libraries, you need to make sure they are kept up-to-date. Also, because oxd provides a higher level API than OpenID Connect itself, it can implement new features of Connect or OAuth without changing the interface to your application, which may break something or trigger a new QA cycle. It's likely that attacks will be discovered against OAuth and Connect. An abstraction layer makes it easier to update the client code quickly.

Installation instructions for `oxd-server` can be found on `https://gluu.org/docs/oxd/install`. You don't need to create a client manually because the `oxd-server` uses dynamic client registration. You may want to extend the registration of oxd registered clients, so they don't expire in the default one day time period for dynamic clients.

There are two configuration files that you'll need to configure in the /etc/oxd folder: oxd-conf.json (which contains basic configuration information for the service) and oxd-default-site-config.json (where you should add the URL of your OP). Make sure that you start the oxd service and see it listening on the default port 8443.

oxd is not a proxy—it is middleware. For front-channel calls (authorize and logout), it returns a URL that's used by your application to redirect the person's browser to the OP. However, oxd makes back-channel calls directly to the Token and Userinfo endpoints. That's why in Figure 5-16, there are lines both from the person and between oxd and the OP. oxd validates the id_token, caches the nonce and state parameters, uses private key authentication at the token endpoint, and is constantly being updated and improved to support the latest and greatest Connect and OAuth security features.

Originally, Gluu published client libraries for oxd in Python, Java, php, Ruby, and several other popular languages. However, it was a challenge to maintain all these libraries. Luckily, a better solution emerged: OpenAPI (i.e., Swagger). The advantage of publishing a OpenAPI document for oxd APIs is that you can generate client libraries in your favorite language. It's easy to do using a platform like SwaggerHub, or your favorite code generator.

There is one caveat to calling oxd APIs: they are protected with OAuth. That means you'll need to obtain a client access token before you call them. Luckily, the oxd-server has an API that makes this easy to do—there is also an API for this. So the basic flow for using oxd is as follows:

1. Obtain OAuth client token with scope oxd.

2. Call the get_authorization_url endpoint, which returns the URL to which your application should redirect the person's browser. Make sure you obtain the state and code from the OP response.

3. Call the get_tokens_by_code endpoint and present the code and state from the previous step.

4. Call the get_user_info endpoint using the access token returned from the previous step.

5. Call the get_logout_uri endpoint when you're done and send the person's browser to the returned URL.

The oxd-server also has APIs for UMA and OAuth and is used as a component of the Gluu Gateway, which is discussed at the end of Chapter 6 on web proxies.

OpenID Connect Glossary and IANA Registry Terms

Just like OAuth, Connect has introduced many terms that were registered at IANA. Tables 5-4 to 5-9 show summaries of these terms. For an updated list, see http://www.iana. org/assignments/oauth-parameters/oauth-parameters.xhtml.

Table 5-4. *OpenID Connect OAuth Authorization Endpoint Response Type (Specified in OAuth 2.0 Multiple Response Type Encoding Practices)*

Parameter	Description
id_token	Implicit flow
id_token token	Implicit flow
code id_token	Hybrid flow
code token	Hybrid flow
code id_token token	Hybrid flow
None	No client access credentials returned

Table 5-5. *OpenID Connect OAuth Extensions Errors (Specified in OpenID Connect Core)*

Parameter	Description
interaction_required	OP requires end user interaction of some form to proceed, but prompt=none
login_required	OP requires end user authentication, but prompt=none
account_selection_required	OP requires end user to select account, but prompt=none
consent_required	OP requires the end user to authorize, but prompt=none
invalid_request_uri	OP cannot read request object specified at URI
invalid_request_object	OP cannot parse the JSON request object
request_not_supported	OP does not support request objects
request_uri_not_supported	OP does not support request URIs
registration_not_supported	OP does not support registration parameter

Table 5-6. *OpenID Connect OAuth Parameter (Specified in OpenID Connect Core Specification, Except session_state, Which Is Defined in the Session Management Specification)*

Parameter	Parameter Usage Location	Description
nonce	Authorization request	Per-session state and be unguessable to attackers
display	Authorization request	Client preference for end user authentication and consent user interface
prompt	Authorization request	Client preference for end user interaction
max_age	Authorization request	Maximum authentication age
ui_locales	Authorization request	End user's language preference for UI
claims_locales	Authorization request	End user's language preference for claims
id_token_hint	Authorization request	Hint by client about an end user's past session
login_hint	Authorization request	Hint to the OP about the end user's preferred identifier or account
acr_values	Authorization request	Space-separated string specifying the acr values requested by the client
claims	Authorization request	Used to specify specific claims
registration	Authorization request	Used to request client registration simultaneous with authorization request
request	Authorization request	Specify request object JSON
request_uri	Authorization request	Specify location of request object JSON
id_token	Authorization response, access token response	JWT returned with information about the subject and authentication event
session_state	Authorization response, access token response	session_state value at the OP

Table 5-7. *OpenID Connect Dynamic Client Registration Metadata (All These Parameters Are Defined in the OpenID Connect Dynamic Client Registration 1.0 Incorporating Errata Set 1)*

Parameter	Description
application_type	Kind of the application: native or web
sector_identifier_uri	URL using the https scheme to be used in calculating pseudonymous identifiers by the OP
subject_type	subject_type requested for responses to this client: pairwise or public
id_token_signed_response_alg	JWS alg algorithm REQUIRED for signing the ID token issued to this client
id_token_encrypted_response_alg	JWE alg algorithm REQUIRED for encrypting the ID token issued to this client
id_token_encrypted_response_enc	JWE enc algorithm REQUIRED for encrypting the ID token issued to this client
Userinfo_signed_response_alg	JWS alg algorithm REQUIRED for signing userinfo responses
Userinfo_encrypted_response_alg	JWE alg algorithm REQUIRED for encrypting userinfo responses
Userinfo_encrypted_response_enc	JWE enc algorithm REQUIRED for encrypting userinfo responses
request_object_signing_alg	JWS alg algorithm that MUST be used for signing request objects sent to the OP
request_object_encryption_alg	JWE alg algorithm the RP is declaring that it may use for encrypting request objects sent to the OP
request_object_encryption_enc	JWE enc algorithm the RP is declaring that it may use for encrypting request objects sent to the OP

(*continued*)

Table 5-7. (*continued*)

Parameter	Description
token_endpoint_auth_signing_alg	JWS alg algorithm that MUST be used for signing the JWT used to authenticate the client at the token endpoint for the private_key_jwt and client_secret_jwt authentication methods
default_max_age	Default maximum authentication age
require_auth_time	Boolean value specifying whether the auth_time claim in the ID token is REQUIRED
default_acr_values	Default requested authentication context class reference values
initiate_login_uri	URI using the https scheme that a third party can use to initiate a login by the RP
request_uris	Array of request_uri values that are pre-registered by the RP for use at the OP

Table 5-8. *OpenID Connect OAuth Token Endpoint Authentication Methods*

Parameter	Reference	Description
client_secret_jwt	RFC 7591	Mechanism to send client credentials as JWT
private_key_jwt	RFC 7591	Mechanism to send client credentials as JWT, using previously registered public key to verify client identity

Table 5-9. *OpenID Connect JSON Web Token Claims (Specified in OpenID Connect Core Specification)*

Parameter	Description
given_name	Given name(s) or first name(s)
family_name	Surname(s) or last name(s)
middle_name	Middle name(s)
nickname	Casual name
preferred_username	Shorthand name by which the end user wishes to be referred
profile	Profile page URL
picture	Profile picture URL
website	Web page or blog URL
email	Preferred email address
email_verified	True if the email address has been verified; otherwise false
gender	Gender
birthdate	Birthday
zoneinfo	Time zone
locale	Locale
phone_number	Preferred telephone number
phone_number_verified	True if the phone number has been verified; otherwise false
address	Preferred postal address
updated_at	Time the information was last updated
azp	Authorized party: the party to which the ID token was issued
nonce	Value used to associate a client session with an ID token
auth_time	Time when the authentication occurred
at_hash	Access token hash value
c_hash	Code hash value
acr	Authentication context class reference
amr	Authentication methods references
sub_jwk	Public key used to check the signature of an ID token

Conclusion

Hopefully you now have a better idea of what OpenID Connect is. Whether you have a consumer facing application with low security requirements, or a top-secret application with high security requirements, Connect is a good choice as the interface to centralize identity. Over time, it's likely we'll see fewer applications that add support for SAML, and more applications that add support for OpenID Connect. Federated identity is a moving target, but Connect and OAuth seem well positioned to adapt to new technology and meet new requirements as they arise.

References

1. "OpenID Connect Discovery 1.0 incorporating errata set 1," http://openid.net/specs/openid-connect-discovery-1_0. html, Sakimura, Bradley, Jones, Jay, November, 2014.

2. "OpenID Connect Dynamic Client Registration 1.0," http:// openid.net/specs/openid-connect-registration-1_0.html, Sakimura, Bradley, Jones, May 2015.

3. "OAuth 2.0 Dynamic Client Registration Management Protocol," https://tools.ietf.org/html/rfc7592, Jones, Bradley, Machulak, July 2015.

4. "OpenID Connect Dynamic Client Registration 1.0 incorporating errata set 1," http://openid.net/specs/openid-connect-registration-1_0.html, Sakimura, Bradley, Jones, November, 2014.

5. "OAuth 2.0 Multiple Response Type Encoding Practices," http:// openid.net/specs/oauth-v2-multiple-response-types-1_0. html, de Medeiros, Scurtescu, Tarjan, Jones, February 2014.

6. "OpenID Connect Implicit Clint Implementer's Guide 1.0," http://openid.net/specs/openid-connect-implicit-1_0. html, Sakimura, Bradley, Jones, de Medeiros, Mortimore, August 2015.

7. OAuth 2.0 Form Post Response Mode, `http://openid.net/`
   `specs/oauth-v2-form-post-response-mode-1_0.html`, Jones,
   Cambell, April 2015.

8. "OpenID Connect Core 1.0 incorporating errata set 1,"
   `http://openid.net/specs/openid-connect-core-1_0.`
   `html#RequestUriRationale`, Sakimura, Bradley, Jones, de
   Medeiros, Mortimore, November 2014.

9. "OAuth 2.0 for Native Apps," `https://tools.ietf.org/html/`
   `draft-ietf-oauth-native-apps-06`, Denniss, Bradley November
   2016.

10. "OAuth 2.0 Multiple Response Type Encoding Practices," `http://`
    `openid.net/specs/oauth-v2-multiple-response-types-1_0.`
    `html`, de Medeiros, Scurtescu, Tarjan, Jones, February 2014.

11. "OpenID Connect Core 1.0 incorporating errata set 1," `http://`
    `openid.net/specs/openid-connect-core-1_0.html`, Sakumura,
    Bradley, Jones, de Medeiros, Mortimore, November 2014.

12. OpenID Connect Session Management 1.0 - draft 27," `http://`
    `openid.net/specs/openid-connect-session-1_0.html`, de
    Medeiros, Agarwal, Sakimura, Bradley, Jones, August 2016.

13. "OpenID Connect Dynamic Client Registration 1.0 incorporating
    errata set 1," `http://openid.net/specs/openid-connect-`
    `registration-1_0.html`, Sakimura, Bradley, Jones, November
    2014.

CHAPTER 6

Proxy

A proxy is a web server middle-man. It receives an HTTP request from a client, forwards
it to another web server, and after receiving a response, returns it to the client (see
Figure 6-1). Proxies should be "transparent," meaning they don't impact either the
client or the backend web service.

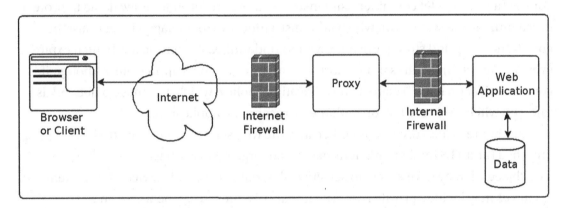

Figure 6-1. *Proxy overview*

In some cases, the proxy uses a path to map the upstream web service. For example,
consider the URL https://www.example.com/myService. In this case, the proxy answers
to the hostname www.example.com, but myService is used as a "junction" to the location
of the upstream web resource. Alternately, a web server could use a hostname to map an
upstream service. For example, https://myservice.example.com.

You may hear your peers use the term "reverse" proxy. As proxies, by definition, go
in both directions, you may have trouble figuring out what's reverse about it. You're not
alone. Maybe people used the term "proxy" to describe the type that is used to intercept
web browser traffic within an organization. If they considered this the "normal" direction
for a proxy, i.e., outbound web requests, then proxying inbound traffic is reverse.

205

© Michael Schwartz, Maciej Machulak 2018
M. Schwartz and M. Machulak, *Securing the Perimeter*, https://doi.org/10.1007/978-1-4842-2601-8_6

Many web application frameworks include a web server component. For example, J2EE applications are deployed inside a servlet container (i.e., a web server). Python Flask builds in a web server implementation. Many system administrators feel uncomfortable exposing these web servers directly to the Internet. Although fairly secure—most vulnerabilities are identified and patched quickly by the community—correctly configuring any web server requires familiarity with the platform. Thus, in a heterogeneous environment, with developers using many web frameworks and tools, it's hard for system administrators to know them all. It's a good practice to minimize the number of Internet-facing web server implementations, so administrators have a smaller surface area to protect from the riskiest network segment.

Configuration of Internet-facing web services is not a trivial task. Many web servers utilize security plugins that prevent attacks. As a result, although a platform like Apache Tomcat (a J2EE servlet container) isn't insecure, there are fewer tools available to protect it. Minimizing the systems on which administrators have to manage TLS may also be a goal. Generating and storing private keys and updating X.509 certificates (which expire every few months) requires more effort than many developers appreciate. Although if your organization has a "secure communication" policy, which assumes no network is safe, you will have to use SSL on both the proxy and the application.

Another reason to use a proxy is because the web server is "dumber". If TLS is breached (and TLS implementations have been targeted in the past, such as by Heartbleed), it may have access to sensitive files, databases, and services. File system resources may include private keys. The impact of a breach can be worse on the application server than on the web proxy. The proxy may have lot of data going through it, so a breached proxy is bad too, but if you have to pick your poison, many security experts will choose the proxy.

From a pure network standpoint, most large organizations want to put Internet-facing proxies on a different network segment, i.e., the "DMZ". An Internet-facing firewall protects the DMZ, and a second firewall protects the private network. This strategy prevents Internet-connected servers from directly communicating with internal databases, or other services that require additional security.

While security was the initial driver, proxies created new opportunities to do some other handy stuff. The following is a discussion of those features.

Load Balancing

If you are building a robust web service, you need to eliminate single points of failure. Figure 6-2 is a high-level representation of a typical approach.

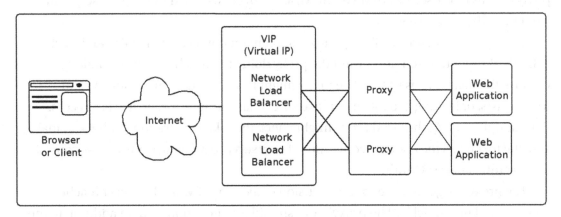

Figure 6-2. *Overview of load balancing*

When a browser or client makes an HTTP request, the host portion of the request resolves to one IP address. We don't want the proxy itself to be a single point of failure. The network load balancer infrastructure normally handles this requirement and routes the request to an available proxy. At this point, the proxy has to route the request to the "upstream" web server. It would be silly to fail if another server could handle the request.

The proxy infrastructure also provides a path to upgrading the upstream applications without incurring downtime. For example, you can take an upstream server out of the available pool, upgrade it, and then add it back.

Network load balancers and proxies normally can handle timeouts automatically. The sophistication of health checks vary. At the simplest level, you can look at the TCP/IP connection—can you connect to the host and port? Of course, a service might listen on a port and still be non-responsive (i.e., hang). Some proxies and load balancers implement "active health checks" to a predetermined URL. "Passive health checks" monitor every request and response. The health checks operate as circuit breakers by switching traffic from an unhealthy service instance to a healthy one. The proxy must use active health checks to restore the circuit breaker automatically, since there is no regular traffic to monitor. Alternately, an administrator can manually reset the circuit breaker.

Access Control and Security

As a funnel for incoming web requests, the proxy is a very good place to enforce security policies. In fact, several early commercial web access management products used the proxy for this purpose, e.g., IBM WebSEAL and Novell Access Manager (subsequently NetIQ and then Micro Focus).

The proxy makes an excellent policy enforcement point (PEP) in a P*P architecture (PEP, PDP, PAP, etc.). You don't want the proxy doing too much policy evaluation because the main goal is speed. The proxy might be checking to make sure a valid token exists, or looking at a token to make sure it has the appropriate level of access. For example, an OAuth-based proxy might check the token expiration or check to make sure the token has the correct scopes. But of course a proxy can use any access control architecture, not just OAuth.

The proxy is a good place to run intrusion detection software. If it gets breached, you want to know quickly. The proxy's logs should also be monitored, in addition to the upstream web server logs. If an attack happens, the logs will contain vital information, such as the network source of the web request.

There is also a security benefit to masking the upstream servers. In security, you always want to expose as little information as possible to potential attackers. By proxying, you hide potentially useful information such as the web server type and network information.

Rate Limiting

An organization may have a mix of web performance requirements. For example, an organization's web services may handle requests from internal departments, partners, customers, or even anonymous Internet clients. Each of these client classes may have different expectations, or even service level agreements. To appropriately deliver web content, it may be necessary for an organization to prioritize certain requests. Proxy implementations can either block requests beyond a threshold amount or delay them. Rate limiting can also help prevent data scraping—although attackers may still attempt to scrape data while living within the rate limit.

Rate limiting can also be an important security feature. Hackers may launch a denial of service attack (DoS) by overloading your web services. By specifying maximum traffic limits, the proxy can prevent overloading the upstream web services. However, the proxy by itself might not be enough to protect you from a DoS attack, which can swamp the proxy itself, so you may need to implement hardware and network strategies as well.

Organizations that charge for web services may use rate limiting for monetization. It's not uncommon for companies that sell APIs to offer a certain number of calls for a given time period. For example, two requests a minute are free.

Proxies use different algorithms to implement rate limiting. There is a tradeoff between performance and precision. A discussion of rate-limiting algorithms is beyond the scope of this book, as there is a large existing body of work on this topic. The algorithms are more complex when multiple proxies are deployed in a clustered solution. In this case, communication is needed between the proxies, normally via a high-speed in-memory network cache, like Redis or memcached. This shared state between the systems will obviously incur some overhead and hence add latency to the traffic. As with any database application, the algorithm needs to mitigate the risk of race conditions and blocking. The different algorithms define various mechanisms to minimize latency, usually at the cost of real-time accuracy.

Caching and Compression

The goal of caching and compression is to gain speed, to minimize network traffic, and to reduce load on upstream servers. It is superfluous for the upstream server to generate the same response twice. Caching is a win-win: it's more efficient for the organization hosting the web service, and it results in a faster response for the web client. Caching only makes sense for the HTTP GET method. The POST, PUT, and DELETE methods are write requests and can't be cached.

The client can use the Cache-Control HTTP header to control how the proxy handles caching. The following is not a full discussion of how to use this header, but it should give you an idea of some of the options.

If the client wishes to prevent the proxy from caching a response, such as to protect sensitive information like a credit card number, it can specify:

Cache-Control: no-store

If a client does not want to get back cached results, it can specify:

Cache-Control: no-cache

The client can also specify a maximum age or request that a proxy not return cached response, even if it has expired (a proxy may do this if a backend service is unavailable):

```
Cache-Control: max-age=3600, proxy-revalidate
```

Cache implementations vary—read the documentation for your proxy.

Telemetry

Human evolution favored those of us who were able to detect changes in our visual environment. Was that flash of stripes a tiger? In information technology, we can put our visual acuity to work by looking at graphs and other reports. Due to the complexity of our infrastructures, it is hard to even diagnose problems if you can't literally see them.

Pretty pictures are not possible without data. Telemetry is the process of recording and transmitting the readings of an instrument—in this case our proxy. Web servers create logs with lots of data. These logs must be processed to produce graphs. Newer proxies send the data needed for analytics at runtime and enable integration with visualization tools like Grafana.

Beyond passively capturing data, the proxy can play an active role by inserting tracking identifiers into the request and response. Tools can use these tracking identifiers to report on transactions through their lifecycle, such as using an open source tool like OpenTracing. It's helpful if system administrators can see execution times and latencies of an entire request cycle, and even configure monitoring tools to send alerts if thresholds are exceeded.

Monetization

The API proxy is like the gate at a large concert—someone has to take the tickets before you get to see the rock band! API monetization can integrate with accounting or e-commerce platforms to transform web traffic into currency!

Amazon, the e-commerce juggernaut of the world, does a really good job at this. Amazon Web Service (AWS) enables developers to monetize APIs built with the AWS API Gateway using Amazon bill calculation and collection mechanisms. API usage plans allow developers to set rate limits and quotas, and to create multiple usage plans with different limits (e.g., Silver, Gold, or Platinum) and offer them as different API products on the Amazon Web Service (AWS) Marketplace.

There are three API monetization models:

- **Tiered**—Access is differentiated by either features, response time, rate limits, volume, or data depth. Additional costs may be incurred for overages, or discounts may be applied for volume.

- **Flat fees**—APIs are billed uniformly based on usage.

- **Freemium**—Try-buy-fly. APIs are free for a certain length of time or for a certain quantity of calls.

Points or credits may be used in lieu of fiat currency. For example, maybe you get 2,500 credits for free, but if you pay $50 per month, you get 5,000 credits. The advantage of this strategy is that it reduces some of the financial friction in the technical infrastructure, especially when customers are global and may want to pay in various fiat or crypto currencies.

In some cases, you could build the billing into the code of the APIs themselves. The intersection of monetization and APIs definitely occurs where billing is a factor in access control.

API vs Web Proxy

A front-channel HTTP request is sent from a person's browser to a web server (or user agent). A back-channel request is sent from a software agent—it can even be a machine-to-machine operation that doesn't involve a person. Therefore, front-channel requests require a web proxy, while back-channel requests use an API proxy.

From the perspective of a proxy, this is a subtle difference. You may even wonder why it matters.

Web proxies need to think about the user experience. A web proxy will need to brand messages to a person. If everything goes well, the web proxy is invisible to the person using a browser. However, if there is an error, for example a non-existent page is requested, the response will vary based on who is making it. A response to a user agent will need to format pages appropriately with the right CSS, JavaScript, and images, while error responses to a software agent are informational only. Web proxies need to be smarter about the variety of browsers, perhaps sending a different response based on the type of browser or logging the information.

Web applications use cookies to track sessions. Session validation is an important feature for a Web proxy. It's easier for a software agent to use the path to request parameters or HTTP headers to communicate information to a web service. And software agents are normally stateless—each request is self-contained and, from the proxy perspective, doesn't depend on previous requests. The software agent equivalent of a session is a token, typically sent in the Authorization header.

Protocols like OpenID Connect, which involve multiple steps—they get the code, use the code to get an access token, and then use the access token to get user_info—are more complex to implement in a proxy and require more advanced handling of state across a series of requests. Also if a web proxy is responsible for authenticating a person, it will need to convey the resulting authentication information to the upstream application. For example, the proxy may set the person's username in the HTTP_REMOTE_ USER header variable. Other HTTP headers may convey other user claims (e.g., HTTP_ EMAIL and HTTP_NAME). Alternately, the web proxy may just send the identity assertion (e.g., HTTP_ID_TOKEN and HTTP_USER_INFO).

The security policies may differ for a web proxy. While a user agent primarily specifies the GET and POST methods, software agents may use all available methods, like PUT and DELETE, and even extension methods like PATCH. Web proxies may want to block these methods.

Open Source Web Proxies

The open source web proxies are as follows.

Apache httpd

The first web server to be used as a proxy was Apache httpd. There are two commonly used approaches:

- The ProxyPass and ProxyPassReverse directives
- The Rewrite directive

The upstream API is mapped to a folder or hostname using the Apache Directory or VirtualHost configuration directives.

It's possible to combine directives. For example, you can require authentication and proxy at the same time. This is a common strategy for handling SAML authentication. A Shibboleth SP proxy configuration might look like Listing 6-1.

Listing 6-1. Apache ProxyPass Example

```
<VirtualHost _default_:443>
    ServerName proxy.example.com
    <Location />
        AuthType shibboleth
        ShibRequestSetting requireSession 1
        Require shib-attr memberOf Manager
    </Location>
    ProxyPreserveHost On
    ProxyPass /target https://target.example.com/mySite
    ProxyPassReverse /target https://target.example.com/mySite
</VirtualHost>
```

Here is a summary of the commands:

- `AuthType shibboleth`—This signals to Apache to use the `Shibboleth` filter for authentication.

- `Location`—This directive limits the scope of the enclosed directives by URL, which is different than `Directory`, where you control access rights to a directory (and its subdirectories) in the file system. In this example, we are using base URL `/`.

- `Require shib-attr memberOf Manager`—This directive requires that certain attributes must contain the specified values in the request. In this case, the `memberOf` attribute must be `Manager` in order to pass the authentication.

- `ProxyPass`—This directive allows remote servers to be mapped into the space of the local server. The local server does not act as a proxy in the conventional sense, but appears to be a mirror of the remote server.

- `ProxyPassReverse`—This directive lets Apache Httpd adjust the URL in the `Location`, `Content-Location`, and `URI` headers on the HTTP redirect responses.

In the discussed configuration, the client attempting to access `https://proxy.example.com/target` is first required to be authenticated by Shibboleth, and then Apache makes a reverse proxy request to `http://target.example.com/` to get the final content displayed on the browser.

mod_auth_openidc

This Apache module functions as an OpenID Connect relying party, authenticating users against an OpenID Connect provider, after which it receives user identity information either via the `id_token` or the `UserInfo` JWT.

Sample configuration to use Gluu as an OpenID Connect provider is shown in Listing 6-2.

Listing 6-2. Sample Configuration to Use Gluu as an OpenID Connect Provider

```
<VirtualHost *:443>
    ServerAdmin webmaster@localhost
    DocumentRoot /var/www/html
    OIDCProviderMetadataURL https://idp.mydomain.com/.well-known/openid-
    configuration
    OIDCClientID (client-id)
    OIDCClientSecret (your-client-secret)
    OIDCRedirectURI https://www.mydomain.com/callback
    OIDCResponseType code
    OIDCScope "openid profile email"
    OIDCSSLValidateServer Off
    OIDCCryptoPassphrase (a-random-seed-value)
    OIDCClaimPrefix USERINFO_
    OIDCPassIDTokenAs payload

    <Location "/">
        Require valid-user
        AuthType openid-connect
    </Location>
```

```
    ProxyPreserveHost On
    ProxyPass /target http://target.host.org/resource.html
    ProxyPassReverse /target http://target.host.org/resource.html
</VirtualHost>
```

A summary of the various directives follows:

- OIDCProviderMetadataURL—The URL for the OP configuration metadata, i.e., the location of the .well-known/openid-configuration file.

- OIDCClientID—The client identifier (client_id) issued by the OP.

- OIDCClientSecret—The secret corresponding to the client_id.

- OIDCRedirectURI—This path will be used by mod_auth_openidc to receive the callback from the OP with the response. It should not map to content on the website.

- OIDCResponseType—The response type expected from the authorization endpoint. Use code for code flow and code id_token for hybrid flow.

- OIDCScope—The scopes requested from the OP.

Nginx

Many system administrators prefer Nginx as a lightweight web server, especially for proxying. A basic nginx.conf file for proxying would look something like Listing 6-3.

Listing 6-3. Sample Nginx Proxy Configuration

```
events {
        worker_connections 1024;
}
http {
  server {
    listen      80;
    server_name  proxy.example.com;
    return      301 https://proxy.example.com$request_uri;
  }
```

```
server {
  listen        443;
  server_name proxy.example.com;
  ssl on;
  ssl_certificate         /etc/nginx/ssl/cert.crt;
  ssl_certificate_key     /etc/nginx/ssl/key.key;

  location / {
    proxy_pass https://backend.example.com/
  }
  location /items {
    proxy_pass https://backend.example.com/items
  }
 }
}
```

Some explanation:

- The worker_connections directive under the events context defines how many clients can be served simultaneously by Nginx. The default is 1024.

- The server directives under the http context are where we define the behaviors of the Nginx web server and see how to handle different requests.

- As you can see in the first server directive, requests are automatically redirected from http calls to https. This is done by listening on port 80 and returning a 301 redirect to the port 443 equivalent of the web server.

  - Inside the following server directive block, we defined our SSL/TLS capabilities with the following declarations: ssl on, ssl_certificate, and ssl_certificate_key.

  - Next is the location directive, which defines what should happen to client requests. For example, a client request to https://proxy.example.com/items will proxy on the backend to https://backend.example.com/items. This will also route traffic to all "children" of this directory, unless another hardcoded

location is defined. For instance, /items/shoes/ will be handled
by this directive unless you have a location /items/shoes/ {}
directive, which will override this one.

A way to further enhance the proxying capability with more complex requirements
is to use the upstream context. In that block, multiple servers can be pooled together
with more complex redundancy processes and load balancing. For an example, see
Listing 6-4.

Listing 6-4. Sample upstream Context

```
http {
  upstream backend_items {
  server backend01.example.com:443 max_fails=2 fail_timeout=10s;
  server backend02.example.com:443 max_fails=2 fail_timeout=10s;
  }
  upstream backend_users {
  server backend03.example.com:443 max_fails=2 fail_timeout=10s;
  server backend04.example.com:443 max_fails=2 fail_timeout=10s;
  }
  server {
    listen        80;
    server_name  proxy.example.com;
    return        301 https://proxy.example.com$request_uri;
  }
  server {
    listen        443;
    server_name proxy.example.com;
    ssl on;
    ssl_certificate        /etc/nginx/ssl/cert.crt;
    ssl_certificate_key    /etc/nginx/ssl/key.key;

    location / {
      proxy_pass https://backend.example.com/
    }
    location /items {
      proxy_pass https://backend_items/items
```

```
      proxy_next_upstream      error timeout invalid_header http_403  http_404
      http_500 http_502 http_503 http_504;
      proxy_connect_timeout    2;
  }
  location /users {
    proxy_pass https://backend_users/users
    proxy_next_upstream      error timeout invalid_header http_403  http_404
    http_500 http_502 http_503 http_504;
    proxy_connect_timeout    2;
  }
}
```

Some explanation:

- To expand on our previous configuration, the upstream directives
  were added to the http context. Here, we define the server pools,
  backend_items and backend_users. These blocks contain each
  server in that proxy pool. By default, Nginx handles the server pools
  in a round-robin fashion: each server is requested in order until it
  rolls back to the first server and the process begins again.

  - Note that each server added must begin with server followed by
    the path to the server. Optional ports can be defined as well. In
    our example, 443 is used.

  - To control failover, Nginx provides max_fails and fail_timeout.
    The former sets the maximum amount of connection failures
    a server can have before it's considered unavailable. The latter
    defines how long Nginx should wait for a connection and also
    how long the server should be considered unavailable.

- Now moving to the location blocks, the proxy_pass directive for
  /items and /users points to the upstream pools defined previously,
  as opposed to any single URL. Anytime a user or agent tries to access
  https://proxy.example.com/users, Nginx will route that request to
  one of the servers defined in the backend_users pool
  (https://backend03.example.com/users for example).

- The proxy_next_upstream directive will forcefully route traffic to the next server in the upstream block if any of the following conditions are met. So if the server that Nginx is trying to route a request to presents an error, has a timeout, returns an invalid_header, or returns any of the HTTP response codes 403, 404, 500, 502, 503, or 504, Nginx will then switch to the next server in the pool.

These are only some of the tools available with Nginx. Let's examine a more complex example and extend the functionality to limit access to people authenticated using OpenID Connect. This example uses the lua-resty-openidc module, written by Hans Zandbelt (who also wrote the Apache module mod_auth_openidc plugin). The instructions for installation can be found at https://github.com/zmartzone/lua-resty-openidc. At this point you should have two servers: one is the OpenID Connect provider, which is idp.example.com in our example. The other server hosts the Nginx web server (tested with version 1.11.2.5) with the lua-resty-openidc dependency properly configured. This second server will be called rp.example.com.

The lua-resty-openidc Nginx library uses the OpenID Connect Authorization Code Flow. The Nginx OpenResty server in this example is the OpenID Connect RP. After navigating to the Nginx OpenResty server, the user will be redirected to the OP. After authentication and authorization, the RP will gather user information from the OP and send the user to the proxied content.

First, let's register the OpenResty client with the OpenID Provider, in this case the Gluu Server. Navigate to your Gluu Server, and on the left panel, click OpenID Connect, and then Clients. Click the Add Client button. Choose a descriptive name for your client, like lua-resty-openidc for convenience (this is only for human readability). Jump down to the bottom, where you will choose Add Login Redirect URI, Add Scope, Add Response Type, and Add Grant Type. For our example, our Redirect Login URI will be https://rp.example.com/welcome to match the hostname of the OpenResty server we will configure shortly.

Now, click Add Scope and Search to display all scope options. Check email, openid, and profile. Next, click Add Response Type and check Code. Click Add Grant Type and check authorization_code. For our simple example, this is enough, and we can click the Add button at the bottom of the page. Once we've done this, we can gather our inum of the client we just created from the OpenID Connect -> Clients dashboard next to the Display Name. OpenResty's Nginx configuration will use this inum as the client_id and the secret we created before will be our client_secret. That's all we need to configure the Gluu Server as the OP.

Take a look at the OpenResty Nginx configuration. By default OpenResty installs their build of Nginx at /usr/local/openresty/nginx/conf/nginx.conf. We want to replace this configuration with our own, as shown in Listing 6-5.

Listing 6-5. OpenResty Nginx Configuration

```
events {
  worker_connections 1024;
}

http {

  lua_package_path "/usr/local/openresty/?.lua;;";

  resolver 8.8.8.8;

  lua_ssl_trusted_certificate /etc/ssl/certs/ca-certificates.crt;
  lua_ssl_verify_depth 5;

  # cache for discovery metadata documents
  lua_shared_dict discovery 1m;
  # cache for JWKs
  lua_shared_dict jwks 1m;

  server {
      listen 80 default_server;
      server_name _;
      return 301 https://$host$request_uri;
  }
  server {
    listen 443 ssl;

    ssl_certificate /usr/local/ssl/nginx.crt;
    ssl_certificate_key /usr/local//ssl/nginx.key;

    location / {

      access_by_lua_block {

          local opts = {
              redirect_uri_path = "/welcome",
```

```
        discovery = "https://idp.example.com/.well-known/openid-
        configuration",
        client_id = "$INUM",
        client_secret = "$SECRET",
        ssl_verify = "no",
        scope = "openid email profile",
        redirect_uri_scheme = "https",
    }

    -- call OIDC user authentication
    local res, err = require("resty.openidc").authenticate(opts)

    if err then
      ngx.status = 500
      ngx.say(err)
      ngx.exit(ngx.HTTP_INTERNAL_SERVER_ERROR)
    end

    ngx.req.set_header("X-USER", res.id_token.sub)
  }
 }
 }
}
```

There are a couple of things to be aware of with this configuration. lua_package_
path must point to the proper location of lua-resty-openidc.lua and its dependencies.
If you installed the packages with the OpenResty Package Manager, this can be left as
shown in Listing 6-4. The ssl_certificate and ssl_certificate_key options should
point to the web certificates for this web server. Creating self-signed certificates isn't
difficult and is the reason we have the ssl_verify option set to no. Replace the $INUM
and $SECRET terms with client_id and client_secret we created earlier in the Gluu
Server.

That's it. Now you can start OpenResty from OpenResty's bin directory. After that,
navigate to https://rp.example.com and you should be redirected to the IDP where you
can log in. After giving consent, you'll be redirected to the default OpenResty landing
page in the /usr/local/openresty/nginx/html/index.html directory.

Looking through the examples and issues in the `lua-resty-openidc` GitHub repo will give you a better understanding of the robust nature of what you can achieve with these tools.

Kong

Kong is an open source API gateway that is free to use (see Figure 6-3). It originated from the Mashape API marketplace (now RapidAPI), where it served tens of thousands of APIs. After the API Marketplace was sold to RapidAPI, Kong Inc. (rebranded from Mashape) focused on extending the API gateway as an open source project.

Figure 6-3. *Kong*

There are two versions of the product. One is the Enterprise Edition, which includes additional tools for documentation and analytics, as well as additional features on the gateway itself. There is also the Community Edition of Kong, which is the bare gateway.

Some of Kong's key features are:

- Very fast, sub-millisecond latency on the core gateway

- Small footprint, suitable for sidecar patterns

- Extensible through custom plugins

- Open source, no black box

- Extensive and active community

- Over 60 plugins available

Kong Technical Component Overview

Kong as a gateway is built on top of the well-known Nginx web server. It is written in Lua (with the OpenResty framework) and as such is easy to extend. For its configuration, it uses a database. You can choose either Postgres or Cassandra. Many Kong nodes can be connected to the same database, and they will then form a Kong cluster. A Kong cluster scales horizontally; all you need to do is add Kong nodes. The Kong configuration is dynamic, which means that any changes made to the configuration will automatically propagate over the entire Kong cluster and take effect within seconds, without having to deploy and push configurations.

Kong is available in packages for more than 12 platforms, from Docker images to source code.

Kong Functional Component Overview

The relationship between several entities determines how you can configure Kong. The entities are: `route`, `service`, `consumer`, `plugin`, `upstream`, and `target`. The last two, `upstream` and `target`, are specific for load-balancing and health-check purposes. We'll not address those here, but the Kong website has excellent documentation.

- Route—A route is a set of matching rules. Whenever a request is received, its characteristics will be matched against the configured `route` entities, and the best match is assigned as the route for this request. Matching can be done on the requested hostname (`host-header`), the requested path, and/or the requested HTTP method. Every route is always connected to one `service` (services can have multiple routes).

- **Service**—A service is the representation of the backend service, where the request will be routed. This means that a service contains all properties for an upstream connection, including host, port, path, connection timeouts, connection retries, and other information to control Kong's proxy behavior. A service can contain many routes.

- **Consumer**—Software that is calling the API. In OAuth, this is mapped to a client. In more primitive API access control implementations, you might use HTTP Basic Authentication, or some other type of shared secret (e.g., an API key or a signed JWT).

- **Plugin**—Plugins add functionality to Kong. Plugins can be attached to any combination of service, route, or consumer. A plugin will be executed when a request is received for any of the items it is attached to. When plugins are not attached to anything, they are global and will be executed on every request. Many standard plugins are included for functions like authentication, security, traffic control, serverless, analytics/monitoring, transformations, and logging. There are also many community-contributed plugins. It is possible to write your own plugins if you're up for learning about Lua and publishing some Lua rocks!

Getting Started with Kong

To get started with Kong, you can use the Docker distribution to quickly create a setup that is fully functional without too much hassle. We'll take the following steps here: (1) Set up Kong and database, (2) Create an API in Kong, and (3) Enable authentication on that API, using plugins.

To get started with Docker, execute the following shell commands.

Step 1: Set up a local PostgreSQL instance (see Listing 6-6).

Listing 6-6. Installing Dockerized Kong

```
> docker run -d --name kong-database \
-p 5432:5432 \
-e "POSTGRES_USER=kong" \
-e "POSTGRES_DB=kong" \ postgres:9.5
```

The command will start a new container running PostgreSQL version 9.5. The container goes by the name kong-database and exposes a single port 5432 to connect to the database. kong is both the username and password.

Step 2: Initialize the Kong database by running Kong migrations up (see Listing 6-7).

Listing 6-7. Initializing the Kong Database

```
> docker run --rm --link kong-database:kong-database \
-e "KONG_DATABASE=postgres" \
-e "KONG_PG_HOST=kong-database" \ kong:latest \
kong migrations up
```

This will start an ephemeral container with Kong running its migrations up command. When completed, it will simply exit. The command will pull the latest version of Kong (as per kong:latest).

The previously created PostgreSQL container kong-database is made available as hostname kong-database. The two environment variables, KONG_DATABASE and KONG_PG_HOST, are passed to Kong to tell it to use PostgreSQL as the database and connect to it as kong-database.

We do not need to pass the port nor any credentials, as Kong defaults to port 5432 and kong for both the username and password (all according to the previously created PostgreSQL container). Obviously, they can be altered and passed along using other settings from Kong's configuration file.

Step 3: Start Kong (see Listing 6-8).

Listing 6-8. Starting Kong

```
> docker run -d --name kong --link kong-database:kong-database \
-e "KONG_DATABASE=postgres" \
-e "KONG_PG_HOST=kong-database" \
-e "KONG_PROXY_ACCESS_LOG=/dev/stdout" \
-e "KONG_ADMIN_ACCESS_LOG=/dev/stdout" \
-e "KONG_PROXY_ERROR_LOG=/dev/stderr" \
-e "KONG_ADMIN_ERROR_LOG=/dev/stderr" \
-e "KONG_ADMIN_LISTEN=0.0.0.0:8001, 0.0.0.0:8444 ssl" \
-p 8000:8000 \
-p 8443:8443 \
-p 8001:8001 \
-p 8444:8444 \
kong
```

This will now actually start Kong and run the container as a daemon (the -d option). From the previous command, there are a few new options passed along. First of all, exposing the Kong ports for the proxy (8000 for http and 8443 for https traffic) and for the Kong administrator interface (8001 for http and 8444 for https). Second, the log files are set to stdout and stderr as per Docker best practices.

Finally, there is the KONG_ADMIN_LISTEN option that tells Kong to listen on all interfaces for the administrator interface. The default here is to only listen on localhost, but since it runs inside a container, that would make it unreachable from outside the container, and hence prevent us from configuring anything.

Step 4: Check your installation.

Run the command docker ps and it should show two containers running, kong and kong-database. To test Kong itself, try making an HTTP GET request on the Kong proxy port 8000 using the following command:

```
> http get :8000
```

This uses the http command provided by httpie (see https://httpie.org), which is a utility that is similar in functionality to curl but provides an easier command line and nicer output, shown in Listing 6-9.

Listing 6-9. Testing Kong

```
HTTP/1.1 404 Not Found Connection: keep-alive
Content-Type: application/json; charset=utf-8 Date: Thu, 19 Apr 2018
18:09:14 GMT
Server: kong/0.13.0 Transfer-Encoding: chunked
{
"message": "no route and no API found with those values"
}
```

The output (despite being an error) clearly shows that Kong is running but cannot find a matching route for the simple test request.

Step 5: Create a service and route.

To actually start using the system, we need to create a route (to catch incoming requests) and a service (where to send them).

```
> http post :8001/services name=test url=http://mockbin.org
> http -f post :8001/services/test/routes hosts[]=myapi.com
```

The route catches any request destined for host myapi.com, then the service will forward it to mockbin.org (a test service to create and debug test requests)

Step 6: Test the activated API.

Make the following request to get a returned copy of your request from mockbin.org.

```
> http get :8000/request host:myapi.com
```

This inserts a host header that matches the route we created earlier. This makes Kong forward the request as expected, and we get a result with a body containing all details of the request we send.

Step 7: Add client authentication using HTTP basic.

By using the `key-auth` plugin, we can quickly secure our test API. Execute the following:

```
> http post :8001/services/test/plugins name=key-auth
```

If you now test the API again (Step 6), you'll get a `401 unauthorized` response. The API is now protected and can only be accessed by providing proper credentials.

Step 8: Add a consumer and credentials.

Since credentials are bound to consumers, we first create a consumer, and then provide credentials for that consumer.

```
> http post :8001/consumers username=aladdin
> http post :8001/consumers/aladdin/key-auth key=OpenSesame
```

Now we can test again (same as Step 6), but we only need to add our key to the request:

```
> http get :8000/request host:myapi.com apikey:OpenSesame
```

Step 9: Examine the response.

When examining the response from Step 8, there are a number of artifacts inserted by Kong into the request and the response.

If you look at the response headers, you'll notice some extra headers:

```
Via: kong/0.13.0
X-Kong-Proxy-Latency: 0
X-Kong-Upstream-Latency: 114
```

The `Proxy-Latency` header shows the latency it took Kong to process the request/response (in milliseconds, so 0 means less than a millisecond). The `Upstream-Latency` is the time it took the upstream to respond.

In the response body, you'll see that our `mockbin.org` test API returned a copy of the request we sent it. And here you can find the details of the authenticated consumer:

```
"apikey": "OpenSesame",
"x-consumer-id":  "3469667b-f4e0-44ca-8356-120563e7c897", "x-consumer-
username": "aladdin",
```

The backend does not have to do its own authentication; it can just grab the details it needs from the headers of the request.

Step 10: Consider some warnings.

These example steps demonstrate the basics of Kong, although obviously this is not a recipe for a secure production deployment. Here are some obvious points to consider:

- All requests are plain HTTP—all APIs should be HTTPS.

- The example backend is reachable by bypassing Kong. Your network firewalls should only allow access through Kong.

- The `apikey` header is forwarded to the backend—configure Kong to remove it.

- Kong's admin API is accessible.

Istio

Launched in 2017 by IBM, Google, and Lyft, Istio is setting the bar for a containerized proxy platform. Istio requires Kubernetes v1.9 or newer. In addition to the elasticity that comes with Kubernetes, Istio provides a few compelling features:

- **Traffic management**—The ability to route requests based on flexible rules is a compelling advantage of Istio. For example, let's say you want to route 10% of your traffic to version 1.1 of your API, while routing 90% to version 1.0. You can implement these kinds of rules in Istio quickly, which is quite difficult in other API gateway platforms.

- **Telemetry Istio**—It's built on a new web server, Envoy (see `https://envoyproxy.io`), which provides quite a bit of telemetry out of the box. This enables you to use a tool life Grafana to provide a visual representation of what's happing in your proxy deployment.

- **Mutual TLS**—You can configure mutual TLS on a per service basis. You can also configure role-based access control (RBAC) for each service.

Istio facilitates accurate monitoring of the health and activity of your micro-services. It also makes it possible to apply policy across dozens or hundreds of micro-services all at once. This is where powerful tooling helps give you control and an accurate picture of your service ecosystem.

For more information on Istio, see the website at `https://istio.io`. Because it's so new, there wasn't enough time to provide a detailed overview here. But given its potential, it seemed remiss not to mention it. Check it out!

Conclusion

Proxying is a powerful technology that keeps getting better. New tools are getting faster, more flexible, more reliable, and easier to manage. Controlling access to web content via the proxy is an essential part of any IAM strategy. In Chapter 8, we'll introduce one more proxy: the Gluu Gateway. This is an open source distribution that uses Kong community edition, but adds some extra IAM management components.

CHAPTER 7

Strong Authentication

Wouldn't you rather stop a security breach than detect it? So why do organizations have a love affair with intrusion detection systems and neglect strong authentication? While an IDS system can detect a breach, the authentication may stop it entirely. Numerous surveys done over the years have shown that passwords are the most common cause of information security breaches. Upgrading authentication may be the best investment you can make in enterprise security in terms of effectiveness.

Attackers have many good options for defeating passwords. Easy passwords are guessable. Sloppy programmers write clear text passwords to the file system or registry, or hard-code them in applications. People reuse passwords at many sites. One hacked website leads to others—especially if hackers sell the stolen passwords on the dark web. Hackers trick people into revealing their passwords via phishing. Key loggers and other malware snoop passwords. Attackers record passwords sent unencrypted over a network (for example, via public WiFi networks). Cross-site scripting (XSS) vulnerabilities may expose your password in the browser. Hackers may have inserted spyware in your hardware. These examples are only the beginning of a list of potential problems with passwords.

Early on, security experts realized that combining passwords with another factor (or factors) increases our confidence in the authentication. As such, MFA (Multi-Factor Authentication) was born. In the 90s, one-time password (OTP) hardware tokens and X.509 browser certificates seemed unbreakable. OTPs allow a user to authenticate to a system with an algorithmically-generated numeric password that changes periodically (every 30 seconds or so). X.509 web certificates enable a web browser to present a person's digital certificate, stored either in the browser or on an external smartcard, to the server and authenticate based on this certificate.

© Michael Schwartz, Maciej Machulak 2018
M. Schwartz and M. Machulak, *Securing the Perimeter*, https://doi.org/10.1007/978-1-4842-2601-8_7

Twenty years later, there are many new authentication technologies beyond OTP and X.509 certificates. The rate of innovation has not slowed—authentication technologies are rapidly emerging. Mobile phones have new sensors and websites have access to behavioral analytics that can mitigate the risk of fraud. But there is a tradeoff in usability. Albert North Whitehead, an English mathematician and philosopher, said "Civilization advances by extending the number of important operations which we can perform without thinking about them." The best usability would be not authenticating at all! My device should just know it's me and send that information over the network. But unfortunately, we're not there yet (although behavioral biometrics and continuous authentication methods are becoming increasing popular). Today, digital authentication balances a tradeoff between security, usability, and cost (or deployability). If there was a technology that was secure, super easy to use, and cheap for organizations to implement, we would be using it. In fact, in many ways, passwords seemed to offer one of the most attractive "triangles" out there (see Figure 7-1).

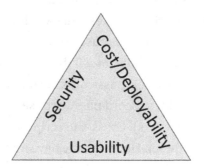

Figure 7-1. *Triangle of trust*

In this chapter, we provide a technical overview of some of the available technologies and standards for strong authentication, such as OATH, Mutual TLS, Fast Identity Online (FIDO), and W3C Web Authentication. Some of these standards can even help protect us against phishing, man-in-the-middle attacks, and replay password attacks. For ideas on how to provision and de-provisioning strong credentials, see Chapter 9 on identity management.

One-Time Passwords (OTPs)

OTPs are not susceptible to replay attacks, meaning an attacker cannot use a stolen OTP code later to impersonate someone. As the name suggests, the usability of an OTP is like a password—something that the person enters in addition to their username. OTPs are not inherently two-factor—the token value is only one factor. One common strategy to make OTP solutions two-factor is to prefix a PIN number before the OTP. This combines the "something you know" (PIN number) with the "something you have" (whatever software/hardware supplied you with the OTP). OTPs are also often used in combination with a password (your first authenticate "as usual" and then you need to provide an OTP).

One of the easiest ways to implement OTP is to generate a random number and send it to the person via email, SMS, or some other messaging platform. One way to accomplish this is to use an algorithm based on some cryptographic material stored on that server (preventing attackers from guessing the one-time passwords).

For example, the server can use the HMAC-SHA-1 algorithm, as defined in RFC 2104, and combine it with the truncation method defined in RFC 4266. The algorithm takes a secret as the seed and a second variable (e.g., time) to produce a hash and truncates that hash to produce a code of a desired length. The length of the code should allow the end user to easily read it and type it back at the site during authentication, hence the length is often of six-eight digits long and contains numbers only to be easily usable on a mobile phone. It is then the responsibility of the server to match the code with the one that has been generated. It's a good idea to make sure the code is only used once, and that the code expires. Such an OTP flow is depicted in Figure 7-2.

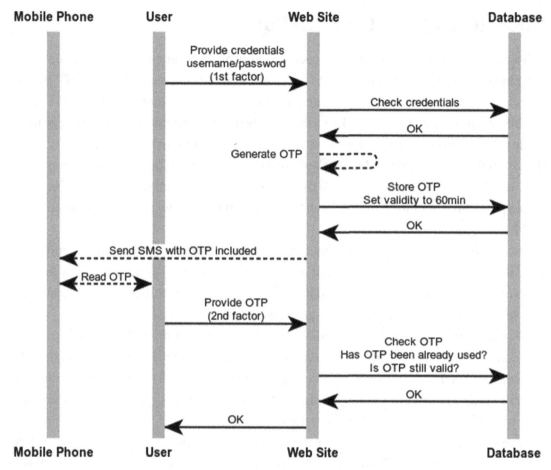

Figure 7-2. *One-time passwords delivered using SMS—example flow*

OTPs delivered via SMS or email don't prove possession of something, they simply prove access to a communication channel. First, you must trust the channel—that an attacker cannot intercept the message. Internet email is hard to trust because it not encrypted—few email transfer agents support TLS. Email clients make a secure connection to the server, but the emails are sent in the clear from one MTA to another. Attackers can use malware installed on the person's device to intercept the code sent via email. When targeting a specific person, attackers can hack the mobile operator by convincing one of the thousands of people or agents to issue a replacement SIM card for a certain num ber.

OTP does not protect you against phishing and allows for man-in-the-middle or man-in-the-browser attacks. If an attacker tricks a person into interacting with the attacker's website (e.g., through phishing), the attacker can replay messages on the legitimate site (e.g., a bank) and proxy back the actual content without the person knowing.

HOTP and TOTP

HMAC-based One-Time Passwords (HOTPs) and Time-based One-Time Passwords (TOTPs) are other types of OTPs. Both types of one-time passwords are examples of a hash-based message authentication code (HMAC) that's computed based on a secret and some other value, either a counter for HOTP or time for TOTP. There are both software and hardware implementations of HOTP and TOTP (see Figure 7-3). We discuss both types in subsequent sections of this chapter.

(a) HOTP and TOTP hardware token examples | (b) HOTP and TOTP software token example

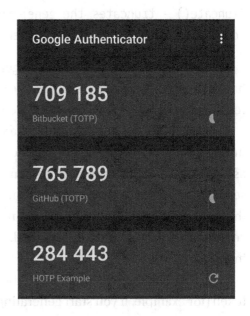

Figure 7-3. *Examples of HOTP and TOTP hardware and software tokens*

HOTP

The HMAC-based One-Time Password method allows for a one-time password to be generated independently by the client using a cryptographic function, which takes a secret and a counter as input. The client and server share the secret and counter. The counter is often set to 0, or a known fixed value, to minimize deployment complexity. However, to mitigate more risk, the counter should be set to a random value for each token in a production environment.

The Initiative for Open Authentication (OATH) incubated HOTP, specified in RFC 4226. The design goals were end-consumer usability, as well as ease of implementation on low-cost hardware with minimal user interface. HOTP codes contain only numeric characters, so people can easily enter one on their mobile phones. The math behind HOTP is as follows:

```
HOTP = Truncate(HMAC-SHA-1(s,c))
```

where

```
s - secret value (seed)
c - counter value
Truncate() - truncates the generated HMAC-SHA-1 to extract 6-8 digits
(depending on the actual deployment)
```

A hardware or software token can generate an HOTP. Organizations decide to use hardware or software depending on the security requirements of a deployment (you may recall examples of such tokens depicted in Figure 7-3).

For hardware tokens, an administrator usually provisions the secret and counter during a centrally-governed account administration process. For software tokens, such as Google Authenticator (which is open source), the server typically generates the secret and counter, and then renders an TLS protected web page, which is scanned by the software token. The server can verify an HOTP because it knows the secret and the counter used to compute the password. Every time an HOTP is generated, the counter increases by one.

You may wonder what happens if the counter on the server gets out of sync with the token (for example, if you start generating HOTPs but are not using them to sign in to the account). HOTP can deal with such situations through its re-synchronization algorithm, which uses something called a look-ahead window. Such windows define a number of acceptable retries for the server to verify an HOTP until giving up and they are usually set somewhere between 10-20. If the server cannot find an acceptable counter to produce a valid OTP, the server can then ask for another authentication pass of the protocol to take place and this happens until the maximum number of authorized attempts is reached. It is common that the server would accept several attempts. In fact, during re-synchronization of an OTP, to minimize the possibility of a fraudulent activity, the server may ask for multiple passcodes to be provided by the user.

If the user fails to resynchronize a token and the maximum number of authorized attempts is reached, the HOTP RFC document suggests locking the person's account.

Importantly, when an HOTP is generated, it can be used on the server for an unknown amount of time. This opens a potential window for an attack, where the OTP is used by the attacker prior to its legitimate use (e.g., the person generates an HOTP but fails to use it for a long time, at which point the OTP can be used on the server by an attacker). This drawback is addressed in another version of one-time passwords, which is TOTP, or Time-based OTP.

TOTP

Time-based OTP was also incubated by the OATH initiative and specified in RFC 6238. It is an example of a hash-based message authentication code (HMAC) and is a variant of HOTP. This algorithm uses a shared secret and time instead of a counter. Because the server and the token are affected by network latency, and their clocks may be slightly out-of-sync, it's not a precise time that is used for calculating the HMAC, but rather a time interval. Half-minute intervals are recommended in RFC 6238 as a balance between security and usability. TOTP is calculated as follows:

```
TOTP = Truncate(HMAC-SHA-1(s,TC))
```

where

```
s - secret value
TC - time counter value which can be calculated as TC =
floor((unixtime(now) — unixtime(T0)) / TI),
Truncate() - truncates the generated to HMAC-SHA-1 to extract 6-8 digits
(depending on the actual deployment)
```

If you compare TOTP with HOTP, you will notice that in fact TOTP can be represented as follows:

```
TOTP = HOTP(s,TC)
```

TOTP is provisioned to the end user in the same way as HOTP—a shared secret is established between the token and the authentication server. During provisioning, clocks need to be synchronized as well.

Verifying a TOTP is similar to the verification done for HOTP. The main difference is that the server must also calculate the current time counter and use it for calculating its own TOTP for comparison. The authentication server can typically accept TOTPs generated from timestamps that differ by one time interval from the client's timestamp, but this depends on the actual configuration of the server.

For TOTPs, the problem of desynchronization between the token and the server is largely alleviated because of the use of time and not a counter. Of course, the clocks can still go out-of-sync significantly and some form of token resynchronization may be required. For example, two TOTP values can be used to search for those passcodes in a larger window back and forth for resynchronization purposes. Furthermore, it may also be possible to do auto-resynchronization.

For example, if the OTP value does not match during authentication, the server can save this passcode. When the user tries to sign in by providing the next generated passcode, then the server can use both OTPs (previous and current) to perform synchronization to a bigger time window. Such a method allows the use of TOTP even for those users who use 2FA very rarely.

Because TOTP is generally usable for only a known and limited amount of time, it can be considered more secure than HOTP. (It is still only a one-time password so if it is used in a single window then it cannot be reused in that window again.) An example of a software token (Google Authenticator) with registered TOTPs and HOTP is depicted in Figure 7-4. You can see that an HOTP can be regenerated at the user's will, while a TOTP changes at each interval automatically.

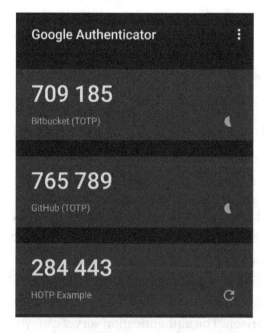

Figure 7-4. *Google Authenticator with two TOTPs and one HOTP*

Both HOTP and TOTP have nothing that binds these tokens to a session between the person's browser and the server, hence there is a possibility of man-in-the-middle or man-in-the-browser attacks.

An example is depicted in Figure 7-5 that shows a man-in-the-middle attack where the victim is tricked into accessing the attacker's website, which is pretending to be a legitimate banking site. The victim may have checked for a secure SSL connection (green lock), but this might not help if the attacker hacked the target organization's DNS server, added an A-record pointing to their malicious site, and obtained a valid SSL certificate from a trusted CA. In one such attack, a hacker intercepted the credentials (username/password) as well as the OTPs (which was either HOTP or TOTP) and reused them to steal a bundle of cash. The aforementioned attack vector is addressed in standards from the FIDO Alliance, presented later in this chapter. It could also have been prevented with mutual TLS.

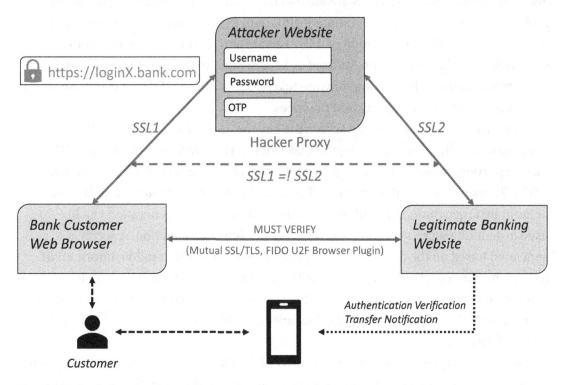

Figure 7-5. *Man-in-the-middle attack on one-time-passwords*

HOTP and TOTP can be susceptible to brute force attacks as the lengths of OTPs are relatively small (typically between six to eight digits), where the attacker tries to guess the value of the OTP. Therefore, it is necessary to ensure that the server accepting OTPs implements some form of throttling and can detect these kinds of attacks. For example, after a few attempts, the server may force a delay before accepting another OTP or can lock the account and fall back to another authentication method. Importantly, HOTP and TOTP specifications, as defined in RFC 4228 and 6238 respectively, contain extensive sections on security considerations. These are worth a read for anyone seriously considering a deployment of these technologies.

Both HOTP and TOTP rely on a secret shared between the token and the server. As discussed earlier, hardware tokens usually have the secret (seed) already baked into them during the manufacturing process or need to be programmed using specialized software. Such tokens are designed to be tamper-resistant to deter reverse engineering and avoid leakage of the secret. Software tokens, which are commonly deployed on mobile phones, rely on the secret shared with them from the server. It is paramount that such tokens utilize encryption of those secrets and rely on existing technologies, such as Secure Element (SE) on Android or Secure Enclave (SE) for iPhone for such encryption. Fortunately, existing software tokens that support HOTP or TOTP use strong cryptography following security best practices.

In terms of the authentication server, the key that is used for HOTP and TOTP needs to be stored securely. It is a good idea to use a Hardware Security Module (HSM) for that purpose, which prevents export of cryptographic material. Interestingly, the RFC 4228 proposes two different ways of generating and securely storing such secrets: deterministic generation or random generation. Deterministic generation can be used to generate secrets on the fly during provisioning and validation. A secret is generated based on the master key (secret value) and some other public information (e.g., identifier of a token). The token itself holds the generated shared secret. Random generation is used only during provisioning and the generated secret must be kept on both the token and the server. See the "Security Considerations" section of RFC 4228 for more information.

Note that it is possible to improve security of the shared secret by using a composite shared secret, i.e., augmenting the seed value with some additional information. For example, the token would only store a basic seed and would also require the user to enter a PIN. The token would leverage the PIN, the stored seed, and the counter/time to calculate the required OTP. Such functionality is available on both software and hardware tokens.

Mutual SSL/TLS

Nearly every user of the Internet has been exposed to the SSL (Secure Sockets Layer) and TLS (Transport Layer Security) protocols, which have been securing transactions on the Internet since SSL has been introduced by Netscape to the public in 1995. Both SSL and TLS allow for authentication and encryption of interactions between two different systems—the client and the server. TLS is the successor of the SSL protocol and provides the same functionality, allowing for two parties to communicate securely. Because of the differences in how these two protocols work, TLS does not interoperate with SSL, although the certificates used in SSL and TLS are the same.

When a user accesses a website over SSL or TLS with any modern web browser, the browser makes a secure connection to that website. The web browser aims to achieve two things when making an SSL/TLS connection:

- Check that the server is the correct one.

- Provide encrypted channel between the browser and the server.

When making a connection with the server, the web browser first obtains an SSL/TLS certificate from the server. This certificate, encoded in X.509 format, contains the issuer of the certificate, the subject including the FQDN (Fully Qualified Domain Name) of the server, the public key of the subject, and the signature of the issuer, among other information. Listing 7-1 shows an example of a X.509 certificate.

Listing 7-1. Sample Certificate

```
Certificate:
Data:
    Version: 3 (0x2)
    Serial Number: b7:41:8a:d5:00:5e:45:b6
    Signature Algorithm: sha256WithRSAEncryption
    Issuer: CN=GlobalSign CA - SHA256 - G2
    Validity
        Not Before: Nov 21 08:00:00 2016 GMT
        Not After : Nov 22 07:59:59 2017 GMT
    Subject: O=SampleCo,cn=A
    Subject Public Key Info:
        Public Key Algorithm: id-ecPublicKey
```

```
    Public-Key: (256 bit)
    pub: 04:c9:22:69:31 [...omitted for brevity...]
    ASN1 OID: prime256v1
    NIST CURVE: P-256
       [...omitted for brevity...]
Signature Algorithm: sha256WithRSAEncryption
 6f:af:40:72:bd:1e:18:5e:30:54:23:35:
 [...omitted for brevity...]
```

The browser can easily check the identity of the server based on the certificate that it receives. First, the browser knows which URL is being accessed and it can compare it against the FQDN specified in the X.509 certificate. Second, the SSL/TLS contains an issuer signature, which allows the client to verify if the certificate is valid or not. The certificate must be signed by an certification authority (CA) that's trusted by the browser and this is where the chain of trust kicks in—it defines which CAs are trusted and which are not (this prevents anyone from creating a certificate for any domain).

Once the web browser authenticates the server, an encrypted channel can be established. This channel uses a symmetric key that can be shared between the browser and the server, leveraging the public key from the certificate (for more information we refer the reader to the TLS protocol specification).

Mutual SSL/TLS differs only slightly from a typical SSL/TLS handshake, as it involves sharing of the client certificate and additional verification (see Figure 7-6). First, the server not only shares its certificate with the client, but it also requests client's certificate. The server does that by sending a `CertificateRequest` message to the client. Importantly, the server needs to be configured to send such messages (i.e., it is not the client that communicates to the server that it wishes to authenticate with a certificate). The `CertificateRequest` message indicates to the client that the server would like the connection to be mutually authenticated and that the client should authenticate using an SSL/TLS certificate. The server also sends the list of Distinguished CA names.

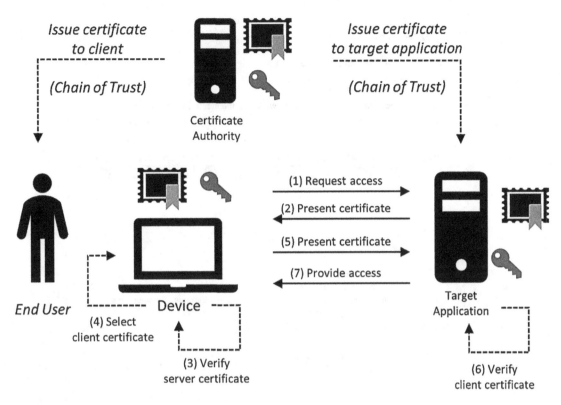

Figure 7-6. *Mutual SSL/TLS*

Upon receiving these messages, the client either sends a pre-configured certificate to the server or asks the person to select the certificate that should be sent (we visualize this in Figure 7-7). The browser only selects the certificates that have been issued by a CA trusted by the server. Once a certificate is selected, the browser responds to the server with a certificate message, which contains the client's certificate. In most cases, the user can ask the browser to remember their decision and use the same certificate on subsequent logons. In such cases, the user would not need to explicitly authenticate to the server but instead this process would happen in the background.

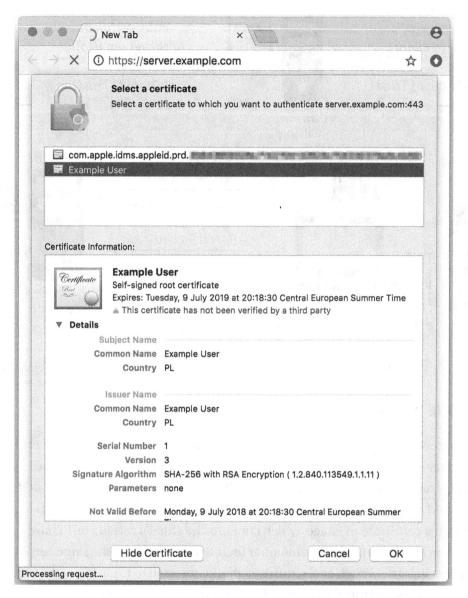

Figure 7-7. *A web browser requests a user to select a client certificate for authentication (self-signed certificate example)*

The client certificate is similar to the certificate of a server, i.e., it contains the same set of fields. However, there are two key differences between these two types of certificates. First, the certificate's Enhanced Key Usage field has the OID set to (1.3.6.1.5.5.7.3.2), which represents "Client Authentication". Second, the subject in a client certificate describes the identity of the user and most likely differs from the FQDN. For example, the subject may contain a DN of the person or their email address.

Based on the subject identifier from the certificate, the server can establish the identity of the person—possession of the certificate (and the corresponding private key) is evidence of identity.

You may wonder why the server would trust the certificate presented from the client. After all, this certificate can be public as it contains the public key, among other information. However, the server authenticates the client based on a challenge-response protocol, which requires control of the private key corresponding to the public key in the certificate. During the TLS negotiation, the client also sends a `CertificateVerify` message. This message contains a signature of some session related information, and this signature is created using the private key owned by the client. The server can use the corresponding public key from the certificate to verify the signature (see Step 6 in Figure 7-6). We refer the reader to RFC 5246 for more information regarding TLS as well as client certificate authentication. Importantly, the server should use an Online Certificate Status Protocol (OCSP) to query the certificate authority's OCSP and see if the client's certificate is still valid (and not revoked).

One of the advantages of mutual SSL/TLS is that there is no shared secret between the client and server. Because the client first authenticates the server, phishing can be prevented, although the user must check if the server being accessed is the correct one (the browser would flag any anomalies or even prevent accessing a site if such site would rely on SSL certificate pinning). Similarly, the man-in-the-middle attacks can be alleviated, as a secure channel can be established between the browser and the server.

In practice, mutual SSL/TLS is rarely used for authentication on the Internet. This is primarily because of the deployment burden that requires a user to obtain and install an SSL/TLS certificate on their computer. Such installation needs to be done on each machine that the user wishes to use for a particular site. Such certificates may expire, which means that the user would need to update them periodically. Sometimes, certificates may need to be revoked and a new certificate issued to the person. If you think about the amount of support that an average person requires just for their username and password credentials, you can imagine the pain of then managing client certificates.

The exception is government sites and sometimes "intranets" (if such a thing still exists). In the first case, users can obtain digital certificates to access highly sensitive websites that require not only authentication but also non-repudiation. As the number of sites is usually limited, the burden of deploying a client certificate authentication system is somewhat minimized. For the intranet case, browser versions are tightly controlled, and certificates are centrally managed. Furthermore, sometimes such certificates can be distributed on physical devices—e.g., X.509 certificates can be placed on smartcards that must be inserted into a computer for authentication.

Fast Identity Online (FIDO)

Fast Identity Online (FIDO) is one of the most important recent efforts to standardize a technology stack for web and mobile authentication. The FIDO standards, incubated by the FIDO Alliance, includes protocols for token based and biometric authentication, including the Universal Authentication Framework (UAF) and Universal 2nd Factor (U2F).

FIDO provides an abstraction layer between the authenticator and the target application that relies on the authentication process. Normally, during authentication, a person would leverage their device (e.g., laptop or mobile device) to authenticate themselves and this device would be an intermediate between the person and the target application. For example, the web browser would pass information to the server while a mobile application could authenticate locally or remotely.

For simplicity, when discussing FIDO, we refer to an IDP as an example of a target application (within the text as well as in the presented figures). However, the target application in this context is any application that relies on the authentication event, for example, the login page of a SAML or OpenID Connect provider, or even a standalone website that is providing its own authentication service.

In FIDO, the intermediate is the authenticator—software running within a web browser, mobile device, or on a separate hardware token. Such authenticator is responsible for verifying the person's presence. Upon successful verification, this authenticator then communicates with the IDP using a standardized protocol that FIDO defines.

FIDO authentication uses public key cryptography where the private key is stored on a device that has a UAF/U2F software stack installed. Only the public key is registered with the FIDO IDP. Authentication is accomplished by challenging the authenticator to produce a valid signature. The authenticator uses its private key once the verification of the presence of the person is confirmed (e.g., users touch an authenticator or scan their fingerprints).

FIDO UAF and U2F solve different use cases. UAF aims to provide a passwordless experience for authentication, while U2F supports a universal second factor, which can be added on top of existing authentication. Proving the identity of the person is done based on the valid signature of a challenge that is sent by the IDP to the authenticator. The use of the private key on the authenticator is allowed once user verification succeeds. Importantly, the private key never leaves the authenticator and is only used to sign a challenge. Furthermore, a new cryptographic key pair is created for each IDP with which a person interacts.

Using FIDO UAF or U2F requires that the client (e.g., a web browser or a mobile application) used to access the FIDO IDP supports this protocol. At the time of the publication of this book, Google Chrome and Mozilla Firefox natively support FIDO U2F, and a third-party extension exists for Apple Safari. Mobile applications can leverage existing SDKs or frameworks from software and hardware vendors. Android applications can also use the natively provided API for FIDO U2F. The beauty of the FIDO proposal is that it is an open standard, hence mobile developers can use their preferred SDKs without worrying if these will work with third-party FIDO servers.

In FIDO, the application recognizes the person through identity verification but does not recognize the identity of the person. Nor does FIDO authentication leak any correlatable identifier of the person—it simply enables a website or IDP to verify that it is the same authenticator that has been previously registered for this person's account. Binding the authentication event to the identity of the person is therefore done outside of the FIDO protocol and such binding often depends on the actual domain where the protocol is used (e.g., banking, e-commerce, social networks, etc.). During deployment of an IAM solution, it is rarely necessary to think about this issue, as FIDO authentication is a means to identify a known person. But keep in mind that not all websites use a central IDP, and the FIDO token is useful to the person for any site that supports it. We discuss how Gluu has adopted the FIDO technology in further sections of this chapter.

FIDO has several advantages over traditional authentication mechanisms (see Figure 7-8). It allows the IDP to control which authenticators are allowed and which are explicitly forbidden. This functionality is achieved because each authenticator has metadata, which is referenced through a private key (called an attestation key) baked into the authenticator during its manufacturing process. Such metadata can include information such as the version of the authenticator, what modalities it supports, and what cryptographic capabilities it has.

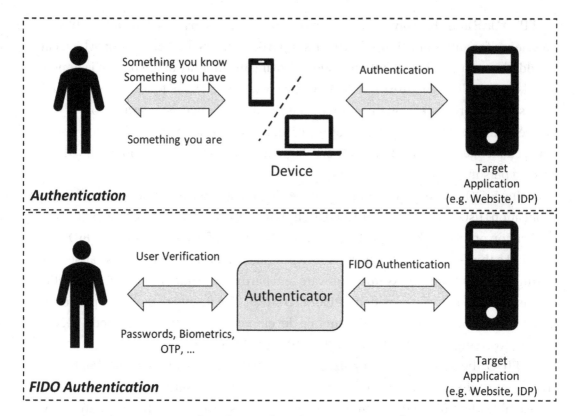

Figure 7-8. *Comparison of traditional authentication and FIDO authentication*

An access-management solution can leverage metadata about authenticators to set authentication policies. For example, a policy may specify that a fingerprint scan is sufficient to access basic functionality, while an iris scan is required to access more sensitive resources. Because the FIDO IDP understands which exact authenticator model is used, one can easily make risk-based policy decisions. For example, an access-management platform may only allow authenticators with a low false acceptance rate.

Because FIDO relies on public key cryptography, there is no secret that is shared between the client and the FIDO server. This prevents several different attacks, which are present for traditional authentication systems. The authenticator would only use the private key to sign a challenge after successful user verification. Such signature is bound to the TLS channel, which is established between the client and that server, hence preventing man-in-the-middle attacks. The FIDO server merely stores a public key associated with the authenticator, so an attack on such a server would not result in any shared secret being revealed. Such public key differs per website, which prevents the correlation of a person with a single authenticator.

FIDO Universal Authentication Framework (UAF)

FIDO UAF aims to provide a passwordless experience for authentication where the person is challenged to verify their presence against a registered authenticator (see Figure 7-9). Like U2F, the person must first register their device (which supports UAF) at the IDP. Then, instead of having to remember a password on that device, the person can authenticate using a local biometric or PIN, which unlocks the private key. UAF also allows experiences that combine multiple authentication mechanisms, hence the remote account can be protected with multiple factors such as fingerprint and PIN.

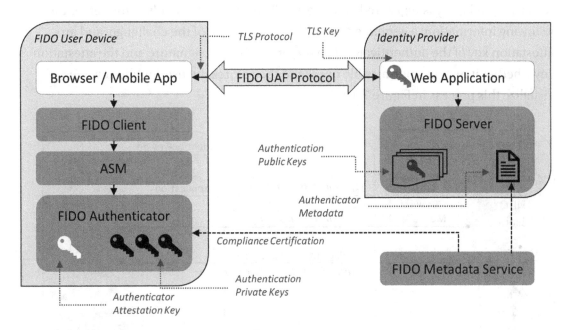

Figure 7-9. *FIDO UAF high-level architecture*

The IDP needs to be able to interact with the FIDO server that can interact with the device using the FIDO protocol. Such FIDO server can allow for specifying authentication policies based on authenticator characteristics (which are defined in authenticator metadata).

UAF authenticators may be connected to a person's device via various physical interfaces, such as SPI, USB, or Bluetooth. The UAF Authenticator-Specific Module (ASM) is an interface on top of UAF authenticators. This interface gives FIDO UAF clients a standard way of accessing specific authenticators and hides the internal communication with these authenticators. For example, a FIDO UAF client would interact with a biometric authenticator in the same way as it would interact with a hardware token (improving the cost and deployability).

The FIDO UAF authentication protocol consists of two main parts: registration and authentication. Registration is initiated by a client, which asks the server to send a challenge as well as policy of permissible authenticators. The client uses the policy to search for an available authenticator and presents it to the end user. The user enrolls depending on the authenticator (e.g., they can scan their fingerprint or provide a PIN). Upon successful enrollment, the authenticator generates a new public/private key pair. The private key is stored securely within an authenticator and is used to sign a challenge while the public key is registered at the server. The client then sends to the server the following information: a generated public key, a signature of the challenge, and an attestation key of the authenticator. The server verifies the signature and the attestation key whether it matches permissible ones, and then stores the user public key. We visualize this process in Figure 7-10.

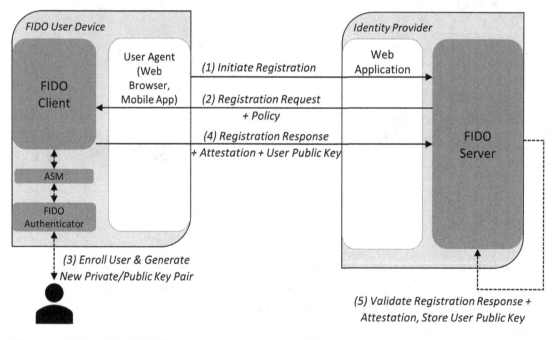

Figure 7-10. *FIDO UAF registration message flow*

During authentication, which is initiated by a client, the server sends a challenge and a policy that defines which authenticators may be used. It is the client's responsibility to then communicate with the correct authenticator that verifies the person's presence and produces a signature of the challenge using a securely stored private key for the person and this target application. The client then responds with the signature. The server checks if the signature is correct and it does that using the corresponding public key of the user. Upon successful verification, the person can be signed in to the relying party. We visualize the UAF authentication message flow in Figure 7-11.

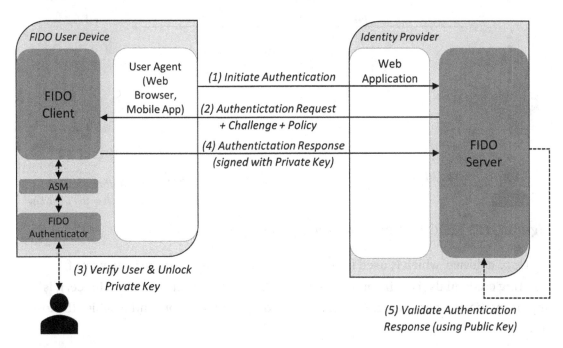

Figure 7-11. *FIDO UAF authentication message flow*

Apart from authentication, the FIDO UAF protocol also enables optional transaction confirmation. Such functionality is of paramount importance for use cases such as banking where information like a payment amount needs to be securely authorized. With a transaction confirmation, apart from sending a challenge, the server also communicates the transaction text to the device, which the person can authorize.

After a successful authentication, the authenticator signs the concatenated challenge and transaction text hash, which is returned to the server. This signature is then verified using the registered public key for the person's account. We visualize the FIDO UAF transaction confirmation message flow in Figure 7-12. For more information on this functionality in FIDO, we refer the reader to the FIDO specification.

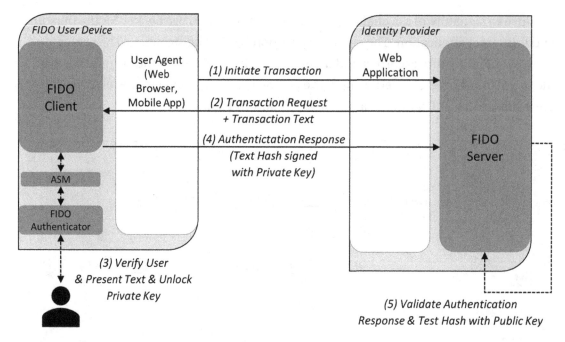

Figure 7-12. *FIDO UAF confirmation message flow*

Once a device, which is used for UAF authentication, is lost there is no way of restoring credentials (i.e., the private keys on that device are kept secure). Hence, it is important that the person registers multiple strong authenticators and disables the lost authenticator.

FIDO Universal Second Factor (U2F)

The FIDO U2F protocol allows for online services to add a second factor on top of an existing authentication. Typically the person would use their password as step one of the authentication, and then the FIDO U2F device in the second step. Because FIDO U2F is built into the browser, it prevents phishing via the MITM attack described in Figure 7-5. Combining phishing resistance, a very low failure rate (compared to OTP which is around 3%), wide availability of USB-A or USB-C interfaces on many devices, and a robust market of vendors producing a variety of token form factors, FIDO U2F is one of the most deployable strong authentication choices available to organizations.

The U2F standard also defines both registration and authentication protocols. Registration is very similar to the one described for UAF. During an authenticated session, a relying party sends a challenge and a policy to the IDP. One of the permitted authenticators must be used to authenticate the person, produce a public/private key pair and then sign the challenge. The signature, along with the authenticator's attestation key and the generated public key is returned to the relying party and checked by the FIDO server. If the verification is successful, then the public key is registered for the person's account.

The FIDO U2F authentication flow is presented in Figure 7-13. After the person submits their credentials, the FIDO server sends a challenge to the client and a policy of permissible authenticators. The client authenticates the person through one of those authenticators. In U2F, the user would press a button on the U2F device, tap it over an NFC reader or scan their finger on a FIDO-compliant mobile fingerprint scanner. This unlocks the private key of the device to be used similarly UAF—i.e., to sign a challenge sent by the server. Once a signature is produced, it is returned to the relying party. The relying party verifies that signature using the corresponding registered public key.

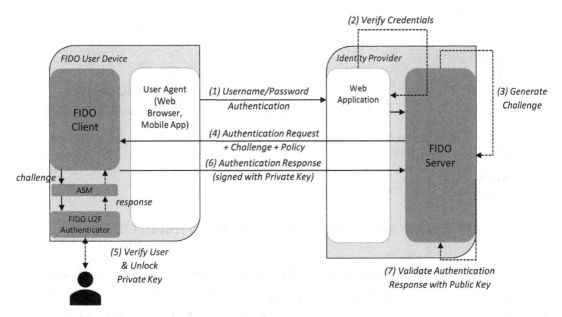

Figure 7-13. *FIDO U2F message flow*

W3C Web Authentication and CTAP

Adoption of the FIDO protocol has been largely dependent on support for this protocol by a specific platform. For example, Android for the last few years has provided the necessary APIs that allow developers to use the functionality of credential creation and subsequent authentication for native applications. On the web, some browsers, such as Google Chrome or Mozilla Firefox, provided support for FIDO U2F, but the lack of ubiquitous browser support was problematic for application developers.

FIDO 2.0 was developed to add features that addressed requirements important to a wider range of browser vendors. It includes two components: the Web Authentication Protocol and the Client to Authenticator Protocol (CTAP). They are complementary and provide a comprehensive suite for strong authentication. Relationships between Web Authentication API and CTAP are visualized in Figure 7-14.

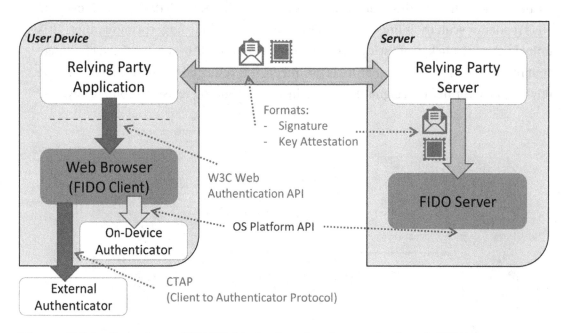

Figure 7-14. *Overview of W3C Web Authentication and related CTAP*

The Web Authentication API, incubated by the FIDO Alliance and standardized by The World Wide Web Consortium (W3C), provides a mechanism for interacting with the FIDO Authenticator. It defines a common and public API which, if implemented by a browser, enables a web application (such as an IDP) to request authentication using the FIDO protocol. Like FIDO U2F, the W3C Web Authentication API defines an API for registration (i.e., enrollment of a credential) and authentication. Vendors such as Microsoft, Google, and Mozilla already support this standard in their web browsers.

In addition to the API, W3C Web Authentication also defines a key attestation format and a signature format. The API is used by the website or web application—a simple JavaScript application can call this API on the user's web browser. Registration communicates data about the authenticator (`makeCredential` endpoint), which is stored on the server and used later for authentication (`getAssertion` endpoint). Much of the heavy lifting is done by the browser, which creates necessary messages and provides error handling. The authenticator performs authentication operations and produces the attestation.

The key attestation format and the signature format are the two elements that define what information is passed between the web browser and the server for registration and authentication. This includes information about the authenticator itself, and the proof of possession of a private key of the FIDO 2.0 credential. We visualize credential registration as well as the use of a scoped credential in Figures 7-15 and 7-16, respectively.

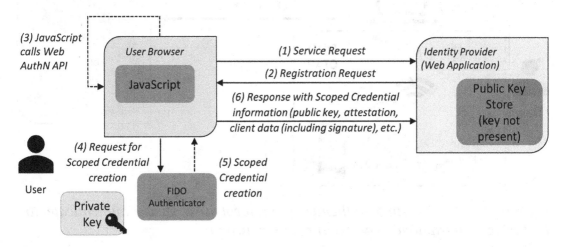

Figure 7-15. *W3C Web Authentication API: registration operation*

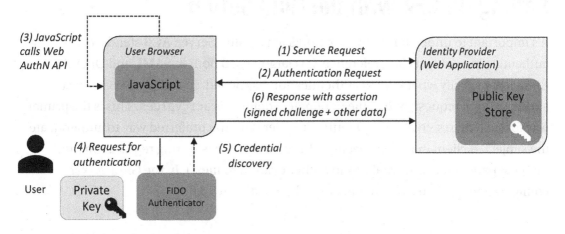

Figure 7-16. *W3C Web Authentication API: authentication operation*

CTAP defines how the FIDO client running on a specific platform, e.g. an operating system or a web browser, can talk to an external authenticator such as a USB-powered security key or a mobile phone that can interact with the computer via NFC or Bluetooth. Combining W3C Web Authentication and CTAP solves a variety of use cases in a simple and standardized way. For example, a person can sign in to a website such as an IDP using their smartphone as an external authenticator, which communicates with the person's laptop over a Bluetooth connection (see Figure 7-17). You should read the specifications of W3C Web Authentication and FIDO 2.0 CTAP for more detailed information.

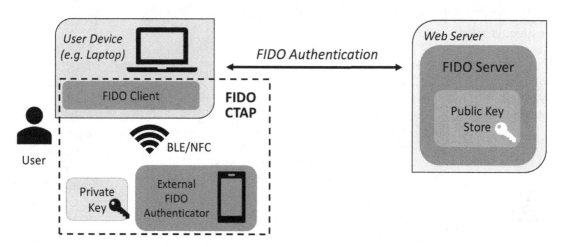

Figure 7-17. *FIDO client to authenticator protocol use case: user authenticates to IDP using a smartphone as an external authenticator*

Setting Up 2FA with the Gluu Server

It's important to understand how acr works in the Gluu Server. ACR stands for authentication context class reference. It is jargon used both in SAML and OpenID Connect to specify what kind of authentication happened. In an OpenID Connect authentication request, one of the parameters defined is acr_values. This is the primary way for a client to signal to the OpenID Provider (OP) the preferred way to authenticate the subject. A client may also specify default_acr_values during registration (and omit the parameter while making an authentication request). In the Gluu Server configuration, acr is used to name the authentication workflow.

Organizations have a wide array of requirements for login—not just how to authenticate the person, but how to log, detect fraud, gather consent, and sometimes even update personal data records on the fly. The diversity of authentication business logic requirements for organizations are so varied, it is difficult (if not impossible) to build a GUI that provides the needed flexibility. Gluu's solution was to create an authentication "interception script"—a standard interface that enables developers to code the exact workflow they need. The goal is to enable extension of the Gluu Server, without forking the core code (which makes it harder to keep current with updates). Gluu uses the interception script approach in several places—not just for authentication. For example, in the next chapter, you see how interception scripts are also used to express policies about when to grant access tokens using the UMA protocol. The interception script that we discuss here is called "Person Authentication".

When you install the Gluu Server, password authentication is enabled by default. You can see this in the oxTrust admin interface, under the Configuration, Manage Authentication section, as shown in Figure 7-18. You can specify the `acr` for oxTrust, which is an easy way to test an authentication workflow, although it's also an easy way to lock yourself out, in which case you may have to change it back to password. In case you forgot your LDAP from Chapter 2, do something like Listing 7-2 (replacing the `inum` to match the entry under `ou=appliances,o=gluu` for your instance).

Figure 7-18. *Configuring the default authentication method in the Gluu Server (oxTrust)*

Listing 7-2. Sample LDIF to Revert to Password Authentication If You Lock Yourself Out

```
dn: inum=@!7A1F!0002!02C3.DD97,ou=appliances,o=gluu
changetype: modify
replace: oxTrustAuthenticationMode
oxTrustAuthenticationMode: auth_ldap_server
```

You then load the `ldif`, as shown in Listing 7-3 (setting the right values for `-j` and `-f` of course).

Listing 7-3. Sample ldapmodify to Revert to Password Authentication

```
$ /opt/opendj/bin/ldapmodify -h localhost -p 1636 \
-D "cn=directory manager" -j ~/.pw -Z -X -f fix-login.ldif
```

If your OpenID Connect script supports setting the `acr_values` parameter, that's a great way to test. If you are using the `oxd-server`, it allows this. In the Apache2 HTTP module, `mod_auth_openidc`, you can send extra parameters:

```
OIDCAuthRequestParams acr_values=u2f
```

Another way to test an authentication script is to set the "Default ACR"—which is the authentication method used if the client fails to specify an `acr`. The Default ACR is also used for all SAML websites. Although in future versions of the Gluu Server, it may support the use of the `AuthnContextClassRef` element in the SAML authentication request.

Although LDAP authentication requires only the completion of the "Manage LDAP Authentication" form (`acr = auth_ldap_server`), if you want to see the other types of authentication available or write your own custom authentication flow, you'll need to look at the Person Authentication tab of the "Manage Custom Scripts" configuration section of oxTrust. You'll notice immediately that the Gluu Server ships with several strong authentication mechanisms, as shown in Figure 7-19.

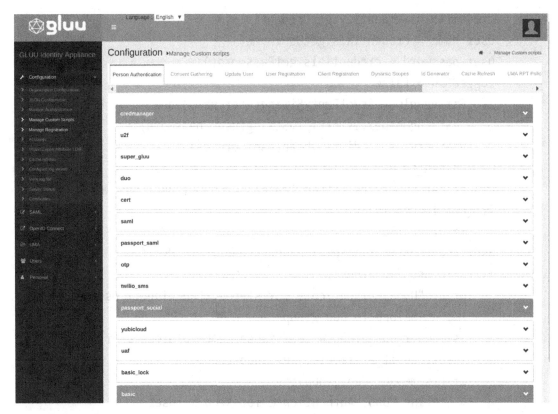

Figure 7-19. *Custom authentication scripts in the Gluu Server (oxTrust)*

Each interception script has a different interface (i.e., what methods are available). For the Person Authentication script, the most interesting method is (not surprisingly) called authenticate, which returns a Boolean depending on success or failure. Listing 7-4 shows the authenticate method for the Duo Security script. Duo is a SaaS authentication provider now owned by Cisco. This script has an interesting example of adaptive authentication.

Listing 7-4. Sample Authenticate Method of a Gluu Server Authentication Script

```
def authenticate(self, configurationAttributes, requestParameters, step):
    duo_host = configurationAttributes.get("duo_host").getValue2()
    authenticationService = CdiUtil.bean(AuthenticationService)
    identity = CdiUtil.bean(Identity)
    if (step == 1):
        print "Duo. Authenticate for step 1"
```

```
            credentials = identity.getCredentials()
            user_name = credentials.getUsername()
            user_password = credentials.getPassword()
            logged_in = False
            if (StringHelper.isNotEmptyString(user_name) and
                    StringHelper.isNotEmptyString(user_password)):
                userService = CdiUtil.bean(UserService)
                logged_in =
        authenticationService.authenticate(user_name, user_password)
            if (not logged_in):
                return False
            user = authenticationService.getAuthenticatedUser()
            if (self.use_duo_group):
                print "Duo. Authenticate for step 1. Checking if user
                        belong to Duo group"
                is_member_duo_group = self.isUserMemberOfGroup(user,
                    self.audit_attribute, self.duo_group)
                if (is_member_duo_group):
                    print "Duo. Authenticate for step 1. User '" +
                        user.getUserId() + "' member of Duo group"
                    duo_count_login_steps = 2
                else:
                    self.processAuditGroup(user)
                    duo_count_login_steps = 1
                identity.setWorkingParameter("duo_count_login_steps",
                 duo_count_login_steps)
            return True
        elif (step == 2):
            print "Duo. Authenticate for step 2"
            user = authenticationService.getAuthenticatedUser()
            if user == None:
                print "Duo Authn step 2. Failed to find user name"
                return False
            user_name = user.getUserId()
            sig_response_array = requestParameters.get("sig_response")
```

```
      if ArrayHelper.isEmpty(sig_response_array):
          print "Duo. Authn step 2. sig_response is empty"
          return False
      duo_sig_response = sig_response_array[0]
      authenticated_username = duo_web.verify_response(self.ikey,
          self.skey, self.akey, duo_sig_response)
      print "Duo. Authn step 2. authenticated_username: " +
        authenticated_username + ", expected user_name: " +
        user_name
      if (not StringHelper.equals(user_name,
                                  authenticated_username)):
          return False
      return True
  else:
      return False
```

Two-factor is not the same as two-step authentication. You could have a two-factor, one-step authentication. For example, many OTP tokens are two-factor, as they require a PIN number to unlock the token (something you know), and then the OTP code is displayed (something you have). However, in this example, OTP authentication is processed in one step. A multi-step authentication workflow is more flexible because it enables you to look at the context in the first step and to decide if you need a second step. If you dynamically adjust the number of steps at runtime, this is called adaptive authentication.

The Gluu Server supports multi-step, adaptive authentication workflows. When the Gluu Server invokes the script, the step is sent to the `authenticate` method as a parameter. In the script, you can switch on the step. That's why there is a large block of code under if (step ==1): and elif (step == 2).

The Duo authentication script provides a nice example of adaptive authentication. The goal of this script was to allow for testing of two-factor authentication for a subset of accounts, before introducing it to the whole organization. After the password is validated, the script checks to see if the person is in a certain group—if so, the person is put through a two-step authentication. If not, the person can proceed with one step.

There are two other important methods that need to support adaptive authentication: `getCountAuthenticationSteps` and `getPageForStep`. The former normally just returns 1 or 2. But for adaptive authentication, it checks a variable. The organization can also customize the two-factor authentication experience by using `getPageForStep`. This determines which JSF page is returned for a given authentication workflow.

Using this approach, the Gluu Server supports a diverse range of authentication requirements. You can call the APIs of 2FA SaaS providers, use custom Java or Python libraries, implement complex conditional logic, look at the security context of the authentication—if you can define an algorithm for authentication, you can implement it in the Gluu Server.

FIDO Support in the Gluu Server

The Gluu Server has built-in FIDO authentication endpoints. Current Gluu Servers publish a configuration document at `.well-known/fido-configuration` (older Gluu Servers used `/.well-known/fido-u2f-configuration`). Published here are the Gluu Server registration and authentication endpoints. Gluu also ships with built-in Person Interception scripts for FIDO U2F. FIDO 2 is supported in Gluu Server 3.1.5 and later.

When a FIDO credential is registered, the Gluu Server stores its metadata and public key in LDAP, under the person's entry, in an organizational unit called `ou=fido`. There is one entry for each FIDO device. Depending on the FIDO protocols used—U2F, FIDO 2, or UAF—the entry may contain a different amount of data. Gluu's Super Gluu application also uses FIDO to authenticate devices and stores phone data in addition to FIDO data.

Storing the FIDO data in one attribute of the LDAP person entry would have made it difficult to index, as FIDO registration data also includes a public key. However, this design also required Gluu to add a FIDO SCIM profile (because it can't be managed as simple user attribute). In Chapter 9, we introduce a user-facing web credential management tool to enable people to add and remove FIDO credentials for their Gluu Server account.

Other Ways to Strengthens Authentication with the Gluu Server

Although some of the technologies are not commercially licensed, no 2FA technology is "free". You always need to consider the cost of supporting people in your organization (who inevitably have questions), the productivity cost of failure, the cost of hardware, and the cost of deployment.

Remember that authentication is about risk mitigation. Strengthening the credential itself is not always the best way to reduce risk. There is a ton of innovation in big data and artificial intelligence. Look for commercial providers of APIs that can help you identify risky transactions. There are various ways this is possible. For example, hackers tend to re-use IP addresses for their attacks. Some security service providers can use the IP as input for a fraud score. You can also look at the credential itself. Sites like `https://haveibeenpwned.com/` will tell you if an email address was part of a breach. Other services, like Vericlouds, hash email address and password combinations purchased on the dark web, enabling you to detect if the credentials themselves have been exposed. With this kind of information, you can improve security by adding an authentication step and forcing the users to change their passwords.

The Gluu Server ships with several other 2FA authentication scripts, and many more are checked into GitHub: `https://github.com/GluuFederation/oxAuth/tree/master/Server/integrations`. You should also check the latest docs for more information on how to write custom Person Authentication scripts if the ones available don't exactly meet your needs.

Conclusion

People are analog. Computers are digital. For a computer to bridge this divide—to positively identify one person with a high degree of certainty—is incredibly difficult. As computers are getting more powerful, and as more hardware is becoming available to increase the sensory capabilities of computers in the analog world, they are getting better at it. But authentication is a moving target, because hackers are getting better at defeating the strategies. You need to think carefully about which authentication workflows to roll out in your organization. But doing nothing (i.e., just using passwords) is becoming less and less of an option. Crossing the digital-analog divide is a core capability for any sizable organization.

References

1. More information on best practices for deploying HOTP can be found in `https://www.yubico.com/wp-content/uploads/2016/02/YubicoBestPracticesOATH-HOTP.pdf`.

2. OATH is an industry-wide collaboration to develop an open reference architecture by leveraging existing open standards for the universal adoption of strong authentication. As of March 2018, members of this initiative include such companies as Symantec, Gemalto, Vasco, Yubico, among others.

3. RFC 4226: HOTP: An HMAC-Based One-Time Password Algorithm. Available at `https://tools.ietf.org/html/rfc4226`.

4. RFC 6238: TOTP: Time-Based One-Time Password Algorithm.

5. Hickman, Kipp, "The SSL Protocol," Netscape Communications Corp., February 9, 1995. Available at `https://tools.ietf.org/html/draft-hickman-netscape-ssl-00`.

6. In the text, we use the term SSL/TLS instead of focusing on any of these two protocols. In reality, we recommend using TLS only as all existing SSL versions have now been deprecated. Readers should use the latest version of TLS, which is 1.2, as specified in `https://tools.ietf.org/html/rfc5246`.

7. RFC 5246: The Transport Layer Security (TLS) Protocol Version 1.2. Available at `https://tools.ietf.org/html/rfc5246`.

8. FIDO Alliance has been set up in 2013 to work on a standard for strong passwordless authentication and strong second factor. More information can be found at `https://fidoalliance.org/`.

9. FIDO UAF specifications can be found at `https://fidoalliance.org/specs/fido-uaf-v1.1-ps-20170202/`.

10. FIDO U2F specifications can be found at `https://fidoalliance.org/specs/fido-u2f-v1.2-ps-20170411/`.

11. The private/public key pair is most typically generated within a secure hardware token (authenticator) that is designed to be tamper-proof, thereby preventing any leakage of the private key.

12. U2F Reference Implementations. Available at `https://github.com/google/u2f-ref-code`.

13. U2F Support Extension for Firefox. Available at `https://github.com/prefiks/u2f4moz`.

14. W3C Web Authentication Specification. Available at `https://www.w3.org/TR/webauthn/`.

15. FIDO Client to Authenticator Protocol. Available at `https://fidoalliance.org/specs/fido-v2.0-ps-20170927/fido-client-to-authenticator-protocol-v2.0-ps-20170927.html`.

16. Anthony J. Nadalin. "New FIDO Specifications Overview - Strong Web Authentication," December 8, 2016. Available at `https://www.slideshare.net/FIDOAlliance/new-fido-specifications-overview-fido-alliance-tokyo-seminar-nadalin`.

CHAPTER 8

User-Managed Access

Today, you use OAuth 2.0 to authorize software to access your own stuff, but what if you want to let someone else access your stuff? We call this "Alice to Bob sharing". This is one of the primary use cases for the User-Managed Access (UMA) protocol. Alice and Bob don't have to be humans—either can be a non-person entity (NPE), such as a software process or company. With UMA, Alice can use any authorization server to share data with Bob. It's up to Bob and the clients he is using, to interact with the authorization servers of Alice's choosing. Moreover, Alice can choose to use the same authorization server for different protected information that she wants to share with Bob—this data can be distributed, yet access to it can be centralized with UMA. An interesting property of UMA is that it also handles asynchronous authorization. For example, Bob may request access to something, and Alice may not approve the request until she's online. Likewise, Alice can also create a policy at the authorization server that gives access to some data to Bob—she does not have to be online for access to be granted.

This chapter covers the second version of the UMA protocol—UMA 2.0. If you are an implementer of UMA software, this chapter provides a conceptual background, but you must still read the actual UMA specifications. The "UMA 2.0 Grant for OAuth 2.0 Authorization" is what you should read if you are implementing an UMA Client. You need to read the "Federated Authorization for UMA 2.0" specification if you plan to implement an UMA Resource Server or Authorization Server.

UMA was eight years in the making. The working group at Kantara Initiative formed in 2009, before the existence of either OAuth 2.0 or OpenID Connect. Previous versions of UMA, although OAuth-like, did not perfectly align with OAuth. One of the main goals of UMA 2.0 was to leverage OAuth wherever concepts and syntax overlapped. UMA 2.0 is complementary to OAuth. It adds new capabilities that are not possible to achieve with OAuth alone.

© Michael Schwartz, Maciej Machulak 2018
M. Schwartz and M. Machulak, *Securing the Perimeter*, https://doi.org/10.1007/978-1-4842-2601-8_8

Like OAuth, UMA uses bearer tokens and scopes to convey the "extent of access". UMA is not a policy expression language. Issuance of an UMA token conveys the successful evaluation of policy by the Authorization Server. But UMA leaves it up to the Authorization Server to decide how to grant access. For example, in the Gluu Server, the oxTrust user management APIs require an UMA access token with the scope `SCIM Access`. To obtain this scope, there is an interception script called `scim_access_policy`, whose authorization method returns a boolean. The SCIM APIs are unaware of the policy—it could have been expressed as XML, it could have involved a human pressing a button—the SCIM API doesn't have to care what happened behinds the scenes at the AS to evaluate the policy.

Alice to Bob sharing has many real-world use cases. An interesting potential use case for UMA is federated document sharing. Google Docs works because everyone has a Google account. However, a service provider could launch an UMA-enabled document-sharing service that allows users to authenticate at any OpenID Connect Provider. Another important use cases for UMA is runtime consent management. The European Union General Data Protection Regulation (GDPR) seeks to give consumers control of their data and require companies to get consent in certain cases, such as sharing personal data with a third party.

Let's use a hypothetical situation: an airline offers you a special deal on a rental car. To complete this transaction, the airline needs to ask you if that's okay, and the car rental company needs a consent receipt that proves you opted into the offer. Both the airline and rental car company create consent records for audit purposes. Let's say there is an API that the rental car company has created specifically for receiving referrals from airlines. The API could require an UMA token with a scope that signifies that an appropriate consent record is present. Without the token, the person's browser redirects to the airline's authorization server to review and approve the release of their personal information.

During development of UMA, the working group considered three possible ecosystems: narrow, medium, and wide. In the narrow ecosystem, one party (like an enterprise) controls the authorization server and resource servers—it is a tightly controlled environment. A medium ecosystem involves the collaboration of a few authorization servers, but the participants manage trust statically—think about a social login environment where you get to choose from a few large consumer IDPs. The wide ecosystem enables autonomous parties to dynamically establish trust as required. For example, in a wide ecosystem, I can access a previously unknown UMA-protected website, introduce a new IDP, and dynamically register my software client to facilitate future transactions. UMA addresses all three ecosystems. The narrow ecosystem perhaps most closely aligns with enterprise identity and access management, so it is the one we focus on in this chapter.

UMA has some special jargon. Let's define it now:

- **Resource owner (RO)**—The entity (person or organization) that grants access to a protected resource (i.e., Alice).

- **Requesting party (RqP)**–The entity, using client software, who is trying to get access to a resource (i.e., Bob).

- **Permission ticket**—An identifier used to correlate a request for access to a resource and a certain client. The permission ticket is similar in function to the code in the OAuth authorization code flow—the UMA client presents the ticket plus client credentials at the UMA token endpoint.

- **Client**—An OAuth client that supports the UMA Grant.

- **Resource server (RS)**—An OAuth resource server that supports the extra requirements specified by UMA, such as registering resources, returning permission tickets to unauthorized clients, and introspecting access tokens. This is sometimes the API software or an API gateway.

- **Authorization server (AS)**—An OAuth authorization server that supports the extra requirements specified by UMA, such as resource registration and the UMA Grant type.

- **Scopes**—As in OAuth, an extent of access. The authorization server uses scopes to map to zero or more policies.

- **Claim**—An attribute about a person (requesting party) or client.

- **Protection API token (PAT)**—An OAuth access token with scope `uma_protection`, used by the RS to call UMA APIs on the authorization server.

- **Requesting party token (RPT)**—An OAuth bearer token used by the client to gain access to a protected resource. This is the most commonly referred to UMA access token! If there is no RPT, the client cannot access an API!

- **Persisted claims token (PCT)**—A reference access token issued
  to the client to represent a set of claims collected during a previous
  authorization process.

As UMA is a profile and extension of OAuth 2.0, Figure 8-1 should look familiar.
The software components (Client, RS, AS) are of course the same as OAuth—it is their
interactions that are slightly different. What is new in this diagram is the placement of
the requesting party (RqP) and the resource owner (RO). In "plain" OAuth, these are the
same person.

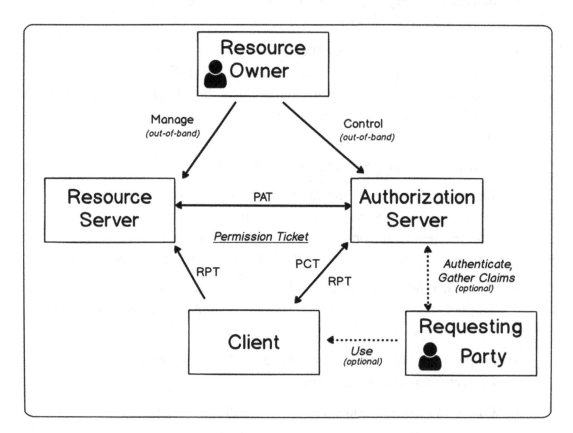

Figure 8-1. *UMA high-level overview*

The PAT is just an OAuth access token with the scope `uma_protection`. It can be
obtained from the AS using the OAuth Client Credentials Grant. The PCT token is not an
access token, but a reference to data.

UMA has two specifications. The first is the "UMA 2.0 Grant for OAuth 2.0 Authorization"; the second is "Federated Authorization for UMA 2.0". For brevity, we will call them UMA Grant and UMA FedAuthz, respectively. UMA Grant addresses the information needed by an UMA client developer. If you are calling an UMA protected resource, and you need to obtain an RPT, then you need to understand the UMA Grant specification. If you are a developer who is writing an API that you want to protect using UMA, then you should read both the UMA Grant and UMA FedAuthz specifications.

One of the innovations of UMA is a loose bundling between the client and the security infrastructure. Look back again at Figure 4-1, which lists the scopes required to access Google APIs. Note that Google must publish each scope. If Google releases a new version of the API, it may impact the required scopes, which means that client developers must update their code. UMA uses permission tickets to hide the scopes from the client. The permission ticket is a guess-resistant alpha-numeric code, used as a handle to reference the required scopes. After the AS returns the permission ticket to the RS, the RS sends it to the client. Importantly, the client never sees the scopes—just the permission ticket (hence, scopes are internal to the client-AS interaction). In this way, the RS is in control of the scopes and can update them without impacting existing client software.

UMA still allows for the client to explicitly request scopes. Of course, the RS will need to communicate these scopes out of band with the client. As in OAuth, clients must register "requested" scopes prior to specifying them. Figure 8-2 uses a Venn diagram to represent the relationship between scopes associated with a ticket, scopes requested by a client, and scopes registered by a client. You could express this as: ticket scopes ∪ (requested scopes ∩ registered scopes). For a more detailed discussion, see the "Interpreting Authorization Assessment Set Math" section of the *UMA Implementer's Guide*.

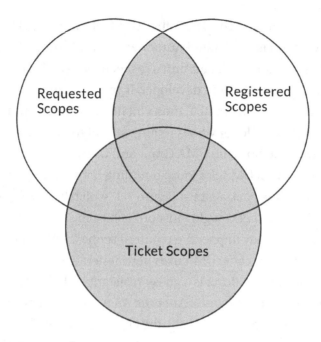

Figure 8-2. *Scopes set math*

You may have heard of a standard called XACML, the "eXtensible Access Control Markup Language". Unlike XACML, UMA does not specify syntax for policy expression. If you want to use XACML to express polices and an UMA authorization server to issue access tokens —that's possible! The UMA AS can gather the claims, generate an XACML request, and return an authorization decision based on the response from an XACML policy decision point. A structured policy expression language is useful in situations where there are many policies, and you need to either perform analysis on policies, or perhaps auto-generate them. If you're a small organization, you probably don't need this.

UMA does not enable fine-grained access control. This does not mean that policy centralization is not useful. If several APIs share a policy, using an UMA access token to implement this policy centrally makes sense. There is a tradeoff between speed and centralization. For example, if you're building an auction website with an Update button, visible only to the item seller, should you use UMA to control rendering this button? Probably not. But what if the Update button requires the seller's consent? In cases like this, centralization may make sense.

In the next few sections, we introduce the UMA 2.0 standard and follow up with some real-world examples of how you can put UMA to work to protect APIs and web applications.

UMA Grant

UMA registers a new `grant_type` in the IANA OAuth Registry: `urn:ietf:params:oauth:grant-type:uma-ticket`. From the name of this grant type, you can see how important the permission ticket is to UMA. At the risk of over-simplifying, instead of using a code to obtain a token at the token endpoint, as in the OAuth Authorization Code Grant, you use a permission ticket. UMA does not support token issuance at the authorization endpoint—there is no UMA implicit flow. In most OAuth profiles, policy evaluation happens at the authorization endpoint (the "policy" is normally "did the person approve?"). Policy is in quotes because synchronous human approval is not a policy as we would normally understand it. The AS iterates through the scopes and maps each to a set of policies. Policy enforcement happens at the RS, which maps the request to a resource identifier (`resource_id`) and ensures that the required scopes are present in the RPT.

UMA RPT Requests with Interactive Claims Gathering

Figure 8-3 is a sequence diagram for the UMA Grant when the AS is using interactive claims gathering. The following is a description of each step for additional context.

1. A person (the RqP) uses a client to access an UMA protected resource at the RS.

2. Without an access token, the RS will return HTTP code 401 (Unauthorized) with a permission ticket (obtained from the AS after registering a resource with certain scopes). The RS will also return the URI of the AS at which to obtain an access token.

3. The client presents the permission ticket at the token endpoint (along with client credentials). In this example, let's imagine that the AS needs the RqP to authenticate.

4. The AS returns 403 (Forbidden) with an error message contained in a JSON object called `needs_info`. The AS also provides a hint as to where the client can obtain authorization, which in this case is the interactive claims gathering endpoint at the AS.

5. The client redirects the RqP's browser to the claims gathering endpoint at the AS. This is the equivalent of redirecting to the authorization endpoint in the OAuth code flow. The request must include the `client_id` and ticket and should include the `claims_redirect_uri` and state.

6. Which claims the AS needs is outside the scope of UMA. For GDPR compliance, the AS may need the person to consent to the release of personal information. It is possible that the AS may need the person to provide government issued license information. Or the policy may require step-up authentication. The possibilities are endless.

7. The RqP supplies the necessary information (or the flow stops).

8. The AS processes the information and redirects the RqP's browser back to the client's previously registered `claims_redirect_uri` with a new permission ticket. Note: the client should check the state parameter to prevent cross-site request forgery attacks.

9. The client requests a new RPT by presenting the new permission ticket.

10. In our example, the AS returns the access token (RPT) on successful evaluation of the policies. Optionally, the AS may return a PCT, which is a token that references the information obtained during interactive claims processing. The client can present this in the future to avoid any redundant interactive claims processing.

11. With a valid access token in hand, the client again tries to obtain the resource.

12. The RS is responsible for validating the access token. In our example, it's good, and the RS returns the protected resource.

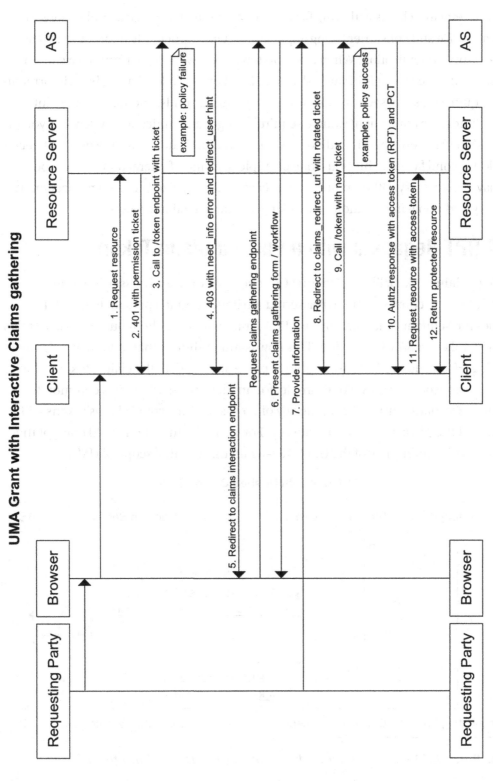

Figure 8-3. UMA Grant sequence diagram (with interactive claims gathering)

The interactive claims gathering flow is very powerful. It has many applications for both enterprise and consumer facing applications. One particularly important use case is for step-up authentication. When a person traverses a website, performing a certain transaction may require additional risk mitigation. For example, viewing bank information might require one set of security policies, and to transfer funds, another. At the point you transfer funds, the bank might want to require stronger authentication by sending you to the bank's IDP to perform this additional step-up authentication (e.g., the user will need to provide a second factor). This is just one example of a kind of interaction with the person that may be necessary. Other important use cases are formalized consent management, providing additional information, or invoking a fraud detection process.

UMA RPT Requests with a Pushed Claim Token

Pushing a claims token, like an OpenID Connect JWT or a SAML assertion, is an expedient way to convey some IDP asserted attributes about a person. Figure 8-4 provides the sequence diagram for the UMA Grant when the client pushes a claim token, like an id_token or SAML assertion. This flow is much shorter than interactive claims gathering. However, the AS must be able to parse and validate the claims token, which is outside the scope of UMA. For example, for an identity assertion, it is common to validate the signature using the public key of the issuer. Encrypted claims tokens will work only if the AS has the right private key. For example, the client could encrypt the assertion with a public key of the UMA AS—again this is out of scope of UMA.

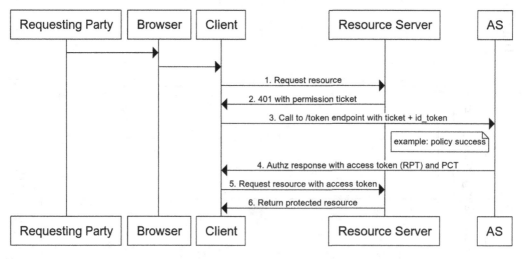

Figure 8-4. *UMA Grant sequence diagram (with pushed claim token)*

RPT Request Options

As mentioned earlier, the client can request a specific scope, using the `scope` parameter, if such scopes are pre-registered by the client. The AS will add this candidate scope to all resources that appear in the permission ticket.

It is possible that the client already has an RPT from a different transaction. The client may include this previously issued RPT using the `rpt` parameter. The client developer should be careful, as the newly issued RPT will contain the previously granted permissions. Unlike OAuth, there is no way to down-scope an UMA RPT. Also, keep in mind that the client may not know the associated scopes for an RPT, as a permission ticket may reference scopes of which it is not aware—there is no requirement to pre-register scopes associated with a permission ticket. However, the UMA FedAuthz spec does recommend in Section 4 that the RS "document its intended pattern of permission requests in order to assist the client in pre-registering for and requesting appropriate scopes at the authorization server".

The client can use the `claim_token` and `claim client_token_format` parameters to specify the presence of a base64-encoded identity assertion. One issue that may arise is that the assertion may have an audience for a party other than the UMA Authorization Server. How the client and AS determine how to align with audience restrictions is also out of scope of UMA.

Finally, there is the `pct` parameter, which is used to send a PCT token returned from a previous authorization workflow. The client must only send the PCT token for the same RqP. The point of the `pct` parameter is to save the requesting party from the effort needed to provide the same required information. The AS can still initiate interactive claims-gathering based on the context of the situation.

Client Credentials

Clients must present credentials (i.e., `client_id` and `client_secret`) at the RPT (token) endpoint, but UMA does not define any mechanism for this to happen, except mentioning that RFC 7591 and OpenID Connect also define client registration. Depending on the security requirements, an OAuth client may choose different mechanisms for client authentication. If you are using OpenID Connect client registration, you should consider using `private_key_jwt`, which avoids any shared secrets between the AS and client.

UMA Federated Authorization

The resource owner (RO)—whether a company or person—can manage access at multiple resource servers. The ability to use multiple autonomous resource servers and authorization servers is why we call it "federated authorization". While the UMA Grant specification provides a protocol for client developers, the UMA FedAuthz specification details the protocol between the RS and AS. How are permission tickets requested, how are resources associated with scopes, and how does the AS enable the RS to request UMA protection for a resource? UMA FedAuthz defines the back-channel communication between the AS and RS. Note: AS and RS developers need to read both UMA Grant and UMA FedAuthz.

Authorization model in UMA offers some of the capabilities of its web access management predecessors. While in OAuth the client must know the scopes it needs, in older web access management platforms, that wasn't the case. The clients just requested a certain URL. See Figure 8-5 for an illustration of how a web access management platform could utilize UMA. In this case, the RS is mapping resources to a combination of a certain URL and HTTP method (or methods). This isn't a requirement—the RS has a lot of flexibility as to "what is a resource". For example, it may only use UMA tokens when it encounters a certain transaction value, or when required to obtain personal consent.

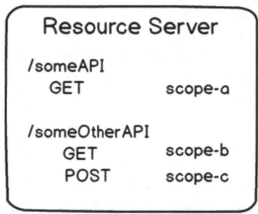
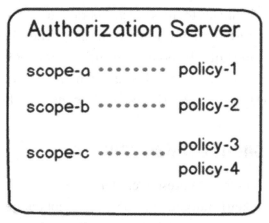

Figure 8-5. *Mapping resources to scopes and policies with UMA*

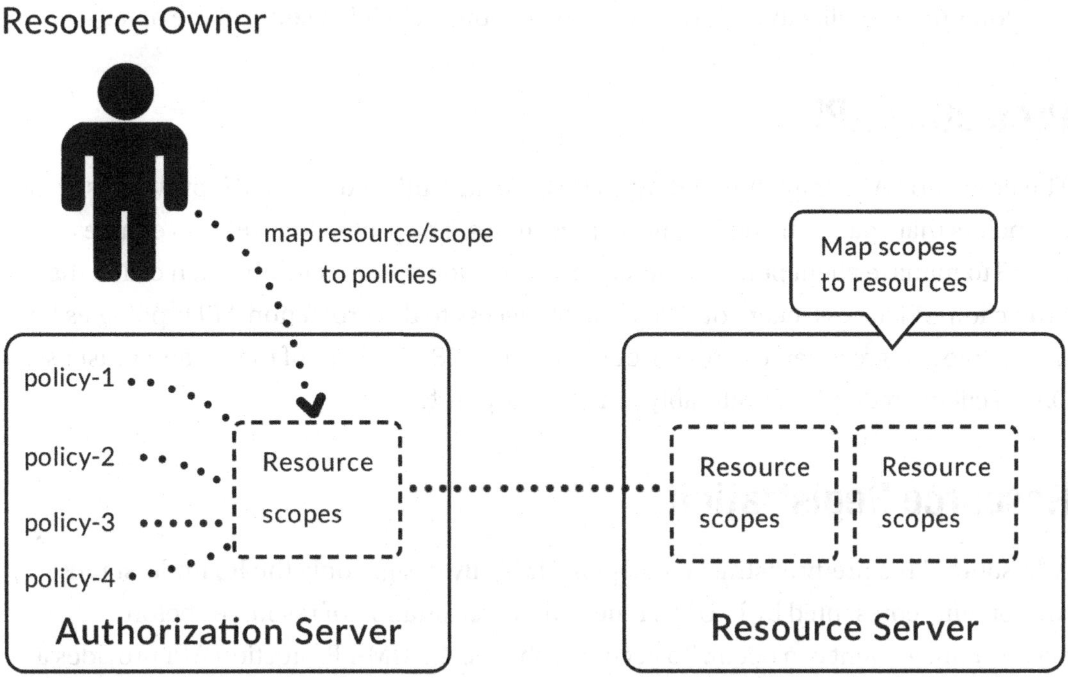

Resource Owner

Figure 8-6. *Resource owner's role: mapping policies to scopes*

Saving the details for later, let's say that in Figure 8-5, the RS has two APIs: /someAPI and /someOtherAPI. To do an HTTP GET request on /someAPI, you need an RPT with scope-a. On the AS, the resource owner determines what scope maps to which policies (as shown in Figure 8-6). This process is also not in scope of UMA. But just as an example, Policy One could state that the person must authenticate locally, and that the role of the person must be "manager". In this case the RS is the policy enforcement point—it must ensure that the token is active and contains the proper authorizations for each resource ID. The AS is the policy decision point—it alone knows the policies, and it must have sufficient information to make a policy decision.

One difference between UMA and web access management is that with UMA, the RS can add extra security as it sees fit. This might not be desirable if you want policy centralization, but it's possible. In UMA, the RS can be a little "smarter" than your typical web access management "agent"—— which as its name suggests, always does the policy server's bidding.

How does this all happen? The next few sections help fill in some of the details.

Protection API

The Protection API, implemented by an UMA AS and utilized by the RS, provides several endpoints that enable the registration of resources. The protection API also enables the RS to manage client permission requests for resources. An OAuth token called the Protection API access token, or PAT, controls access to the Protection API (apologies for the tautology—great names are self-defining). The RS is a client of the AS and must use OAuth client credentials, preferably `private_key_jwt`.

Resource Registration

A "resource" is a pretty abstract concept in UMA. By design, only the RS understands the content represented by it. UMA relies on the registration of resources before access management can occur. To accomplish this, the UMA Protection API provides a resource registration endpoint. The UMA authorization server publishes the URLs for all endpoints in the configuration metadata document found at the issuer URL plus `/.well-known/uma2-configuration`. The RS specifies `resource_scopes`, which are all those possible for access to this resource. A client can request one or more `resource_scopes` during the authorization phase. The AS returns a resource ID on resource creation. The RS needs the resource ID for future calls to the Protection API. Figure 8-7 provides a sequence diagram for resource registration. For more details on resource registration, read the resource registration section of UMA FedAuthz.

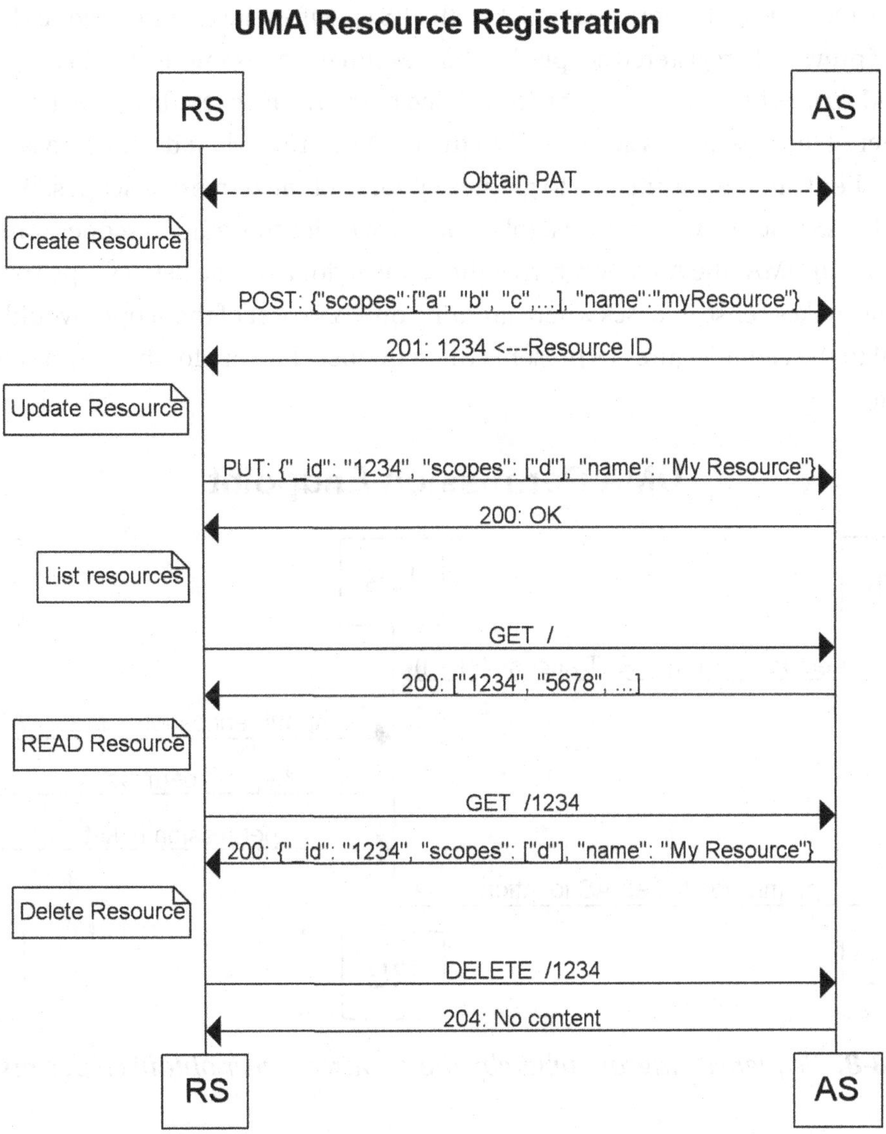

UMA Resource Registration

Figure 8-7. *Resource registration sequence diagram example*

Permission Endpoint

If a client requests a resource without an RPT access token, if the token is invalid, or lacks sufficient scopes, the RS uses the permission endpoint to obtain a new permission ticket. The RS returns the permission ticket, along with the URL of the AS to the client.

While requesting the permission ticket, the RS specifies the required scopes from the list of previously registered scopes for that resource. For example, the RS might have registered scopes `https://as.example/all` and `https://as.example/view`. Let's say that either of those scopes is acceptable to the RS. Note, that when deciding to issue an RPT to a client, the AS may decide to grant only some of the requested scopes. While in OAuth, the AS would always return a token authorized for the granted scopes (omitting the others), in UMA, the AS may return either a token for a partial list of scopes or an error. This makes sense in cases where granting only a subset of the scopes would not be useful to the client. Figure 8-8 presents the sequence diagram for the permission endpoint.

UMA Permission Endpoint

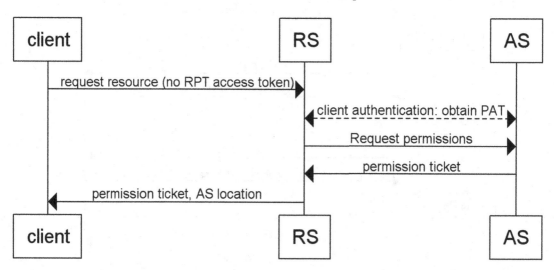

Figure 8-8. *Sequence diagram whereby the resource server obtains a permission ticket*

By now, you are probably wondering what one of these elusive permission tickets looks like during registration. Listing 8-1 shows an example of an HTTP POST request that RS makes to AS to register permission (and get permission ticket back).

Listing 8-1. Sample UMA Permission Ticket Request

```
POST /perm HTTP/1.1
Content-Type: application/json
Host: as.example.com
Authorization: Bearer 74b57da9-b12a-49cc-8026-a97f5a1e8234
...

[
   {
      "resource_id":"c746d6d4-992f-4d93",
      "resource_scopes":[
         "https://as.example/view"
      ]
   },
   {
      "resource_id":"8c799def-cd4d-46ee",
      "resource_scopes":[
         "https://as.example/view",
         "https://as.example/all"
      ]
   }
]
```

The RS should use HTTP headers to communicate the ticket and the AS location to the client. Listing 8-2 is the example from the UMA Grant of a response to a client from the RS with the ticket obtained from the AS permission endpoint.

Listing 8-2. Sample UMA Permission Ticket Response

```
HTTP/1.1 401 Unauthorized
  WWW-Authenticate: UMA realm="example",
    as_uri="https://as.example.com",
    ticket="016f84e8-f9b9-11e0-bd6f-0021cc6004de"
```

Token Introspection

An UMA RPT is an OAuth bearer token. The RS needs to know if this token is active, and what permissions it grants. While a bearer token could be a base64-encoded JWT, in many implementations, it is just a non-guessable string—a reference to an object stored at the AS. In order to retrieve the corresponding object, UMA aligns with OAuth token introspection (RFC 7662), but adds an UMA specific response parameter: permissions. Also, an UMA token introspection response must not return a scopes parameter. This would be confusing to an RS, because scopes are bound to resources (instead, it returns the aforementioned permissions parameter). For example, we could have scopes called https://as.example.com/view and https://as.example.com/all. Let's say you have two files, file1 (resource identifier is c746d6d4-992f-4d93) and file2 (resource identifier is 8c799def-cd4d-46ee). It's conceivable you could grant someone https://as.example.com/view on file1 but on file2 you would grant both https://as.example.com/view and https://as.example.com/all (or just the latter one). Listing 8-3 shows an example of a response containing the introspection object with the permissions parameter.

Listing 8-3. Example of a Response Containing the Introspection Object with the Permissions Parameter

```
HTTP/1.1 200 OK
Content-Type: application/json
Cache-Control: no-store
...

{
   "active":true,
   "exp":1256953732,
   "iat":1256912345,
   "permissions":[
      {
         "resource_id":"c746d6d4-992f-4d93",
         "resource_scopes":[
            "https://as.example/view"
         ],
         "exp":1256953732
      },
```

```
{
    "resource_id":"8c799def-cd4d-46ee",
    "resource_scopes":[
        "https://as.example/view",
        "https://as.example/all"
    ],
    "exp":1256953732
}
]
}
```

In a nutshell, UMA provides a way for a client to obtain an access token to access a resource. How the AS authorizes the access token is the only thing that changes versus "normal" OAuth. In the next few sections, we describe how to put UMA to work.

UMA Authorization Server Software

This section focuses on how to configure the Gluu Server (specifically the oxAuth component) as an UMA authorization server. Some of these features require no configuration by the administrator. For example, the Gluu Server shows the resources registered by the RS, but there is nothing for the AS administrator to do. Likewise, oxAuth implements the UMA configuration endpoint, but it requires no configuration by the administrator. The primary UMA configuration responsibility of the administrator is to define UMA scopes, RPT policies, and claims gathering workflows.

Managing Scopes

Scopes represent the "extent of access". In UMA, the RS manages access to a resource by specifying the required scopes. When evaluating whether to grant access to a client, oxAuth calculates all the policies associated with the scopes for that permission. Let's say Alice is sharing a document with Bob. When Bob tries to read the document, the RS makes a request for a permission ticket with the view and search scopes. Bob's client must obtain an RPT at the UMA token endpoint, at which point the AS looks up all the policies associated with the view and search scopes (corresponding to the ticket). Policies vary—maybe the AS checks a database to see if Alice has given Bob access to this document, and if Bob has authenticated using a strong two-factor authentication mechanism. In oxAuth, you define Python interception scripts to express policies. The most important method in the UMA RPT Authorization script is the `authorize` method, which returns a boolean. All policies associated with all scopes must evaluate to true for the oxAuth to return an RPT. In the oxTrust administration interface, the admin defines the policies. Figure 8-9 shows an example of scope management.

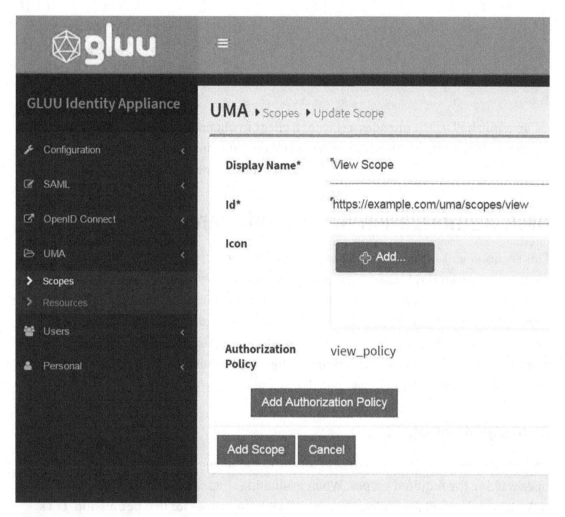

Figure 8-9. *oxTrust screenshot of UMA scope*

You can use the Gluu Server oxTrust interface to map policies to scopes. The AS must define the scope before an RS can use it. The RS does not know what policies map to the scope. The AS can update the policies, or even add new policies without impacting the RS or client code. It's recommended to use a URI as the ID of the scope, to avoid collisions in the event of a merger with another organization.

286

Managing Authorization Policies

Interception scripts are the standard mechanism for customizing business logic in oxAuth. Administrators enter scripts directly into the oxTrust web interface, as shown in Figure 8-10, in which case oxTrust stores them in the LDAP server. Administrators can author scripts directly on the file system, although LDAP storage is more convenient for clustered deployments. Figure 8-10 describes the interface for an UMA RPT policy interception script. As you might expect, init is called before the authorize method, and destroy is called after. The authorize method must return either true or false. The policy may have access to the requesting party's identity if the client pushed claims (for example, an OpenID id_token or Userinfo JWT), the PCT token, or a previously issued RPT sent with the token request. The Gluu Server administrator can create many interesting policies about the requesting party, for example if she has a certain role or used a certain type of authentication. You can make policies based on client claims— perhaps internal and third-party clients have access to different APIs. Policies can call external APIs, for example to obtain a fraud score based on the IP address of the client (the AS can determine the IP address in the HTTP Request object).

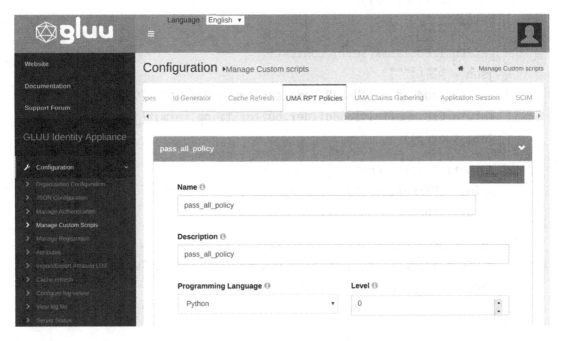

Figure 8-10. *RPT policy interception script screenshot*

If a policy fails, the AS may want to provide a hint to the client as to what went wrong. The AS has two ways to communicate this information to the client: via the need_info response, or as a parameter to the claims gathering endpoint. After all the policies have been evaluated, the response will be returned by oxAuth. See Listing 8-4.

Listing 8-4. UMA RPT Policy Interception Script

```
class UmaRptPolicy(UmaRptPolicyType):
    def __init__(self, currentTimeMillis):
        self.currentTimeMillis = currentTimeMillis

    def init(self, configurationAttributes):
        print "RPT Policy. Initialized successfully"
        return True

    def destroy(self, configurationAttributes):
        print "RPT Policy. Destroyed successfully"
        return True

    def getApiVersion(self):
        return 1

    def getRequiredClaims(self, context):
        json = """[]"""
        context.addRedirectUserParam("customUserParam1", "value1")
        return ClaimDefinitionBuilder.build(String.format(json, context.
        getIssuer()))

    def authorize(self, context):
        print "RPT Policy. Authorizing ..."
        return True

    def getClaimsGatheringScriptName(self, context):
        context.addRedirectUserParam("customUserParam2", "value2")
        return "sampleClaimsGathering"
```

Interactive Claims Gathering Workflows

Sometimes the AS may need to interact with the RqP to make an authorization decision. Using the UMA claims gathering workflow, the AS may present forms or even redirect the RqP to another website. During this interaction, the AS may look at the context and decide it needs to mitigate additional fraud risk. To do this, it might require a more secure type of authentication. Or it's even possible the AS may need to facilitate local registration, or to get the consent of the RO to share personal information. The AS may need to communicate instructions for some offline activity. There are many possible use cases where the answer to "can you get a token" is not simply "yes" or "no".

Gluu Server administrators control claims gathering by writing a custom script. Claims gathering is like an authentication script, which is also front-channel. The getStepsCount method determines the number of steps. For example, step one could be to authenticate the user more strongly, and step two to present a form to request additional information from the RqP. Unless the step involves a redirect, oxAuth will display the page specified in getPageForStep. The getClaims method processes the information submitted by a form presented in a step. If there is information it wants to attach to the PCT token, it uses the storeClaimInPCT method. The getClaims method returns the PCT after each step. For examples of claims gathering, see the default scripts included with the Gluu Server. See Listing 8-5.

Listing 8-5. Claims Gathering Interception Script

```
Class ClaimsGatheringScript(ClaimsGatheringType):
    def init(self, configAttrs):
        return

    def destroy(self,configAttrs):
        return

    def process(self, claimsGatheringContext, configAttrs):
        return pct

    def prepareForStep(self, configAttrs):
        return True
```

```
def getExtraParametersForStep(self, configAttrs, step):
    return None

def getStepsCount(self, configAttrs):
    return 1

def getStepsCount(self, configAttrs):
    return 1
```

UMA Resource Server Software

As UMA 2.0 is a relatively new standard, there is not a lot of client software at this time of this first edition. Of course, the RS can implement the protocol directly, but having client software makes the job a lot easier. Chapter 5 introduced the oxd client middleware server for OpenID Connect. This software also provides interfaces for UMA, for the UMA client, the RS, and the OAuth client credential grant (to call oxd APIs and the RPT endpoint). You can use the oxd OpenAPI document (i.e., Swagger document) to generate client libraries for Python, Php, Node, Java, C#, Ruby, Go, and many other languages using code generators or SaaS services like SwaggerHub.

The two oxd methods that an API developer needs to use are uma_rs_protect and uma_rs_check_access. The protect method is used to register resources and associate scopes. The check_access method is used to validate access tokens, before content from an API is returned.

Gluu Gateway as UMA Resource Server

In Chapter 6 we introduced the Kong API gateway. In this section, we describe how to turn it into an UMA RS, which verifies that tokens are active and have the scopes required to call certain APIs. Gluu accomplished this by writing two Kong plugins (see Figure 8-11). The first filters HTTP requests and inspects the Authorization header for a valid token. The second looks at the requested URL and HTTP method and verifies that the right scopes are present.

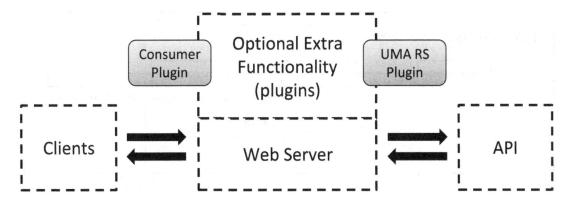

Figure 8-11. *Gluu Gateway plugin overview*

The Gluu Gateway package integrates several components:

- Kong Community Edition

- Konga administrative web GUI

- oxd

- Postgres

- Setup script

Like the Gluu Server, the goal of Gluu Gateway is to supply a Linux package to make these components easy to install by providing a straightforward deployment process. The Gluu Gateway is MIT licensed. It should be noted, however, that it uses the oxd client middleware, which is commercial (although up to 10 licenses are free). See the Gluu Gateway and oxd documentation sites for more information on licensing: `https://gluu.org/Docs`.

Gluu Gateway has three modes: OAuth, UMA, and Mix (see Figure 8-12). In OAuth mode, the client obtains a token from the OAuth token endpoint and calls OAuth protected endpoints; in UMA mode, the client obtains a token from the UMA token endpoint (RPT) and calls UMA protected endpoints; in Mix mode, the client obtains an OAuth token, but the Gluu Gateway switches it for an UMA token prior to calling the upstream web server. In this section, we cover the UMA mode only. The purpose of Mix mode is to keep it simple for developers—they just need to think about client credential grant (i.e., they don't need to read the UMA Grant specification). For more information about Mix mode, see the Gluu Gateway docs at `https://gluu.org/docs`. This feature may be removed from a future version of Gluu Gateway.

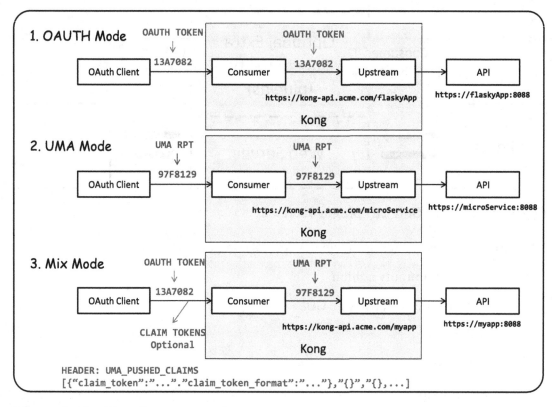

Figure 8-12. *Gluu Gateway modes*

One of the most important features of the Gluu Gateway is to provide a GUI to enable administrators to specify which UMA scopes are required to call a certain endpoint with a certain method. The Gluu Gateway uses scope expressions, a draft UMA extension, to enable administrators to use complex boolean statements to control access to APIs. Figure 8-13 shows a sample configuration for a test API.

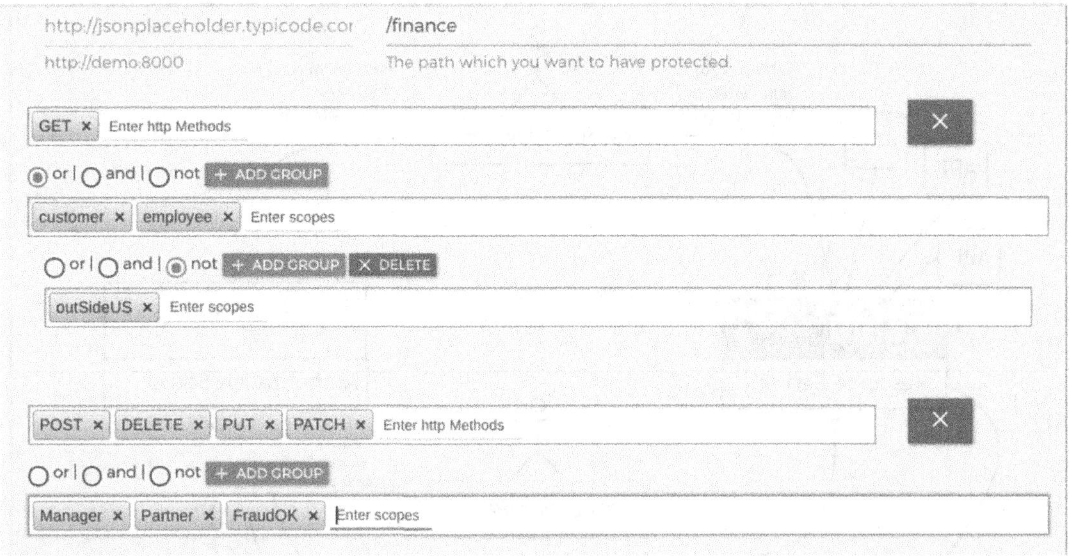

Figure 8-13. *Gluu Gateway RS security*

UMA Client Software

As mentioned, using the oxd middleware is your best bet for client software. There is a useful sample application included in the gg-demo folder of the Gluu Gateway GitHub project: https://github.com/GluuFederation/gluu-gateway.

This project walks you through each step of what an UMA client needs to do, both with and without claims gathering. The demo deploys as a simple cgi-script and requires some setup on the AS and RS, which is described in the README.
Figure 8-14 provides an overview of the components. Notice that oxd is handling all of the back-channel calls for the client and RS. It's effectively the same as the standard UMA protocol, except oxd is doing some of the heavy lifting.

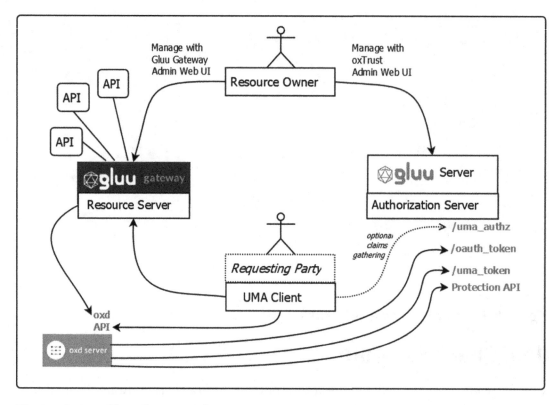

Figure 8-14. *Gluu Gateway demo overview*

The following sequence provides an overview of UMA from the perspective of an UMA client using oxd. In the first step, the client calls an API hosted by the Gluu Gateway acting as an UMA RS (see Figure 8-15). As the request does not contain a bearer token in the `Authorization` header, the RS returns a `HTTP 401 Unauthorized` response, but includes a permission ticket in the `WWW-Authenticate` header.

Request url:	http://demo.gluu.org:8000/posts
Request headers:	{'Host': 'non-gathering.example.com', 'Connection': 'keep-alive', 'Accept-Encoding': 'gzip, deflate', 'Accept': '*/*', 'User-Agent': 'python-requests/2.5.2 CPython/2.7.6 Linux/3.13.0-149-generic'}
Request body:	""
Response status:	401
Response headers:	{'transfer-encoding': 'chunked', 'server': 'kong/0.11.0', 'connection': 'keep-alive', 'date': 'Sat, 30 Jun 2018 21:44:13 GMT', 'content-type': 'application/json; charset=utf-8', 'www-authenticate': 'UMA realm="rs",as_uri="https://demo.gluu.org",error="insufficient_scope",ticket="9a2e6d48-edc6-4d39-b3d8-bad657fce8ea"'}

Response body:	{
	    "message": "Unauthorized"
	}

Figure 8-15. *Step 1 of UMA client*

In Step 2, the client obtains a plain OAuth client token (see Figure 8-16). This will be needed when the client calls the oxd APIs, and when the client tries to obtain an RPT. Note the AS returns scopes `uma_protection` and `openid`. This is only because they are configured as default scopes on the Gluu Server—they serve no purpose in this demo. What's really needed is the access token in the response body.

Request url:	https://demo.gluu.org:8443/get-client-token
Request headers:	{'Content-Length': '260', 'Accept-Encoding': 'gzip, deflate', 'Accept': '*/*', 'User-Agent': 'python-requests/2.5.2 CPython/2.7.6 Linux/3.13.0-149-generic', 'Connection': 'keep-alive', 'Content-Type': 'application/json'}

```
{
    "client_secret": "f57c07fd-729b-40e5-a8e3-cf0aa6482451",
    "oxd_id": "313c7d38-ad6c-47eb-8991-62a1a950092f",
    "scope": [
        "uma_protection",
        "openid"
    ],
    "client_id": "@!7A1F.7A69.7E9A.EFBA!0001!AD32.2532!0008!3498.AD16.F1E5.42A4",
    "op_host": "https://demo.gluu.org"
}
```

Response status:	200
Response headers:	{'date': 'Sat, 30 Jun 2018 21:44:13 GMT', 'content-length': '148', 'content-type': 'application/json'}

```
{
    "status": "ok",
    "data": {
        "access_token": "ac654b2e-cbbd-4895-b36b-fa51dcf0832c",
        "scope": "openid uma_protection",
        "expires_in": 299,
        "refresh_token": null
    }
}
```

Figure 8-16. *Step 2 of UMA client*

In Step 3, the client attempts to get an RPT by calling the oxd `uma-rp-get-rpt` endpoint (see Figure 8-17). It presents the ticket from Step 1 and uses the access token from Step 2 in the `Authorization` header. The AS evaluates all the policies for the scopes required by the respective permission ticket. In this case, they must evaluate to true, as the response contains a new access_token—the RPT!

Request uri:	https://demo.gluu.org:8443/uma-rp-get-rpt
Request headers:	{'Content-Length': '157', 'Accept-Encoding': 'gzip, deflate', 'Accept': '*/*', 'User-Agent': 'python-requests/2.5.2 CPython/2.7.6 Linux/3.13.0-149-generic', 'Connection': 'keep-alive', 'Content-Type': 'application/json', 'Authorization': u'Bearer ac654b2e-cbbd-4895-b36b-fa51dcf0832c'}
| Request body: | ```
{
    "scope": [
        "demo_scope_non_gathering",
        "uma_protection"
    ],
    "ticket": "9a2e6d48-edc6-4d39-b3d8-bad657fce8ea",
    "oxd_id": "313c7d38-ad6c-47eb-8991-62a1a950092f"
}
``` |
| Response status: | 200 |
| Response headers: | {'date': 'Sat, 30 Jun 2018 21:44:13 GMT', 'content-length': '241', 'content-type': 'application/json'} |
| Response body: | ```
{
    "status": "ok",
    "data": {
        "access_token": "6cbdb6de-653b-4fe2-ab47-c80f83ea65e9_D8C4.FB90.171B.6E5B.F02D.1190.ED83.3507",
        "token_type": "Bearer",
        "updated": false,
        "pct": "462477a3-4eaf-4a2c-a532-bb199448743d_E340.AEED.89E1.E338.BD94.B1FB.DF2F.0F1B"
    }
}
``` |

Figure 8-17. *Step 3 of UMA client*

In Step 4, the client uses the RPT to populate the Authorization header of the request (see Figure 8-18). The RS introspects the token and evaluates the permissions. Everything is okay, because the RS returns content!

Request url:	http://demo.gluu.org:8000/posts
Request headers:	{'Accept-Encoding': 'gzip, deflate', 'Connection': 'keep-alive', 'Accept': '*/*', 'User-Agent': 'python-requests/2.5.2 CPython/2.7.6 Linux/3.13.0-149-generic', 'Host': 'non-gathering.example.com', 'Authorization': u'Bearer 6cbdb6de-653b-4fe2-ab47-c80f83ea65e9_D8C4.FB90.171B.6E5B.F02D.1190.ED83.3507'}
Request body:	""
Response status:	200
Response headers:	{'expect-ct': 'max-age=604800, report-uri="https://report-uri.cloudflare.com/cdn-cgi/beacon/expect-ct"', 'access-control-allow-credentials': 'true', 'via': 'kong/0.11.0', 'x-content-type-options': 'nosniff', 'x-powered-by': 'Express', 'transfer-encoding': 'chunked', 'set-cookie': '__cfduid=d8c1ee42f829f23df30852680a4c988471530395051; expires=Sun, 30-Jun-19 21:44:11 GMT; path=/; domain=.typicode.com; HttpOnly', 'cf-cache-status': 'HIT', 'expires': 'Sun, 01 Jul 2018 01:44:11 GMT', 'vary': 'Origin, Accept-Encoding', 'content-encoding': 'gzip', 'x-kong-proxy-latency': '163', 'connection': 'keep-alive', 'etag': 'W/"6b80-Ybsq/K6GwwqrYkAsFxqDXGC7DoM"', 'pragma': 'no-cache', 'cache-control': 'public, max-age=14400', 'date': 'Sat, 30 Jun 2018 21:44:11 GMT', 'cf-ray': '4333d010e87706e2-LHR', 'server': 'cloudflare', 'content-type': 'application/json; charset=utf-8', 'x-kong-upstream-latency': '20'}
| | ```
[
    {
        "body": "quia et suscipit\nsuscipit recusandae consequuntur expedita et cum\nreprehenderit molestiae ut
        "userId": 1,
        "id": 1,
        "title": "sunt aut facere repellat provident occaecati excepturi optio reprehenderit"
    },
``` |

Figure 8-18. *Step 4 of UMA client*
```

But what if all the policies don't evaluate to true? If you call the `demo-client` CGI script with the parameter `claim=true`, you can see such an example (see Figure 8-19). Instead of getting back an RPT, as in Step 2, you will get back a `need_info` error. The response also details required claims, which could be useful information for the client. And importantly, the client gets back a `redirect_user` value, where it can redirect the user to interact with the AS.

```
Response status:    200
Response headers:   {'date': 'Sat, 30 Jun 2018 22:03:56 GMT', 'content-length': '911', 'content-type': 'application/json'}

                    {
                        "status": "error",
                        "data": {
                            "error_description": "The authorization server needs additional information in order to determine wheth
                            "details": {
                                "ticket": "71091942-70cf-4811-9cd6-7ce9819c1c9f",
                                "redirect_user": "https://demo.gluu.org/oxauth/restv1/uma/gather_claims?customUserParam2=value2&cus
                                "required_claims": [
                                    {
                                        "claim_type": "string",
                                        "friendly_name": "country",
                                        "name": "country",
                                        "claim_token_format": [
                                            "http://openid.net/specs/openid-connect-core-1_0.html#IDToken"
                                        ],
                                        "issuer": [
                                            "https://demo.gluu.org"
                                        ]
Response body:                      },
                                    {
                                        "claim_type": "string",
                                        "friendly_name": "city",
                                        "name": "city",
                                        "claim_token_format": [
                                            "http://openid.net/specs/openid-connect-core-1_0.html#IDToken"
                                        ],
                                        "issuer": [
                                            "https://demo.gluu.org"
                                        ]
                                    }
                                ],
                                "error": "need_info"
                            },
                            "error": "need_info"
                        }
                    }
```

Figure 8-19. *The need_info error*

In this demo, there is a two-step claims gathering process. In the first step, shown in Figure 8-20, the AS presents a form for the RqP to enter a country. This is a simple example, but the AS could do anything here. Just a few examples would be to authenticate the RqP, query external fraud detection APIs, or ask the RqP to consent to sharing personal information. Figure 8-21 shows Step 2 of the sample claims gathering workflow, asking for the RqP to enter a city.

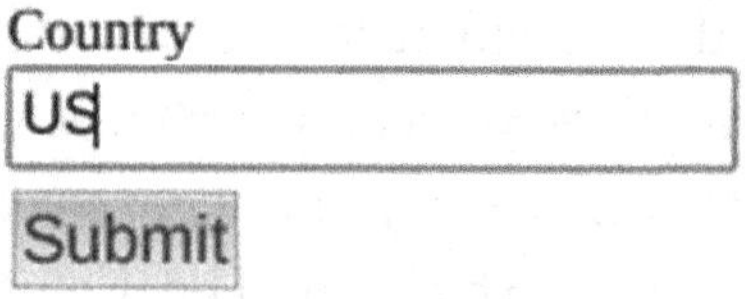

Country

```
US
```

Submit

Figure 8-20. *Claim gathering Step 1 by the AS*

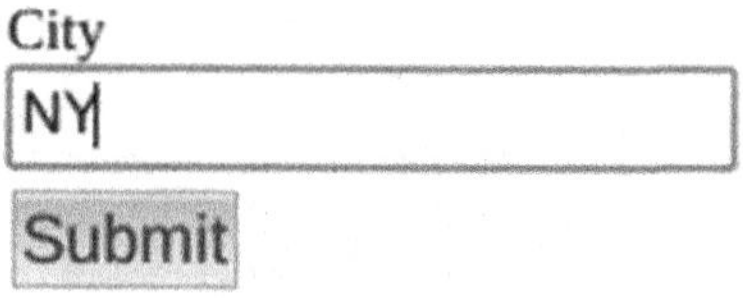

City

```
NY
```

Submit

Figure 8-21. *Claim gathering Step 2 by the AS*

The claims gathering script is similar to authentication, which also allows for a multi-step front-channel (browser) interaction. In claims gathering, instead of an `Authenticate` method, there is a method called `gather`.

Once claims gathering is done, if the policies now evaluate to true, a new ticket is generated, which the client can present to the RPT endpoint, or if using oxd, to call the `uma-rp-get-rpt` endpoint. Information gathered during claims gathering is stored and referenceable in the future when the client uses the PCT (see Figure 8-22).

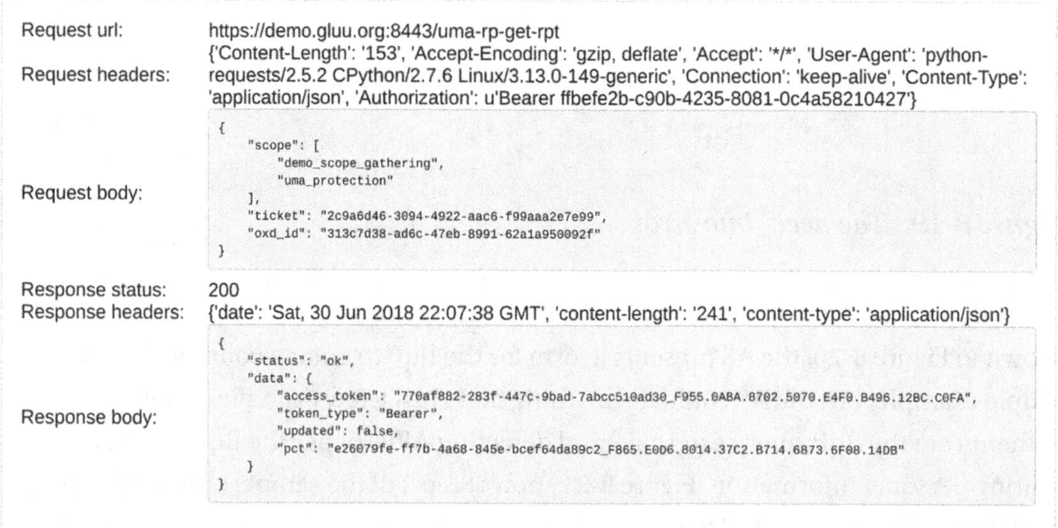

Request url:	https://demo.gluu.org:8443/uma-rp-get-rpt
Request headers:	{'Content-Length': '153', 'Accept-Encoding': 'gzip, deflate', 'Accept': '*/*', 'User-Agent': 'python-requests/2.5.2 CPython/2.7.6 Linux/3.13.0-149-generic', 'Connection': 'keep-alive', 'Content-Type': 'application/json', 'Authorization': u'Bearer ffbefe2b-c90b-4235-8081-0c4a58210427'}

Request body:	<pre>{
	    "scope": [
	        "demo_scope_gathering",
	        "uma_protection"
	    ],
	    "ticket": "2c9a6d46-3094-4922-aac6-f99aaa2e7e99",
	    "oxd_id": "313c7d38-ad6c-47eb-8991-62a1a950092f"
	}</pre>

Response status:	200
Response headers:	{'date': 'Sat, 30 Jun 2018 22:07:38 GMT', 'content-length': '241', 'content-type': 'application/json'}

Response body:	<pre>{
	    "status": "ok",
	    "data": {
	        "access_token": "770af882-283f-447c-9bad-7abcc510ad30_F955.0ABA.8702.5070.E4F0.B496.12BC.C0FA",
	        "token_type": "Bearer",
	        "updated": false,
	        "pct": "e26079fe-ff7b-4a68-845e-bcef64da89c2_F865.E0D6.8014.37C2.B714.6873.6F08.14DB"
	    }
	}</pre>

Figure 8-22. *Successful claims gathering response*

Conclusion

UMA is useful. Hopefully this chapter has given you a basic understanding.

UMA and OpenID don't overlap. In fact, UMA relies on the identity layer provided by OpenID, as well as its advanced client registration and authentication features. In some ways, UMA is backward OpenID Connect. A developer writing an OpenID client always calls the authorization endpoint first, and then if necessary calls the token endpoint. With UMA, the token endpoint is called first, and then if necessary, the RqP is redirected to the authorization endpoint.

UMA is very different kind of standard than OpenID. By 2011, many large consumer identity providers were using OAuth for authentication and to enable people to authorize access to their personal information. OpenID aligned the various implementations so developers didn't have to learn ten different ways to do the same thing. UMA is a "build it and they will come" standard. There is always the risk that such standards are a field of dreams that never become a reality, especially if something else comes along that solves the same problem and gains more adoption. Luckily, this hasn't happened. Authorization is very much an unsolved problem today, and UMA presents our best chance at an interoperable solution, which resulted from a truly consensus based standards organization. The ball is in our court now to drive adoption!

CHAPTER 9

Identity Management

Although this book is primarily about IAM, not IDM or IAG, it would have been a missed opportunity not to provide a short overview of some of the free open source software tools for IDM: Evolveum MidPoint, Apache Syncope, Wren:IDM, and Gluu Casa.

MidPoint, Syncope, and Wren:IDM offer traditional enterprise IDM features like approvals, workflows, synchronization connectors, and self-service password management. Casa extends the traditional capabilities of self-service password management, enabling people to manage their strong authentication credentials (two-factor). It also supports optional plugins for non-authentication self-service features, like enabling a person to revoke prior authorizations or manage client credentials.

To implement a quality enterprise identity infrastructure, the importance of IDM cannot be ignored. The cliché "garbage in, garbage out" is particularly relevant. If the underlying data used by the IAM platform is wrong, bad things will happen. The IAM platform is just one consumer of identity data from an IDM system. Many systems require up-to-date identity data. Failure to implement quality identity management processes will result in security problems and lost productivity.

As an organization grows, it becomes critical to exert control over the flow of identity information between systems. On the path from startup to enterprise, organizations organically assemble processes to keep identity information in systems up-to-date. In the beginning, there may be one person who is responsible for adding and removing accounts in various systems. They may write some scripts to make their job easier. But eventually, home-grown processes become hard to maintain, unreliable, and too manual. They don't offer the operational leverage needed for efficiency, accuracy, and legal compliance. Enter IDM and IAG software.

© Michael Schwartz, Maciej Machulak 2018
M. Schwartz and M. Machulak, *Securing the Perimeter*, https://doi.org/10.1007/978-1-4842-2601-8_9

IDM and IAG are not exclusively technical challenges. Deploying software is only part of the solution—there are business challenges that need to be resolved too. It is not uncommon for IDM and IAG projects to require a significant investment of time by everyone in the organization. There is no quick fix, and all levels of management should be involved in crafting the IDM strategy. End user behavior may need to change—thus IDM is cultural too.

Implementing IDM and IAG systems can require a fair amount of configuration and customization. The tools are powerful, and the learning curve can be steep. You don't have to implement a comprehensive solution on the first try. It may be best to keep the scope tight and roll out additional functionality as you go.

This overview of MidPoint, Syncope, Wren:IDM, and Casa is just an appetizer to whet your appetite for more information. You should visit each respective website, dive into the documentation, and try out the software to get a more thorough understanding of the capabilities and business models behind the software.

MidPoint

MidPoint is a comprehensive open source IDM and IAG platform. The project is led by Evolveum, who offers professional support subscriptions to organizations using the software. MidPoint is a Java application that leverages the Spring framework for its internal structure. The source code is released under the Apache license. Evolveum engineers are the primary developers, leading a vibrant and growing community of individual and organizational contributors.

MidPoint includes the following features:

- Identity provisioning and synchronization
- Role management
- Organizational structure management
- Approval process management
- Auditing
- Access certification
- Policy rules
- Web interface
- Web services

Identity Provisioning and Synchronization

At its core, MidPoint has a powerful connector-based IDM engine. A connector is a simple piece of code that moves identity data (e.g., an account) from a source system to a target system. MidPoint connectors are based on the Connectors for Identity Management (ConnId) framework that is used by many open source and commercial IDM software products. This is handy because connectors are interoperable across any ConnId-based IDM system, including MidPoint.

Connectors are relatively simple blocks of code that implement a standard interface. There is almost no IDM logic in the connector. The synchronization business logic is located inside MidPoint, reducing bloat in the connectors themselves. The same logic is reused for all connectors.

MidPoint saves the account-to-person link information in its database and continuously keeps data synchronized. Once a data mapping is configured, it is reused for provisioning, synchronization, data import tasks, and other IDM functions. This unifies IDM policy and simplifies maintenance.

MidPoint can also map data to populate account attributes. A mapping can pass values unchanged or can transform values with a script (Groovy, JavaScript, or Python). Conditional mapping provides flexibility for propagating data based on context, such as a role or association with an organizational unit. Administrators can also define manual processes to supplement data with information provided by business people.

Synchronization can be configured to work in "both directions". For example, MidPoint can push information about a person from a Human Resources system to an LDAP server. The LDAP server itself may be authoritative for other information, like the person's password. MidPoint can aggregate the data and synchronize it to all required systems.

MidPoint can synchronize data about any object type that is accessible by a connector, not just user attributes. For example, MidPoint can read data from a relational database table and create an LDAP subtree or a nested group, use the location of an entry in the LDAP tree to provision data in a relational database table, or automatically create an LDAP role entry based on group.

Connectors can also be configured to send notifications to alert people that their account was provisioned. They can also perform system administration tasks, such as the creation of home directories, mailboxes, or password policies. The possibilities are almost limitless.

Role Management

Roles are used by most IDM platforms and are central to how MidPoint organizes privileges. Role Based Access Control (RBAC) is a strategy used by many organizations to authorize access to resources. However, RBAC has a dark side: if roles are used to reference each unique access requirement, the number of roles can grow exponentially. In fact, some organizations have more roles than people! This is known as "role explosion". MidPoint uses several strategies to reduce the impact of role explosion, such as enabling dynamic expressions inside roles to make roles conditional, so one role is included in another role only if a specific condition is satisfied.

MidPoint roles may be based on specific user data, or a parameter of the role itself. For example, roles such as Sales Assistant, Engineering Assistant, and Logistics Assistant can be simplified with one generic Assistant role, where the organizational unit (sales, engineering, or logistics) is just a parameter to that role.

In MidPoint, role evaluation can be applied to the roles themselves, enabling the creation of meta-roles. For example, it is common for roles to be divided into several types, such as application roles, business roles, or technical roles. Roles may share common characteristics such as an approval process or lifecycle policy. Instead of duplicating common attributes, business roles may be assigned a meta-role to define common characteristics across all business roles.

Organizational Structure

Traditional IDM is primarily concerned with synchronizing changed information about people, but many important changes aren't about the person, rather their place in the organization. Organizational structure such as regions, divisions, departments, work groups, projects, sub-projects, ad hoc teams, faculties, classes, realms, tenants, and domains all affect which systems a person should be able to access. Many parallel organizational structures can be modeled in MidPoint. For example, there may be one big tree that represents a functional organizational structure, and a semi-flat structure of projects, ad hoc groups, and so on. A person may belong to any number of organizational units in any organizational structure. Mathematically speaking: if your structure can be expressed as an acyclic oriented graph, it can be modeled in MidPoint.

Membership in an organizational structure may include privileges to access certain resources. Therefore, organizational units can be used to control access in the same way as roles. However, the leaders of a business unit may have different access than ordinary members. In MidPoint, the organizational unit manager is a specific relation a user can have to the organizational unit and is decoupled from organizational unit membership itself. This enables a person to be a manager of an organizational unit of which they are not a member.

Organizational structure can be synchronized in the same way as a person's accounts. MidPoint mappings can be used to transform organizational structure and maintain it in the form of LDAP groups, organizational units (OUs), entitlements, roles, or almost any form.

Approval Processes

MidPoint can assign roles and organizational units automatically, for example, based on job codes. This is an efficient and scalable approach, but is typically only feasible for a small subset of roles. Administrators can manually assign other roles and organizational units, but this is not scalable. Therefore, most IDM deployments use a process-based approach where the person requests required roles. The request is then routed through an approval process where individual approvers can make decisions about the request.

Frequently, the first stage of the approval process is performed by a person's manager. Further stages may require approval from a business owner, security officer, resource owner, or project manager. In most IDM platforms, the approval process is driven by an internal workflow engine, which is customized using a workflow language such as Business Process Model and Notation (BPMN). This is a very flexible approach, however, approval workflows tend to get extremely complicated and can become difficult to maintain.

Rather than complex custom workflows, MidPoint supports "policy-based" approval processes driven by declarative approval policies. The approval process for each role request is dynamically computed based on associated policies. An approval policy can be defined globally, individually for each role, or for a group of roles (using the meta-role mechanism). A policy may specify approval stages that are mandatory, optional or conditional. Each stage may have different approvers or approver groups. MidPoint also supports approval escalation, delegation, and auditing. Policy-based approval means no programming is needed to set up an approval process, enabling very complex policies to be defined and maintained efficiently.

Even though MidPoint offers strategies to reduce role explosion, there may still be tens or hundreds of roles in the system. To simplify the process of assigning roles, MidPoint offers a role catalog and shopping-cart style request process for people to browse categories, select the appropriate roles, and request approval.

Midpoint Delegated Application Security Model

MidPoint's internal authorization mechanism controls access to MidPoint objects such as users, roles, organizational units and resources. Fine-grain authorization policies can be specified down to the level of individual object properties. The authorization mechanism is aware of the organizational structure, enabling delegation of identity administration within an organizational unit to its respective managers, and the delegation of roles to its owner. The same mechanisms used to access target systems can be used to obtain access to MidPoint itself. Therefore, access to data in MidPoint can be requested, approved, and audited.

MidPoint also enables a person to specify a "deputy" who can temporarily obtain their authorizations and privileges. This can be useful when a person is traveling or on leave. The deputy can access the work items (approval decisions) of the delegating user. The deputy also gains access to entitlements in target systems, for example temporary assignment to the same LDAP groups. Privileges are automatically revoked when the operational time has concluded. Deputy functionality is meant to provide continuity of business processes both inside MidPoint and in target systems.

Auditing

MidPoint can maintain an audit trail for changes to data about people, roles, organizational structure, and configuration. A complete description of changes and any useful metadata is available for any MidPoint object. A feature called "time machine" enables the restoration of any past state. Audit trails are recorded in a database table and can be used to integrate MidPoint with security information and event management (SIEM) or data warehouse systems.

Access Certification

Role request and approval processes tend to result in a person accumulating many roles over time. However, because removal of roles no-longer-needed is often overlooked, it's important for organizations to regularly perform access certification campaigns (i.e., "recertification" or "attestation"). For example, once per year, managers may need to decide if the roles assigned to subordinate employees are still needed. The MidPoint web interface enables managers to efficiently make these decisions. Once certification decisions have been submitted, any superfluous roles are automatically marked for removal and unassigned.

Removal of a non-sensitive role is not an urgent matter. However, certain situations might require faster action, for example if an employee is moved to a different organizational unit with a different manager. The new manager assumes responsibility for the employee's roles and should execute an ad hoc recertification process for that specific user.

Policy Rules

Businesses must abide by certain rules and regulations. Executives are tasked with determining which rules are appropriate. Information technology professionals are responsible for implementing those rules in systems. An example is segregation of duties (SoD). For instance, it may be inadvisable for a person to both write and sign checks. Another example—at an investment banking firm, you can't advise companies about mergers and acquisitions and trade securities.

Midpoint policies express rules governing organizational structures and roles, such as "a project must have at most one manager" or "a role must have at least one owner". Policy rules can express policy-based approvals, which may also govern role lifecycles. The totality of policies determines the governance of the organization.

A single policy rule has two parts: a constraint and an action. A constraint defines a situation or event where the rule applies, such as "A is assigned to a user" or "A is assigned together with B". If the constraint is triggered, then an action takes place. Actions may be as simple as "prohibit such an operation". But actions can also be complex, for example, removing all conflicting assignments or driving a request through an approval process or re-certification.

Policy rules can be combined to form more complex business logic, such as "prohibit assignment of A and B at the same time". MidPoint enables administrators to combine policy rules with meta-roles and approval processes. An example might be: "if any two roles from this set of roles are assigned to the same person, then drive the request through an approval by a security officer". Such combinations are used to implement advanced features like ad hoc recertification and role lifecycle management.

User Interface (UI)

The MidPoint UI can be used for:

- End user self-service management of identity data, for example allowing people to edit their user profiles, change their passwords, or request new roles.

- Identity administration, such as managing user data, roles, organizational structure, approvals, and access certifications.

- Configuration of the MidPoint system.

The MidPoint UI is designed to automatically adapt to custom inputs. For example, an LDAP server may have a custom LDAP attribute called "foo". When MidPoint connects to that LDAP server for the first time, it retrieves its schema, including the custom "foo" attribute. The resource schema is stored in MidPoint and automatically used for all data processing. It is also immediately reflected in the web user interface, automatically rendering an input field for that attribute. No programming or customization is needed to use this functionality. The web interface also automatically adapts to authorizations. Only those pages to which the user has access are displayed, and all inaccessible forms and input fields are hidden or displayed as read-only.

Of course, some customization may be required. MidPoint offers configuration options to specify how certain parts of the web interface behave, for example, to hide widgets or unused features.

Services and Integration

Most MidPoint functionality is available via the following three public interfaces:

- RESTful interface, which is an HTTP-based interface that exposes MidPoint functionality by following applicable RESTful principles. Data is presented in XML, JSON, or YAML data formats.

- SOAP interface specified using WSDL and XSD standards.

- Java interface, which is a natural choice for Java extension code, e.g., when using overlay projects and extensions based on source code modifications.

All three interfaces offer roughly equivalent functionality. The Java libraries are used by the MidPoint UI, therefore, those interfaces can be used to build a custom UI or to integrate MidPoint with other systems for management, advanced tooling, or various other purposes.

Other MidPoint Features

MidPoint offers additional features not included in this overview, including flexible reporting capabilities, self-registration and self-service password reset procedures, self-healing capabilities, and virtual identities (or "personas"). In addition, the IDM system is an ideal place to track and protect identity data, and development is ongoing to add features to enable better protection of data—a key requirement for compliance with the European Union General Data Protection Regulation (GDPR).

Get Started with MidPoint

Visit the Evolveum MidPoint wiki to learn how to get started: https://wiki.evolveum.com/display/midPoint/Introduction.

Apache Syncope

The Apache Software Foundation is the world's largest open source foundation. The Syncope project team is comprised of members and contributors. Members have direct access to the source of the project and actively evolve the code-base. Contributors improve the project through submission of patches and suggestions to the members. Syncope features include:

- Provisioning:

  - Synchronization of users, groups, or other objects (e.g., printers, services, or sensors). Definition of realms—primarily meant for containing users, groups, or other objects. Identity lifecycle management.

  - Full reconciliation and live synchronization from external resources. Workflow based approval.

- Identity Governance and Administration, including:

  - Reports

  - Auditing

- Administrative web application for full system management, delegated administration, self-service registration, and profile management.

- Command Line Interface (CLI) for easy integration with system tools.

- JAX-RS 2.0-compliant, full-fledged RESTful interface to access all services.

Syncope Architecture

Syncope is a Java application that requires the following:

- The latest JDK 8 available

- A Java EE Container, such as Tomcat, Payara Server, or Wildfly

- A relational DBMS, such as PostgreSQL, MySQL, MariaDB, Oracle DB, or MS SQL Server

A bird's-eye view of the architecture is shown in Figure 9-1.

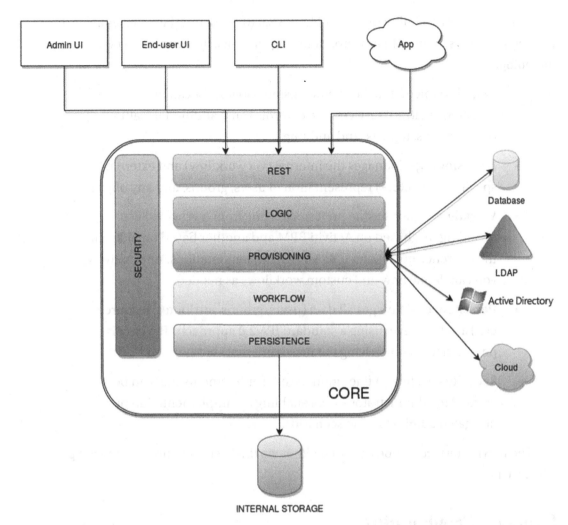

Figure 9-1. *Apache Syncope architecture*

Admin UI is the web-based console for configuring and administering active deployments, with full support for delegated administration.

End User UI is the web-based application for self-registration, self-service, and password reset.

CLI is the command-line application for interacting with Apache Syncope from scripts, particularly useful for system administrators.

Core is the central component, providing all services offered by Apache Syncope.

Syncope exposes a fully-compliant JAX-RS 2.0 RESTful interface that enables third-party applications, written in any programming language, to consume IDM services, including:

- **Logic**—Implements the overall business logic that can be triggered via REST services and controls some additional features (notifications, reports, and auditing).

- **Provisioning**—Manages the internal (via workflow) and external (via specific connectors) representation of users, groups, and any objects.

- **Workflow**—Chooses the preferred engine from a provided list, including one based on Activiti BPM and another based on Flowable, the reference open source BPMN 2.0 implementations. Alternatively, you can define new and custom workflows as needed.

- **Persistence**—Manages all data (users, groups, attributes, resources, etc.) at a high level using a standard JPA 2.0 approach. The data is persisted to an underlying database (internal storage).

- **Security**—Defines a fine-grained set of entitlements that can be granted to administrators, thus enabling the implementation of delegated administration scenarios.

The REST interface can be accessed either via the Java client library or using plain HTTPS calls.

Syncope Provisioning

Like MidPoint, the Provisioning layer for Syncope relies on ConnId. ConnId is the continuation of The Identity Connectors Framework (Sun ICF) project, which used to be part of the Sun Microsystem IDM product and has since been released as an open source project. This makes the connectors layer particularly reliable because most connectors have already been implemented in the framework and widely tested.

The ConnId project features contributors from several companies and meets the requirements for a modern, active open source project, including an Apache Maven driven build, artifacts, and mailing lists (see Figure 9-2). Additional connectors, such as for SOAP, CSV, PowerShell, and Active Directory, are also provided.

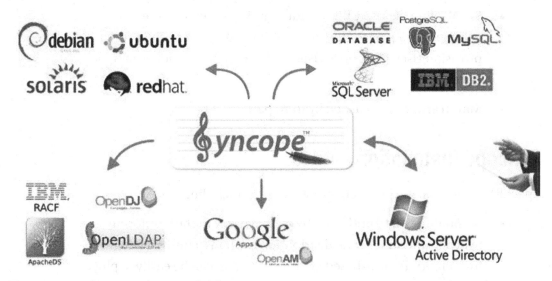

Figure 9-2. *Syncope interactivities*

Syncope Extensions

You can enhance Syncope with useful features via extensions. An extension might add a REST endpoint, manage the persistence of additional entities, extend security mechanisms, tweak the provisioning layer, add features to the user interface, or even add all such features together. Extensions are available from different sources, including: Maven artifacts published from the Apache Syncope code-base, part of the official releases, such as:

- **Swagger UI**—Enables Swagger UI as a web interface to work with Syncope RESTful services.

- **SSO Support**—Provides both OpenID Connect and SAML 2.0 access to the administrative or end user web interfaces.

- **Apache Camel Provisioning Manager**—Delegates the provisioning process execution to a set of Apache Camel routes, which can be dynamically changed at runtime via the REST interfaces or the administrative console. Modifications are immediately available for processing.

- Elasticsearch—Provides an alternate internal search engine for users, groups, and objects, requiring an external Elasticsearch cluster.

- **SCIM**—Provides new REST endpoints implementing the communication according to the SCIM 2.0 standard, in order to provision User, Enterprise User, and Group SCIM entities to Apache Syncope.

- Maven artifacts published by third parties.

Syncope Installation

Apache Syncope can be deployed in several ways, including:

- **Standalone distribution**—The simplest way to start exploring Syncope, the standalone distribution contains a fully working, in-memory Tomcat-based environment that can be easily deployed on a laptop, workstation, or server.

- **Debian packages**—Available for use with Debian GNU/Linux, Ubuntu, and their derivatives.

- **Installer**—A GUI application for configuring and deploying on supported DBMSes and Java EE containers.

- **Maven project**—The preferred method for working with Apache Syncope, the Maven Project provides access to the full set of customization and extension capabilities.

Visit the Apache Syncope documentation to learn how to get a local instance up and running: `http://syncope.apache.org/docs/getting-started.html`.

Wren:IDM

Wren:IDM is a community-developed identity management system with a flexible data model, multiple extension points, and scripting support, including JavaScript and Groovy. It can connect to and manage a wide range of systems through the Identity Connector Framework (Wren:ICF).

Wren:IDM is one of the projects in the Wren Security Suite, a community initiative that adopted open source projects formerly developed by ForgeRock, which has its own roots in Sun Microsystems' products.

The project is also an example of open source philosophy benefits in practice. In 2017, when it became apparent that ForgeRock reduced their open source commitment, the "it's time for a fork" initiative arose. It collected developers and engineers willing to sustain and evolve the latest open source code available before it was closed. ForgeRock no longer releases any of the most recent versions of their software under an open source license and the current ForgeRock's Community Editions are several major versions behind what was previously offered under the CDDL license. But luckily, once code is open sourced, its copies can't be "un-open sourced". The community, which broke away from the closed-source model, was later named Wren Security: `https://wrensecurity.org/`.

The Wren Security Suite projects include:

- Access management in Wren:AM (formerly OpenAM)

- Directory server in Wren:DS (formerly OpenDJ)

- Identity management in Wren:IDM (formerly OpenIDM)

- Identity Connector Framework Wren:ICF (formerly OpenICF and ICF), a special part of the IDM solution, which also provides a set of production-ready connectors—LDAP, Office 365, SPML, SSH, SQL, PowerShell, REST, and many more

Wren:IDM itself is focused on identity management processes and also provides a powerful framework for implementing IAG and a portion of IAM processes. Although the project is based on OpenIDM code, it is not affiliated with ForgeRock in any way. It is based on the very latest code available under a CDDL license (not-yet-released OpenIDM 5.x).

The features of Wren:IDM include:

- **A complete platform**—Used for building IDM and IG solutions using the concepts described next, including roles, mappings, synchronizations, workflows, policies, etc.

- **ICF connector servers**—Services that allow connectors to be run outside of the IDM itself. Useful when a connector needs a specific client environment to talk to the integrated system. Also facilitates security. .NET and Java Connector Servers are available.

- **Administration GUI**—An interface for making changes to data models and configuration using a point-and-click interface rather than Wren:IDM's REST interface.

- **Self-service GUI**—An interface for end users to update their profile information, passwords, and preferences.

Both the Administration GUI and Self-Service GUI are web-based, single-page applications that can be turned off in deployments that do not desire to use them.

Wren:IDM Quick Start

To begin using Wren:IDM, do the following:

1. Visit `https://wrenscurity.org` to get the Wren:IDM package, either by downloading a binary package or building from the latest sources.

2. Make sure you have Java 8+ installed. Both OpenJDK and Oracle JDK work well. Extract the package to a folder and navigate there using your terminal.

3. Run the startup script `startup.sh` (UNIX/Linux) or `startup.bat` (MS Windows).

4. Open `http://localhost:8080/admin` in your web browser, log in with the default credentials `openidm-admin:openidm-admin`, and explore the administration interface (see Figure 9-3).

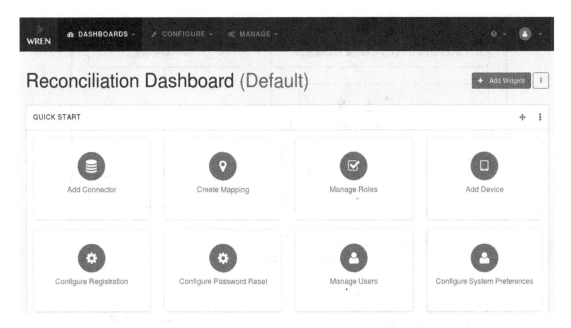

Figure 9-3. *Wren:IDM basic administration dashboard*

System Overview

Wren:IDM provides a JSON-based object model, where objects are treated uniformly using APIs. These objects include:

- **Managed objects**—Maintained in IDM's repository

- **System objects**—Represent external resources such as accounts

- **Configuration objects**—Represent various aspects of IDM configuration

- **Workflow objects**—Represent approval process or other business processes

Working with these objects is pretty straightforward. For example, when you patch a managed object like a user, it is updated in the repository and configured actions take place. When you patch a system object like an account, it is updated in the integrated system. Audit trails will appear in the system in both cases. The main system components are shown in Figure 9-4.

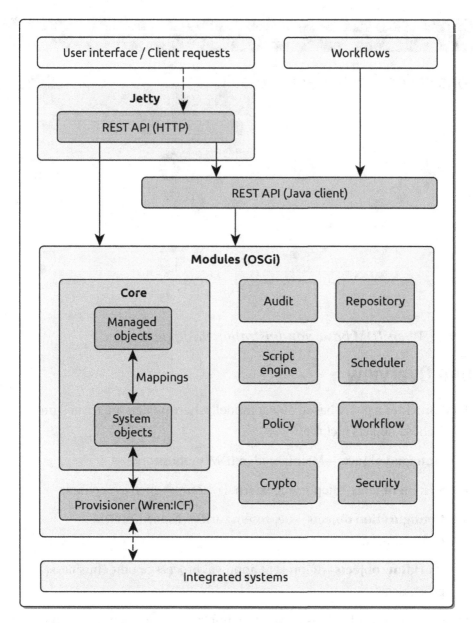

Figure 9-4. *Wren:IDM component overview*

Wren:IDM takes a novel approach by providing access to all components through a unified Resource API. The API is the same—whether objects are being accessed through REST API calls or internally from scripts and other parts of the IDM system itself. For example, consider the following JavaScript Resource API called from within IDM:

```
var users = openidm.query("managed/user", { "_queryFilter" : '/givenName eq
"Peggy"' });
```

And the equivalent query called via the REST API accessed from the outside:

```
$ curl -u openidm-admin:openidm-admin \
'http://localhost:8080/openidm/managed/user_queryFilter=givenName+eq+"Peggy"'
```

Wren:IDM Implementation Basics

JSON-based object model applies to the configuration as well. This is why you'll see so much JSON while examining Wren:IDM. IDM can be managed using an admin GUI, but the admin actions still result in REST API calls. And the configuration ends up in human-readable, structured files.

This way the IDM unites the worlds of GUI-based management, API-based programmatic administration, and config-file-based administration. Organizations may find it useful to abandon the GUI-based (i.e., IDM repository-based) configuration in favor of using file-based configuration management. While the former provides IDM-level auditing, the latter allows leveraging standard SCM tools like git, which may better fit into modern devops environments. You can also combine these approaches.

The components are familiar from most IDM platforms:

- **Audit**—Component for auditing of all triggered events and states

- **Repository**—Persistence layer for storing all managed objects

- **Script engine**—Component for scripts execution (JavaScript or Groovy)

- **Scheduler**—Component for executing scheduled jobs

- **Policy**—Component for executing validations during object modifications

- **Workflow**—Embedded workflow engine based on Activiti

- **Crypto**—Component for data encryption

- *Security*—Component for handling REST API security

- **Managed objects**—IDM managed objects like users, roles, or any objects the organization uses

- **System objects**—Integrated system objects

- **Provisioner**—Abstract layer for integrating external systems

- **Custom endpoints**—REST API endpoints defined by the implementers to provide their own business logic

Wren:IDM takes a path of extension over modification. Every aspect of the system—from the data model to the framework configuration—is configurable. Implementers can use the Wren:IDM framework and its components in whichever way best meets their needs. The domain data model and its database representation are also solely in implementers' hands. Your custom entities don't have to end up in tables like custom_object, custom_attribute, and custom_attr_value, known from common customizable systems. The DB structure can follow your conventions, allowing the data to be better examined by administrators and even transferred to another system in the event of migration.

Using explicit mappings, a custom database schema can be accessed through the IDM's unified API, as shown in Listing 9-1. In addition to giving you a standard interface for access to your data, the configured business rules—like auditing and access control—are also enforced. For example, an update to a custom managed object is done in the very same way like any other update, as shown in Listing 9-1.

Listing 9-1. Wren:IDM Sample Update to a Custom Object

```
$ curl \
 -u openidm-admin:openidm-admin \
 --header "Content-Type: application/json" \
 --request PATCH \
 --data '[{"operation" : "replace", "field" : "ownerWorkforceId",
"value" : "90' \
'http://localhost:8080/openidm/managed/costcenter/42'
```

This translates to the following SQL DML command (according to your schema):

```
UPDATE openidm.managedou SET ownerworkforceid = '90', rev = '4' WHERE
objectid = '42';
```

This then ends up in the audit like any other operation, as shown in Listing 9-2.

Listing 9-2. Wren:IDM Sample Audit Record

```
objectid           | 40f007eb-4479-476e-9989-6aa48098bec3-94
activitydate       | 2018-07-15T08:43:19.507Z
transactionid      | 40f007eb-4479-476e-9989-6aa48098bec3-85
activityobjectid   | managed/costcenter/42
operation          | PATCH
subjectbefore      | {"_id":"42","_rev":"3","ownerWorkforceId":"10","name":
                     "Global Marketing","remarks":"Example by Orchitech"}
subjectafter       | {"_id":"42","_rev":"4","ownerWorkforceId":"90","name":
                     "Global Marketing","remarks":"Example by Orchitech"}
subjectrev         | 4
status             | SUCCESS
```

Wren:IDM Pre-Defined Types

There are a number of pre-defined types in Wren:IDM.

Managed User

This is a pre-defined managed object type representing a user identity and its attributes.

Managed Group

This is a pre-defined managed object type representing a low-level access right in a target system, e.g., an LDAP group. It is optional—organizations that do not use groups may use roles instead.

Roles

These can be either authorization roles, which grant rights within the IDM itself, or provisioning roles, which define how objects are provisioned in target systems. Roles are managed objects, which means they can be extended to contain additional information or invoke scripts, just like any other IDM object.

Role Grants

These relate users and roles. They can be either manual or conditional. For example, they can be triggered automatically based on a matching query. As with any managed object, role grants can carry any number of additional properties—such as temporal constraints (e.g., "users have this role for 90 days").

Effective Roles

These indicate which roles a user ends up with after applying additional logic. By default, the effective role of a user matches his role grants. In more complex deployments, effective roles can also be calculated using a custom script that may alter the result: filtering out some role grants, or adding additional role grants. Such a script might even calculate the resultant roles on-the-fly, without considering any role grants at all.

Role Assignments (aka Assignments)

These set rules for how roles are provisioned in a particular system. For example, they might indicate that a user with the role of "Broker" gets an account created in the CRM system. There can be several assignments defined for a role.

Effective Assignments

These indicate which assignments a user ends up with after applying additional logic, similar in concept to effective roles. By default, a user's effective assignments are the same as the assignments attached to the user's roles. As with effective roles, a script may calculate effective assignments, enabling you to more finely control role assignment.

Relationships

These are managed object attributes used to connect one managed object to another. You can defined them to synchronize data unidirectionally or bidirectionally, one-to-one, one-to-many, or many-to-many. For example, consider an organizational chart in which one person reports to another. Such a relationship is frequently represented as a bidirectional relationship in IDM between two users—the "manager" and his "direct reports". Another example are the roles mentioned previously—each of a user's roles is represented as a predefined "roles" relationship in each user. As is the case for all other IDM objects and attributes, relationships can be retrieved through the API or shown in administration GUI, as shown in Figure 9-5.

Data Types:

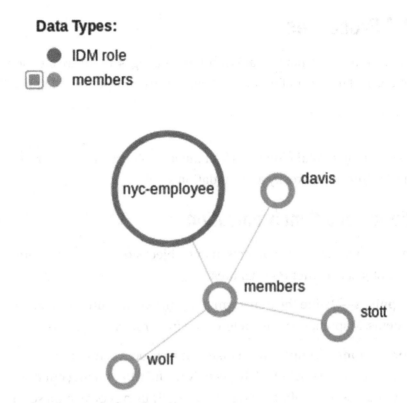

Figure 9-5. *Relationship visualization*

Triggers

These are extension points that allow invoking some logic on a managed object before an operation happens. For example, effective roles are calculated by invoking an onRetrieve script defined on the effectiveRoles attribute of user records. Such logic can be written in either JavaScript or Groovy—depending on whichever best suits the needs of the implementer for the use case.

There is nothing inherently special about the pre-defined types mentioned in this section. In a new installation, these types have some behavior that controls how provisioning is done, but this behavior is defined in the same way that you define behavior for any custom type. Provisioning is simply modeled through managed object definitions, relationships, and triggers. All of this logic is configurable and modifiable by the implementer, giving full control over the logic the system ends up using to manage identities.

Wren:IDM Processes

Beyond the data and entitlements that Wren:IDM manages, there are also several processes Wren:IDM uses to maintain the data. These concepts include the following.

Policies

These processes enforce validation rules for managed objects. They can be enforced automatically and/or used directly as a validation service.

Reconciliation and Synchronization

These processes make the state of objects in one object store match the state of corresponding objects in other object stores.

- **Mappings**—Define the transformations between source and target systems. Mappings are also referenced from role assignments.

- **Correlations**—Define how to match objects between source and target if they are not linked. Especially useful when rolling out the IDM. Can be also defined programmatically using correlation scripts.

- **Synchronization situations**—Represent an evaluated result of source and target comparison, such as FOUND, MISSING, CONFIRMED, etc.

- **Synchronization actions**—Represent the configured reaction to a synchronization situation, such as UPDATE, UNLINK, IGNORE, ASYNC, etc.

- There are subtle but important differences between reconciliation and synchronization:

  - **With reconciliation—**A full synchronization of objects in source and target systems takes place.

  - **With synchronization (aka "LiveSync")—**Just a particular delta is synchronized, allowing it to be run frequently and changes to be quickly reflected.

Scheduling

This process controls when synchronization happens. Without a schedule, systems are only reconciled manually, on-demand.

Password Synchronization

This feature allows users to have the same password among multiple target systems, even when such systems might use different ways to hash or encrypt passwords. Wren:IDM supports plugins that can be installed in target systems to intercept password changes that occur outside of IDM, so that these changes can be propagated to all of the systems that the user needs access to.

Workflows

This process is the key to integrating identity management into business activities, including approvals, escalations, recertifications, and many others. Wren:IDM uses the Activiti BPMN 2 Engine for modeling and executing workflows. Workflows are exposed through the standard IDM resource API. Implementers can use standard Activiti tools— including the Activiti Designer—to define and edit workflows.

Example: Make Your Own Self-Service GUI

You can use the Wren:IDM default user-facing self-service website. However, there might be situations when a custom solution is preferable, either for self-service or for administrative tasks performed by, for example, the help desk staff. The simplicity of implementing such a solution is one of the strengths of the platform. The following steps provide an overview of how to create a custom self-service website.

Step 1: Endpoint configuration (`endpoint-accounts.json`) (see Listing 9-3).

Listing 9-3. Creating an Endpoint Configuration in Wren:IDM Sample

```
{
    "context" : "endpoint/accounts/nyc",
    "type" : "text/javascript",
    "file" : "handle-accounts.js"
}
```

Step 2: Endpoint implementation (`handle-accounts.js`) (see Listing 9-4).

Listing 9-4. Sample Endpoint Implementation

```
/* global openidm */
// Return all AD accounts from 'Pennyworth - New York City' department
return openidm.query('system/ad/account', {
        _queryFilter: '/department eq "us_nyc"'
    });
```

Step 3: Endpoint security (`access.js`) (see Listing 9-5).

Listing 9-5. Wren:IDM Sample Endpoint Security

```
{
    "pattern"    : "endpoint/accounts/nyc",
    "roles"      : "company-admin",
    "methods"    : "query",
    "actions"    : "*"
}
```

Step 4: GUI interface (`index.html`) (see Listing 9-6).

Listing 9-6. Customizing the Wren:IDM User Interface

```
<!DOCTYPE html>
<html>
    <head>
        <meta charset="UTF-8">
        <script src="https://code.jquery.com/jquery-3.3.1.min.js"></script>
        <script type="text/javascript">
            $(document).ready(function() {
                $.ajax({
                    type: 'GET',
                    url: 'http://localhost:8080/openidm/endpoint/accounts/
                    nyc',
                    // You'd use JWT in the real life
                    headers: {
                        'X-OpenIDM-Username': 'company-admin',
```

```
                'X-OpenIDM-Password': 'company-admin'
            },
            data: {
                '_queryId': 'dummy'
            },
            success: function(data) {
                data.result.forEach(function(account) {
                    $("#accounts").append('<li>' + account.
                    sAMAccountName + '</li>');
                });
            }
        });
    });
</script>
</head>
<body>
    <ul id="accounts"></ul>
</body>
</html>
```

Example: Consent Governance

Role and assignment resolution mechanisms also provide a way for various IAG rules to be enforced in real time.

For example, let's imagine a company "H.Q. Pennyworth & Co," which has brokers who work with clients. Imagine that the firm has a business rule that requires brokers to make contact information readily available to those clients. To enforce this rule while complying with local regulations, a Pennyworth broker must consent to sharing his personal contact information. If a broker has not yet consented, you want to restrict either his roles or resource grants. In such a case, having the broker role is a necessary—but not sufficient—requirement for having broker access.

As suggested, the restriction can be made on two different levels and the difference is conceptual (see Figure 9-6):

- **Restriction at the role resolution level**—An employee without consent won't effectively get the broker role even if it is assigned to them.

- **Restriction at the assignment resolution level**—An employee without consent can effectively get the broker role, but they still won't be eligible to get the assigned resources.

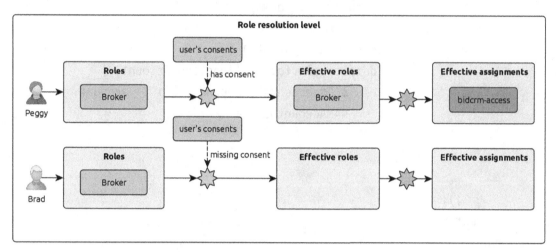

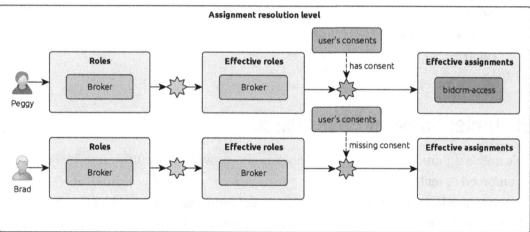

Figure 9-6. Enforcing the consent condition in H.Q. Pennyworth & Co: effective roles or effective assignments

Example: Connector Configuration with Object Mapping Transformations

Let's say we want to set up the mapping suggested in Figure 9-7.

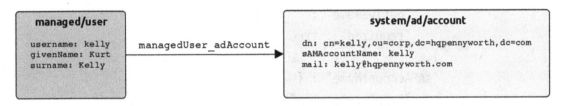

Figure 9-7. *Sample connector and mapping scenario*

The connector configuration might be as shown in Listing 9-7.

Listing 9-7. Wren:IDM Sample Connector Configuration Sample

```
{
    "name" : "ad",
    "connectorRef" : {
        "bundleName" : "org.forgerock.openicf.connectors.ldap-connector",
        "bundleVersion" : "[1.4.0.0,2.0.0.0)",
        "connectorName" : "org.identityconnectors.ldap.LdapConnector"
    },
    "configurationProperties" : {
        "host" : "localhost",
        "ssl" : true,
        "principal" : "cn=root",
        "credentials" : "password",
        "baseContexts" : [ "ou=corp,dc=hqpennyworth,dc=com" ],
        "baseContextsToSynchronize" : [ "ou=corp,dc=hqpennyworth,dc=com" ],
        "objectClassesToSynchronize" : [ "user" ]
    },
    "objectTypes" : {
        "account" : {
            "$schema" : "http://json-schema.org/draft-03/schema",
            "id" : "__ACCOUNT__",
            "type" : "object",
            "nativeType" : "__ACCOUNT__",
            "properties" : {
                "dn" : {
                    "type" : "string",
```

```
                    "nativeName" : "__NAME__",
                    "required" : true
                },
                "sAMAccountName" : {
                    "type" : "string"
                },
                "mail" : {
                    "type" : "string"
                }
            }
        }
    }
}
```

The mapping configuration shown in Listing 9-8 also shows how mapping transformations are applied.

Listing 9-8. Wren:IDM mapping Configuration Sample

```
{
    "name" : "managedUser_adAccount",
    "source" : "managed/user",
    "target" : "system/ad/account",
    "enableSync" : true,
    "validSource" : {
        "type" : "text/javascript",
        "source" : "source.username != null"
    },
    "correlationScript" : {
        "type" : "text/javascript",
        "source" : "var query = {'_queryFilter': '/sAMAccountName eq \"' +
        source.username + '\"'};query;"
    },
    "onCreate" : {
        "type" : "text/javascript",
        "file" : "managedUser_adAccount_onCreate.js"
    },
```

```
"properties" : [
    {
        "source" : "username",
        "target" : "sAMAccountName"
    },
    {
        "source" : "",
        "transform" : {
            "type" : "text/javascript",
            "source" : "source.username + '@hqpennyworth.com'"
        },
        "target" : "mail"
    }
]
}
```

And the OnCreate script is another example of property transformation:

```
/* global source, target */
target.dn = 'cn=' + source.username + ',ou=corp,dc=hqpennyworth,dc=com';
```

When Is Wren:IDM Suitable?

In small to medium organizations that have only a single location —or multiple locations where identity information is owned by a single location—other IDM products that make a lot of assumptions about corporate structure may be faster to implement.

In medium to large organizations, where there are branch offices and/or organizational units that need to have autonomous control over their identity information, Wren:IDM is an excellent fit.

Effectively, Wren:IDM is so flexible that you could end up spending a lot of time on integration when something out-of-the-box fits your model. But if your organization isn't cookie-cutter, and you have some requirements that take you a little outside of the other solutions, then Wren:IDM is a better solution, even if it might take a bit more time to integrate, because it's built to handle the customization. The time spent integrating pays off in flexibility and maintainability of the implementation.

Rolling Out Wren:IDM to Production

Wren:IDM can run with any JDBC-connected database, but has been tested with PostgreSQL, MySQL, Oracle, and Microsoft SQL. In addition, for local development and testing purposes, it also ships with an embedded copy of OrientDB. In general, Wren:IDM shares dependencies common to any lightweight JEE application. It runs both on Oracle JDK and OpenJDK.

A single, commodity-hardware machine with 4GB of RAM would be sufficient to run the whole solution, including a PostgreSQL database server on a Linux operating system. The requirements grow with the number and frequency of scheduled tasks and complexity of the particular actions. The system can be also operated in a cluster. While high availability is usually not a requirement for IDMs, cluster-based deployment can help by distribute reconciliation tasks across several nodes. In addition, if direct access to target systems from the IDM is not possible or desirable (e.g., the target system is local, but IDM is running on Amazon EC2), connector servers can be used to provide an interface from the IDM to the target system.

The limiting factor in most deployments is the I/O throughput of the target system; specifically, how quickly such a system can query records and return them. If you're using existing connectors, take note of options that can reduce the amount of data that a connector will need to request from the remote system (e.g., limit base DNs, filter out objectclasses that are not of interest). If you're developing custom connectors for an IDM project, it is best to optimize the connector to query the target system for as few records as possible.

As far as an overall deployment, the best approach to address performance issues is:

1. Plan out your deployment ahead of time.

2. Integrate with each target system one at a time. Isolation can help to reveal bottlenecks.

3. Test the system as you go rather than testing everything at the end of implementation.

There are several approaches to deploying and testing Wren:IDM. A good implementer can leverage software engineering best practices such as using SCM, test-driven development, continuous integration, and continuous delivery. Wren:IDM works best in such a process.

Gluu Casa

MidPoint, Syncope, and Wren:IDM offer enterprise IDM and IAG tools, and even some handy user-facing self-service functionality. However, data related to a person's web authentication and authorization preferences is outside the scope of traditional IDM and IAG systems.

In addition to managing personal information, people need to:

- Enroll and manage two-factor authentication (2FA) credentials and preferences (e.g., phone numbers, U2F keys, OTP, etc.)

- View and revoke consent decisions (e.g., which applications have what access to personal data)

- Add and remove social login accounts (e.g., Facebook or GitHub)

- Request and manage OAuth client credentials

Gluu Casa (Casa) offers a user-facing, self-service dashboard for managing these newer self-service requirements. It's available under the free open source MIT License.

Architecture

Casa is a Java EE web application that runs inside the Gluu Server's chroot container, although it's distributed as a separate package. Casa interacts directly with Gluu's underlying LDAP server and file system, and uses the `oxd-java` library to leverage Gluu's OpenID Connect Provider (OP) and UMA Authorization Server (AS) functionalities. Casa is built using frameworks such as Weld, ZK, and RestEasy.

Casa's core functionality—self-service 2FA management—is enabled via a Gluu Server custom authentication script written in Jython. The script enables a person to specify their preferences for 2FA—whether to prompt for every authentication, to remember a certain location, or to remember the browser.

2FA Credential Management

2FA can significantly increase account security. However, security is only as strong as its weakest link. If you have a strong authentication mechanism, but you can use email to recover from a lost credential, your security is degraded. Control of email is an even weaker credential than a password! If a human operator can reset a strong credential, people are extremely susceptible to social engineering. Don't hack the crypto—hack the people! Account recovery is the Achilles heel of 2FA, as an authentication mechanism is only as strong as the weakest recovery process.

As there are no widely accepted Internet standards for account recovery and strong authentication, it can be helpful to review and mimic how industry giants like Google support these important security processes. With one billion user accounts, Google has lots of data to determine how to roll out secure and usable 2FA.

Google supports several types of authentication: SMS, OTP, FIDO tokens, and several others. With billions of accounts, strong security can't come at the expense of usability—that's why Google offers a self-service portal where people can enroll, delete, and manage their own strong credentials.

Gluu Casa provides an open source solution that organizations can use to offer a similar user-facing, self-service 2FA experience. In the Casa dashboard, people can enroll and manage their strong authentication credentials to secure their accounts.

Out-of-the-box, Casa supports the same credentials as Google: FIDO, OTP, SMS, and mobile push (using Super Gluu). This combination of 2FA options makes strong security available to anyone with a mobile phone. The self-service dashboard empowers people to enroll multiple strong credentials to thoroughly secure their account.

Net-net, the value of the transaction should drive security enforcement, and in the Casa administration web interface, system administrators can manage which 2FA mechanisms are enabled and supported by the system.

Consent Management

Federated identity enables people to leverage an existing account in an identity provider (IDP) to create and maintain a passwordless account in an external service provider application (SP). For example, when you "Sign in with Google" to an unaffiliated third-party website, Google may send along personal information about you that will be used to create a local profile for you (sans password). In these situations, before allowing you to proceed, the IDP will prompt you to "consent" to the release of personal information (in OAuth jargon, this is the authorization). In addition, Google may prompt you to authorize the third-party website to perform actions on your behalf, for example to access your contacts or update your calendar.

As the user's window into the authentication system, Casa provides a UI for reviewing and revoking previously made consent decisions. For example, if you sign in to Dropbox using your Gluu IDP account, then decide you no longer want Dropbox to be able to control your calendar, you can revoke your consent decision in Casa. The third-party website could (and likely would) retain a copy of any personal data previously shared, but would no longer have authorization to perform actions on your behalf—it would need to re-prompt you for consent if you attempt to access the service again using your external IDP account.

Social Login Account Management

Creating and remembering passwords for each service is not only a terrible user experience, but people tend to re-use passwords in many systems, which can quickly lead to account security issues. Not all systems are secured equally! Spreading your password across the Internet like the seeds of an ailanthus tree certainly increases your risk of compromise.

Casa offers people the ability to enroll and remove social login accounts available to the Gluu Server as a means of authentication. For example, you could create your account by signing in with Google, then enroll a Twitter, GitHub, and Facebook account to provide multiple options for accessing your account. This way, even if you get locked out of Google, you can still access your account.

Developer Portal

In order to support federated authentication and authorization, application developers need client credentials from the IAM system (i.e., `client-id` and `client_secret`). Client credentials enable an application to identify itself to the IAM system. Depending on the scopes granted, client credentials can be used for different purposes. Casa provides an interface for people to request and manage client credentials in the IAM system, enabling a more convenient developer experience and greater transparency and accountability for system administrators.

Getting Started

Gluu Casa can be deployed via Linux packages. Visit the documentation to learn how to get a local instance up and running: `http://gluu.org/docs/casa`.

Conclusion

It's critically important to your organization's security to get IDM right. It's a moving target—there will always be new systems and new business process to which you will need to adapt. It won't be easy—defining and implementing IDM requires a significant investment of time and energy.

CHAPTER 10

Multiparty Federation

"Information security is a fundamentally cooperative endeavor, one in which responsibility and authority are distributed across a wide array of actors."

—Ashwin J. Mathew[1]

Federated identity protocols like SAML and OpenID Connect enable us to authenticate people in other domains, but trust issues quickly surface. For example, if your organization operates a website with valuable content and someone you authenticated at another domain steals the content, what recourse do you have? If your organization operates an OpenID Provider (OP), and a relying party website (RP) is hacked, potentially exposing your account holders' personal information, do you expect to be notified? What rights do you have to update your personal information at identity providers or websites that you use? These related federated trust considerations are aptly described by Scott David, a legal identity scholar, as the "triangle of trust" (see Figure 10-1).

---

[1]https://er.educause.edu/blogs/2018/5/how-can-we-trust

© Michael Schwartz, Maciej Machulak 2018
M. Schwartz and M. Machulak, *Securing the Perimeter*, https://doi.org/10.1007/978-1-4842-2601-8_10

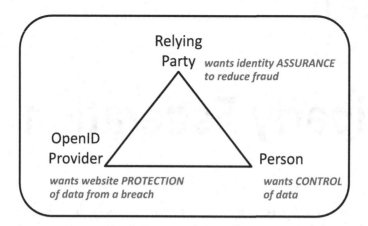

Figure 10-1. *Triangle of trust*

Figure 10-1 conveys what type of trust is needed and by whom. It uses OpenID Connect vocabulary (OP, RP) but you could substitute the equivalent SAML terms (IDP, SP). While you are most likely to hear about "Level of Assurance" of an authentication, you are less likely to hear about the "Level of Protection" or "Level of Control". However, these trust considerations are equally important.

Let's summarize for each vertex:

- Level of Assurance (LOA)—The RP needs assurance from the OP.

    Is the person who is the subject of the assertion really who they say they are? How well did you prove this person's identity? Did you inspect a state issued ID in-person? Did you verify with the issuer that the ID was valid? How well did you authenticate the person (password, OTP, biometric)? How secure are your account recovery procedures? The OP provides assurance, and in some cases, liability protection to the RP. The assertion is only as good as the identity management and security practices behind it. Identity need not be asserted for the necessary assurance to be met. Sometimes the RP only cares "is the person really who they say they are?". In the case of WiFi federation, what the RP wants to know is "are we assured this person will comply with our network rules?". In the case of federated access to licensed resources (e.g., online journals), it's "is this someone whose bill will paid?". LOA) is closely associated with version 2 of NIST 800-63, which defines levels one to four. The current version of 800-63 is updated to reflect a more nuanced view of the vectors of risk. 800-63C contains NIST's digital identity guidelines for federation and assertions and outlines many of the technical considerations for federation operators. You can read it on the web at `https://pages.nist.gov/800-63-3/sp800-63c.html`.

- Level of protection (LOP)—The OP wants the website to protect the data.

  Most RPs will write data to their database. Using federated identity, RPs don't need the secret credentials (e.g., passwords), but it is common for RPs to create a local account for each person to track their history and preferences. Whether or not the person approved the release of information explicitly or implicitly to the RP, most OPs expect a certain amount of diligence for the handling of shared PII. The RP should adopt best practices for data security and the extent to which it does is its LOP.

- Level of control (LOC)—The person wants to update, remove, or otherwise direct the use of their data.

  Today people are demanding control of their data as a human right. However, within an ecosystem, the concept of data ownership gets murky fast, as a person can't necessarily demand the removal for their personal information. For example, if an employee places an order, whose data is it? The employee's? The buyer's? Or seller's? Federation agreements can specify a person's rights to control the use and accuracy of data about them.

Our national, state, and international laws can't be relied on to create a workable trust fabric. At best, they are a patchwork of frequently outdated regulations that tend to inconsistently address issues of assurance, protection, and control. For example, in the United States, the HIPAA regulations specify that data must be protected by encryption. Other government regulations are proscriptive about assurance, but say nothing about protection. The EU GDPR regulations give the person increased control over their data.

Two organizations can achieve trust by describing all the contingencies in legal contracts. For example, the contract can specify acceptable types of authentication, the procedure for breach notifications and obligations to update or remove a person's information upon their request. However, in a large ecosystem with many companies, requiring each pair of organizations to negotiate a bilateral agreement is not efficient. In fact, trust derived from one-off agreements should be the anti-pattern.

A better approach is to define one standard contract that level sets assurance, protection and control within the community. If each federation participant signs a standard participant agreement, one-off agreements can be greatly reduced.

Another federation legal guru, Thomas J. Smedinghoff from the firm Locke Lord LLP describes three levels of law that govern multi-party federations: Level 1: general law (e.g., statutes and regulations); Level 2: law specific to the type of multi-party federation involved (e.g., financial or medical); and Level 3: system specific rules. Federation documents define the Level 3 system specific rules, which may address business (e.g., duties and responsibilities), legal (e.g., allocate risk and liabilities), technical (e.g., how data is formatted and secured), and operational (e.g., process and procedures) considerations. See Figure 10-2 for an illustration of this concept.

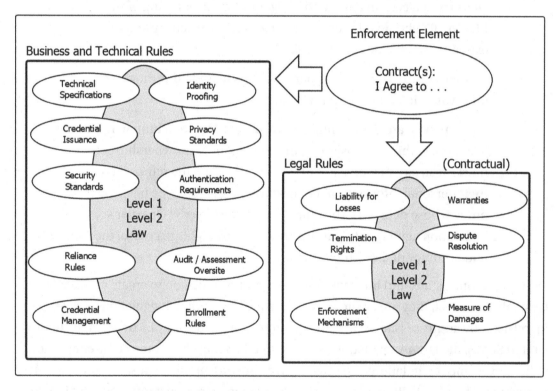

Figure 10-2. *Three level identity system*

Federations have existed for a long time. In government, a federation describes multiple autonomous states ceding authority to a central entity. The United States itself is "federal"—i.e., granted certain powers in the Constitution by the states in the interest of efficiency. The Internet is a federation—those connected agree to use IP addresses. Internet standards enable TCP, UDP, TLS, HTTP, and other communication streams.

There are many existing industry federations. If you are a member of a stock exchange, a sports league, or even a farming collective, you decide that it's worthwhile to give up some autonomy to gain efficiency in an ecosystem.

Federations offer different services depending on the level of trust the participants have in the federation operator and cost. The three existing types of services operated by federations are (1) root of trust to enable a hierarchical service; (2) metadata aggregate publication; (3) proxy.

Figure 10-3 uses DNS as an example of a Root of Trust service. ICANN is a sort of federation where TLDs, registrars, and organizations agree to be governed by some rules in exchange for DNS. Another example of a hierarchical trust service is the EduRoam higher education network, which enables reciprocal WiFi across participating campuses. eIDAS, a set of standards defined in EU regulations, enables interoperable national ID cards.

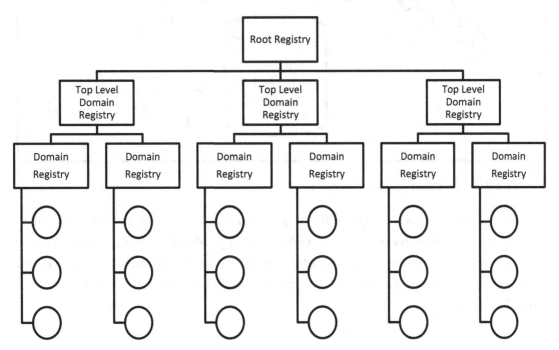

Figure 10-3. *Hierarchical trust service*

For meshed federation, as demonstrated in Figure 10-4, one of the best examples is InCommon (`https://incommon.org`), a federation of U.S. higher education institutions, which currently has approximately 1000 members: 700 universities and 300 websites. InCommon also has an inter-federation agreement with eduGAIN—the EU higher education federation. Government, defense, pharmaceutical, and automotive industries also have created supply chain SAML federations using the metadata aggregate approach.

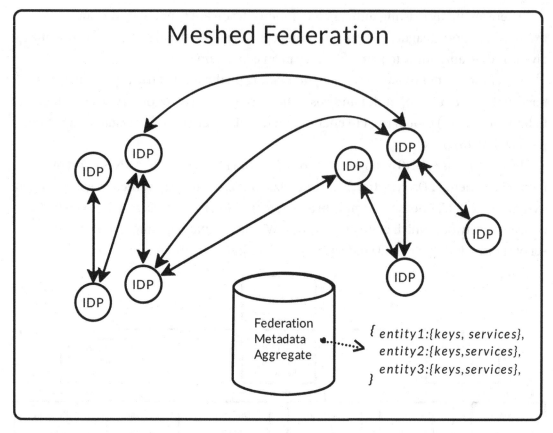

Figure 10-4. *Meshed federation via aggregate*

Proxy services, shown in Figure 10-5, cost the federation operator more to run, but are very convenient for participants. In a SAML identity federation, this means that the IDP has only to import one SP metadata (all the backend SPs are hidden from view). And likewise, the SP only need to know about one IDP (the proxy), so there is efficiency in both directions.

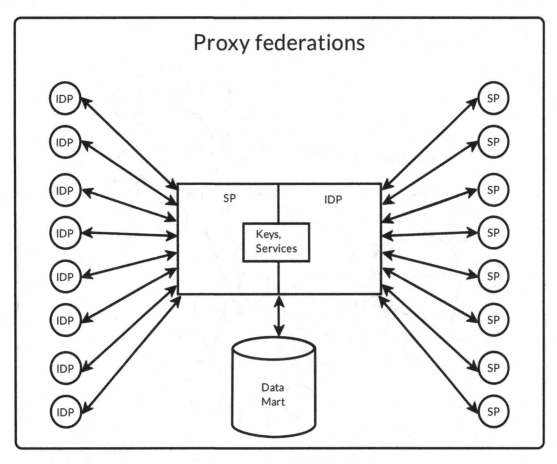

Figure 10-5. *Proxy federation service*

The federation could also offer centralized API proxy service and enforce federation policies. Although no current federations are doing this, it seems likely to happen soon.

Information security federations define the *tools and rules* for trust. See Figure 10-6 for a visualization of trust between federations. Federation "tools" are protocols, data structures, and vocabularies. Imagine how expensive it would be if every website used a different identifier for first name and last name. InCommon specifies that participants must support the eduPerson attributes. Beyond user claims, identity federations could define standard vocabularies for authentication mechanisms, OAuth scopes, and other custom schema.

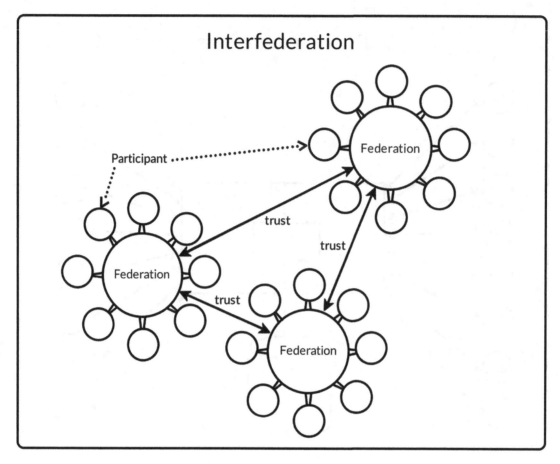

Figure 10-6. *Federation and interfederation trust*

Federation "rules" are the legal agreements that bind the parties together. There are a few legal recipes for how to accomplish this. The following recipe is for three agreements: a "Federation Policy," which defines the top level governance; a "Data Protection Code of Conduct," which defines not just protection, but also privacy responsibility of participants that hold data about people; and finally, the "Network Use Agreement," which should be displayed each time the person is authenticated as a participant.

Federations are not tied to specific protocols or technologies. Technical and legal innovations are inevitable, and effective federations will evolve to address new realities.

Federation Privacy Considerations

When federations offer services (like the publication of metadata or a proxy), they need to consider the ramifications for personal privacy. There are three risks:

- Observability, which refers to collecting data about a person activity

- Linkability, which refers to introducing a common identifier (like your Gmail address)

- Impersonation, as a result of attacks against the SSO mechanisms

The federation is not the only way a person can be tracked, linked, or hacked. For example, device fingerprinting, IP address, and compromised passwords all take their toll. But the federation should design its services in a way to avoid the above as much as possible.

NIST Special Publication 800-63C does a nice job of defining the privacy considerations for federations, and offers advice to minimizing "tracking" and "profiling". Other considerations include:

- Notice and consent

- Data minimization

- Blinding in Proxied federations

- Usability considerations

However, "privacy" can vary depending on your location. The EU has privacy principles:

- Fairness and lawfulness

- Final purpose

- Propotionality

- Data quality

- Information security

- Openness and transparency

- Individual participation

- Accountability

And don't forget the excellent "Privacy by Design" rules:

- Minimal identification

- Disclose/need to know

- Limited Linkability

- Transparency and user control

- Information security

The guidelines in NIST 800-63-C about blinding in proxied federations are particularly interesting. Consider Table 10-1.

Table 10-1. *NIST 800-63C Federation Proxies*

Proxy Type	RP Knows IdP	IdP Knows RP	Proxy Can Track Subscriptions Between RP and IdP	Proxy Can See Attributes of Subscriber
Non-Blinding Proxy with Attributes	Yes	Yes	Yes	Yes
Non-Blinding Proxy	Yes	Yes	Yes	N/A
Double Blind Proxy with Attributes	No	No	Yes	Yes
Double Blind Proxy	No	No	Yes	N/A
Triple Blind Proxy with or without Attributes	No	No	No	No

Does a "Triple Blind Proxy with or without Attributes" actually exist in real life? It's hard to say. But you get the idea here—it's very hard to protect privacy when you operate a proxy. Consult the experts!

Federation Policy

This document describes the governance of the federation. Does the federation have a steering committee? If so, how many members? Serving for how long? Voting in what way? The Federation Policy should also define how the federation is managed. Who will operate the day-to-day services? How should the federation market itself to drive more memberships? The Federation Policy covers a few more important areas like disputes resolution, and how an organization could become a participant. You can find quite a few federation polices on the Internet, as these are public documents, and most large federation operators point you to them.

Data Protection Code of Conduct

With the intent of giving people more control of their data, participants agree to a Data Protection Code of Conduct, regarding the handling of personal information. The federation can define the baseline expectations for consent, notification, and data protection. The document may also detail the data retention period and the rights of a person to access or rectify their data.

Network Use Agreement

Ultimately, the buck stops with people. End users have to take responsibility for their own security hygiene. That includes taking the appropriate level of care to protect their credentials from loss or compromise. The network banner also informs the person about their rights to correct information, to request removal from a service, and sometimes where to direct questions at the federation or participant.

Federation Actors

As this is a book for techies, not lawyers, back to the tools! Figure 10-7 shows the actors that participate in an identity federation.

- **Registration Authority**—Trusted third party that operates the federation technical infrastructure. For example, a hosting company, ISP, or telecommunications provider.

- **Federation Operators**—The organization that makes the rules, specifies the tools, and vets members. The federation should also perform due diligence on the Registration Authority, as the federation is partially liable for its operation.

- **Participant**—An organization who is qualified to join a federation, signs all the necessary legal agreements, and pays all fees.

- **Entity**—A service operated by a participant or the federation. Generally, the service needs to register its cryptographic signing key with the federation, and the web endpoints where its services can be found. It may also register other information that is useful to publish centrally, for example, to help other participants or end users find or better utilize its service. It's not uncommon for a participant to have several entities, for example, a university may operate an SAML IDP and several websites.

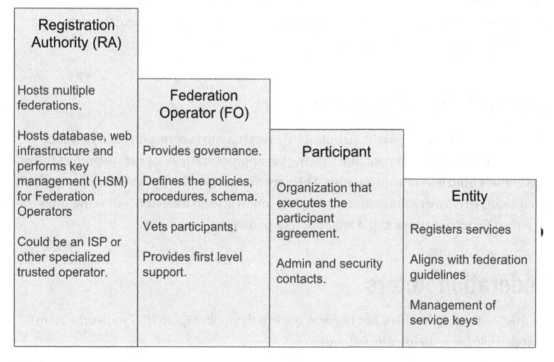

Figure 10-7. *Federation actors*

Joining a Federation

A participant is born once an organization signs the necessary legal agreements and performs all the required duties, such as paying any fees. The federations vet the participant and countersigns the documents. The participant specifies administrative, legal, and technical contacts and shares its technical configuration information, such as web endpoints and the public keys for each of its services. This metadata about its services is filtered and published by the federation. The federation may add configuration information, such as whether the entity qualifies as a certain federation managed category—for example, the Research and Scholarship (R&S) category in the higher education federation community.

Federation Trust Models

In addition to the trust generated by the agreements on a shared set of rules, multi-party federations also use technology to improve security.

The primary trust model used on the Internet today is TLS. We emphasize to consumers: make sure the little green padlock icon in your web browser is green! Some browsers make it difficult to navigate to a website where the SSL certificate is invalid. This trust model relies on the idea that the only organization that controls a domain can get a certificate for that domain from a well-known certification authority—one that has its root certificate installed in the browser. In general, this trust model works, but it's not secure enough for certain organizations that need to mitigate more risk than the average ecommerce transaction.

In addition to SSL, SAML and OpenID Connect define mechanisms to sign and encrypt identity assertions. If you download the public keys via HTTPS, then the trust model is still TLS. However, if the federation provides an out-of-band, highly secure way for the participant to upload its public keys to the federation operator, and the consumer of the identity assertion uses the federation's copy of the public key, it adds security over TLS. To forge the signature, the attacker would need to hack both the participant and the federation.

SAML Federations via Metadata Aggregate

SAML metadata allows for the description of multiple entities. A SAML federation metadata aggregate is a big file with all the entities for all the participants. The federation signs this XML file with its private signing key and publishes it.

A metadata aggregate can get large. Each entity publishes its public certificates. There is also XML needed to describe the endpoints and other SAML options. An already big metadata aggregate can get even bigger as a result of inter-federation—if one federation imports all the entities of another federation.

For many SAML federations, publication of metadata is an automated process that happens every five minutes or so. In terms of operations, the SAML federation metadata can be published as a flat file. This makes global distribution of the document easy, as the federation or registration authority needs no runtime infrastructure other than a web server. The metadata aggregate can just be copied to multiple data centers, enabling robust publication.

In SAML, both IDP and SP entities are treated similarly in the metadata. Both are required to have a stable entityID, which is like a primary key—the entityID must be unique in the metadata. It's a common convention to use the URL of the entity's metadata as the value for the entityID (a URL is collision resistant). The other common convention is to use a URN as the value for the entityID. As mentioned, the metadata published by the entity may or may not be the same as the metadata published for that entity by the federation, as the federation may add extra information about the entity to its aggregate.

There are a few drawbacks of the metadata aggregate approach:

- Interfederation using metadata aggregates does not scale well. A large file can get even bigger if you are including entities from another federation. The process of copying files and perhaps transforming them to meet your federation's metadata conventions can be onerous.

- The metadata aggregate is hard to search. It's very flat, so inevitably, you need to iterate through all the entries (which can be very slow if you're parsing the XML at runtime).

- Size is limited to a few thousand entities.

To solve this scaling problem, some federations are deploying the SAML Metadata Query Protocol (aka, MDQ), which allows for deployments to consume just the metadata they need and still verify the signature on the metadata to ensure trust. Entities which need to perform discovery operations may fetch a list of all entities via this API, extract the information they need for searching and discovery, and cache that information so that users can interact with it easily. Metadata is already cached by SAML software for validity periods defined in the metadata itself, in order to ensure reliability and performance, so this is not much extra work for the software. More information on MDQ is available at `https://datatracker.ietf.org/doc/draft-young-md-query/`.

Federation software that's of interoperating using SAML metadata must take into consideration other factors, including, but not limited to:

- Consuming multiparty metadata (via an aggregate or otherwise).

- Verifying the signature on the metadata.

- Refreshing its cached copy of that metadata on a regular basis (at least daily).

- Configuring itself to exchange identity information based solely on the configuration material contained in the metadata (trustmarks, etc.).

- Handling key-rollover scenarios decrypting assertions using multiple keys (SP) and issuing encrypted assertions using multiple SP public keys with all necessary key material published in the metadata.

- Ignoring parts of the X.509 certificate wrapper that play no role in the federation trust model and relying solely on the key material in the metadata and the metadata signature for trust.

All requirements for SAML software to be able to interoperate in this context are documented in the Kantara Initiative's SAML v2.0 Implementation Profile for Federation Interoperability at `https://kantarainitiative.org/file-downloads/saml-v2-0-implementation-profile-for-federation-interoperability-version-1-0-pdf/`. This profile builds on the core OASIS standards that define requirements for SAML software in general.

Trustmarks

Most of this content is thanks to the Georgia Tech Research Institute (GTRI) with the support of the National Strategy for Trusted Identities in Cyberspace (NSTIC) via the National Institute of Standards and Technology (NIST).

Standard disclaimer: "The views expressed do not necessarily reflect the official policies of NIST or NSTIC; nor does mention by trade names, commercial practices, or organizations imply endorsement by the U.S. Government."

Trustmarks enable organizations to convey security risks in machine readable format. A trustmark can be an assertion about anything! For example, technical interoperability (e.g., vocabularies and protocols), LOA/LOP/LOC considerations, or business. The legal aspects of trustmarks are conveyed not through the trustmarks themselves, but via the trustmark policies and/or trustmark agreements under which trustmarks are issued and used.

This kind of federation is potentially more efficient than a centralized or "monolithic" federation.

Figure 10-8 shows how a trustmark can lower costs. The straight line represents the growth of costs when establishing trust through a series of pairwise (bilateral) trust relationships. Each new pairwise relationship established requires the same amount of time and effort as was required for each previously established relationship. This line represents a worst-case scenario and is an unacceptable strategy for any ecosystem that wishes to establish more than a trivial number of trust relationships with other organizations.

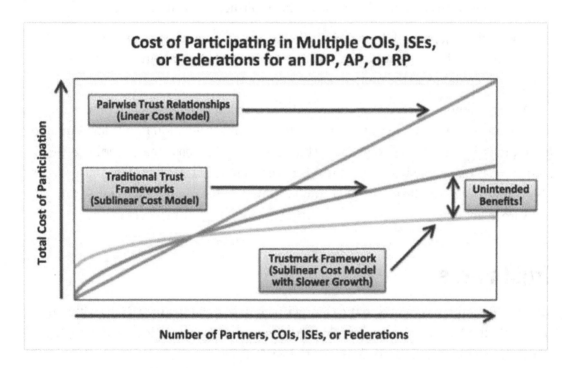

Potential Cost Savings from a Trustmark Framework

Figure 10-8. *Potential cost savings from a trustmark framework, courtesy GTRI*

The "Traditional Trust" curve represents the growth of costs when establishing trust through a series of traditional trust frameworks. The route of monolithic trust frameworks tends to imply joining multiple monolithic trust frameworks over time. The strategy of joining multiple monolithic trust frameworks does not scale as poorly as the bilateral trust strategy; however, it is still suboptimal. Since each new monolithic trust framework is opaque, it is unlikely that a significant amount of the prior work, which was performed during the process of joining previous monolithic trust frameworks, will be applicable when joining the next monolithic trust framework.

The "Trustmark Framework" curve represents the growth of costs when establishing trust through a componentized trustmark framework in which individual trust components tend to be reused between trust frameworks. In this scenario, joining a new trust framework requires three steps.

- Determining which trustmarks are required by the new framework.

- Determining which required trustmarks are already possessed, and which need to be acquired.

- Acquiring the necessary trustmarks that are not already possessed.

Over time, as the organization seeks to join multiple componentized trust frameworks, it is increasingly likely to already possess many or most (or all) of the necessary trustmarks based on its previous efforts to join other trust frameworks. This causes the cost growth curve to become flat, or nearly flat, over time.

This analysis illustrates one of the most important benefits of trustmarks: not only do trustmarks enable componentization and reuse of trust and interoperability criteria, but they also carry the potential for significant cost savings over time as the ecosystem grows to encompass many communities that engage in a variety of cross-COI collaboration scenarios.

For more information on trustmarks, including the trustmark XML specification, a database of existing security trustmarks (many!), and lots of great theoretical information, visit GTRI's trustmark page at `https://trustmark.gtri.gatech.edu/`.

OpenID Federations

OpenID federations are moving in a similar direction as trustmarks—toward a componentized trust model. The proposed OpenID federation specification, which is currently a draft and is likely to change, links together signing keys using a JSON Web Key Set (JWKS) to create a chain of signing keys. Like public key infrastructure (PKI), it provides a way to verify that an intermediate key is trusted by a root key.

OpenID presents some unique challenges when compared with SAML. In SAML, both IDPs and SPs have an entityID, which is a convenient way to reference them in a federation's metadata. In OpenID Connect, it's a requirement that the OpenID Provider publishes its metadata (although they don't call it that) on a URL—the `.well-known/openid-configuration` endpoint. It's common for SAML IDPs to publish metadata on a URL. For example, for a Shibboleth deployment, it can be found at `https://hostname/idp/metadata`.

However, what is the entityID for an OpenID RP? One suggested change to OpenID federation proposes a stable identifier for the RP. During OpenID dynamic client registration, the OP issues a `client_id`, which is different for each OP. One could argue that the `redirect_uri` is a reasonable way to identify a client. However, you need to take into account that `redirect_uri`, may be multi-value, and the RP may update it, so it's not a great primary key. OpenID Federation requires non-public RPs (i.e., websites) to publish a `signed_jwks_uri`. This is impossible for supporting mobile clients and JavaScript applications running in the browser.

Another consideration for OpenID Federation was that OpenID Provider keys used to sign and encrypt assertions are rotated every two days according to current best practices. That's a lot—SAML keys are usually rotated every few months or every year. One of the innovations of OpenID federation is to introduce a stable signing keys for the OP and RP, the location of which is published on the OpenID Provider discovery page. The public signing keys are stored by the client and provide additional trust over TLS (after the key is retrieved). The signing key is used to publish a verifiable OpenID discovery document.

The main innovation introduced in the OpenID Connect federation specification is the idea of `metadata_statements`, a JSON assertion, signed by the federation. The technical mechanics of how `metadata_statements` are created are somewhat complicated—it involves successive cryptographic operations.

Metadata statements are published by the OP or presented by clients during dynamic registration. Think of the metadata statement like a Russian matryoshka doll—where each concentric metadata statement asserts information about a link in the trust chain. For example, a developer creates a metadata statement, signs it, and passes to the organization, who adds information and signs it, and then passes it to the federation that signs it. With the right tooling, such a process could be productive for both developers and security devops.

OpenID Connect Federation specification work is still formative. Feedback from implementations will result in changes to the specification.

OTTO Federation

OTTO is a set of standards under development at the Kantara Initiative. OTTO stands for the "Open Trust Taxonomy for Federation Operators". It is a set of APIs for federation management, and an extensible JSON-LD vocabulary to model federation data. Like the OpenID federation spec, it is waiting for adoption.

OTTO addresses some of the weaknesses of existing SAML federations. The OTTO APIs standardize operation by the registration authority. How does a participant join a federation? How to register or update an entity? How to leave a federation?

OTTO APIs provide a standard way to do these things. In SAML, federation operators either wrote their own operational software or used open source software to manage federation data. Some federations offer participants no automated interface—registration and updates happen via a manual process. If federations become more common, consistency would offer more efficiency to participants and operators alike.

OTTO APIs provide a query mechanism to obtain information from the federation. While this comes at additional operational complexity—the federation operator is no longer just copying a static file to a web server—hosting APIs has become somewhat of a mainstream activity for organizations. And registration authorities who specialize in hosting federations will certainly have the technical capability.

One of the other goals of OTTO was to make inter-federation more scalable. SAML's approach of copying the data from one federation to another is not particularly effective. It results in large files and raises challenges around filtering the data, as the imported metadata may not align perfectly with the metadata conventions of the federation that consumes it and may need to be transformed. The design of OTTO is to use linked data to enable one federation to reference the data of another.

In addition to the APIs, OTTO defines several JSON-LD vocabularies. The OTTO core vocabulary defines the common denominator for the registration authority, federation, participant, entity, and schema. It also defines vocabulary extensions for SAML and OpenID—the two most important initial use cases. But it leaves open the possibility that new protocols and new trust models will evolve, and that it can be extended to meet those new requirements by supporting additional standard or even custom (industry-specific) vocabularies.

OTTO API

The registration authority hosts the OTTO API, which consists of a number of service endpoints.

- **Configuration API** —Returns a JSON document describing the federation services of the registration authority—basically the URLs of all the endpoints described next. This is published as `https://domain/optional-path/.well-known/otto-configuration`.

- **Federation API** —This is the workhorse endpoint. First it is used by the registration authority to add, edit, and delete federations. It is used by an organization that wants to sponsor a federation. The federation uses this endpoint to add and remove participants. It is used by participants to request to join or leave a federation. And finally, it can be used by anyone to search public information about the hosted federations.

- **Participant API** —This endpoint is used by federation software to create a participant, look up information about a participant, or otherwise update a participant's data. It is also used to link a participant to federations and entities. Lookup by reference ID is supported.

- **Entity API** —This endpoint is used by participant software to create, update, and delete entities and to link them to participants (who operate them) or federations. Lookup by reference ID is supported.

- **Metadata API** —This endpoint, hosted by the Registration Authority, enables the management of metadata of the federation. The API requires a `category` (e.g., OpenID or SAML) and allows optional parameters `metadataFormat` and `expiration`. Metadata could be periodically downloaded and published in the traditional way (i.e., copy to a bunch of servers). Or it can be handled more dynamically: the software for a participant will obtain a software statement or metadata statement on the fly.

- **Schema API** —This endpoint, hosted by the registration authority, enables the management of schema available to federations. The `category` property is required. For example, the OpenID vocabulary defines `UserClaim`, `Scope`, and `ACR` as values for schema category. When you create a schema, you have to say if it's required. For example, perhaps an email address is a required user claim in certain federations. The schema endpoint enables software to view, create, and update schema, and to link schema with an entity or federation. The endpoints also enable lookup of a schema by ID and an endpoint to return all available schema categories.

OTTO Vocabulary

JSON-LD 1.0 is a W3C specification, which can be found at `https://www.w3.org/TR/json-ld/`. It is a lightweight syntax to serialize Linked Data in JSON. Since JSON-LD is 100% compatible with JSON, you can use your existing JSON tools and libraries. JSON is better for security. Compared with XML, JSON is simpler, and parser developers are less prone to security snafus.

Although there are many good reasons to use JSON-LD, three features were important to OTTO (see Figure 10-9):

- **Linking**—You can refer to a JSON object in a different domain. Many of the objects are related. For example, entities are operated by a participant, whereas a federation has participants and a registration authority operates federations. This capability can reduce some of the data duplication and filtering challenges in the current metadata aggregate approach.

- **Extensibility**—A JSON-LD class may be a subclass of another class, inheriting its properties. The OTTO Core Vocabulary defines building blocks, with which additional OTTO vocabularies can be built. For example, SAML IDP and OpenID OP both use OTTO Entity as a subclass. Future vocabularies may address UMA, ACE, PKI, and other protocols yet to be invented, and hopefully will not have to reinvent—just supplement.

- **Re-Use**—OTTO used schema from `https://schema.org` as a starting point. This means our vocabulary was almost complete—OTTO defines some additional vocabulary for federation specific stuff. For example, in OTTO a participant is a subclass of schema.org organization, `https://schema.org/Organization`.

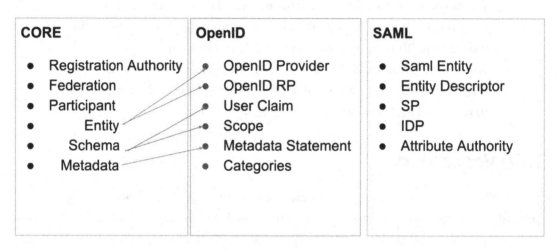

CORE	OpenID	SAML
• Registration Authority	• OpenID Provider	• Saml Entity
• Federation	• OpenID RP	• Entity Descriptor
• Participant	• User Claim	• SP
• Entity	• Scope	• IDP
• Schema	• Metadata Statement	• Attribute Authority
• Metadata	• Categories	

Figure 10-9. *Vocabulary overview*

All core OTTO classes have an `@id` and `name` property. The `@id` is a globally unique identifier—a primary key used for linking data. The issuer of the `@id` should either use a GUID algorithm or a hierarchical name space (such as a URL). The `name` property is a human-readable identifier.

The following is a summary of the information stored in each.

- **RA**—Subclass of schema.org/Organization. Contains the OTTO endpoint URIs (e.g., `federation_endpoint`, `participant_endpoint`). The `registers` property specifies the hosted federations.

- **Participant**—Subclass of schema.org/Organization. Entities are linked by the `operates` property. Federations are linked by the `memberOf` property. Participant contact information can also be published here.

- **Entity**—Subclass of schema.org/Thing. A technical service of a participant. The `operates` property indicates the resource. The `operatedBy` and `federatedBy` properties specify the organization and federation links. The `supports` property can be used to describe schema requirements or to publish trustmarks. The `category` property can be used by the federation to group entities to facilitate trust management (e.g., R&S websites).

- **Federation**—Subclass of schema.org/Organization. The `member` and `federates` properties link participants and entities respectively. The `metadata` property specifies the federation's public keys, certificates, and other cryptographic information to enable verification of federation assertions and encrypted communication. The `sponsor` property specifies the organization responsible for governance. Federation contact information and legal agreements can be listed. The federation can use the `supports` property to publish schema standards, like user claim identifiers (e.g., `givenName` or `first_name?`) and trustmarks (as mentioned in the previous section).

- **Metadata**—Subclass of schema.org/Thing. This class specifies its `metadataFormat`, `expiration`, and `category` (e.g., OpenID or SAML). OTTO extension vocabularies (like OpenID and SAML) subclass metadata, adding the necessary details for their protocols.

- **Schema**—Subclass of schema.org/Thing. Also uses the `category` property to group schema (e.g., `user_claims`, `scope`). The `required` boolean can be used by an entity, e.g., an SP might require the email address attribute. The `sameAs` property can be used to link schema to eliminate overlap.

Retrieving Datafrom OTTO Federations

Using the OTTO Federation API, you can search and retrieve data about entities. An OTTO client can use parameters to signal to return the data.

- `filter`—Enables the OTTO client to use a search expression to limit the results returned. OTTO uses the JSPath query syntax. You can read more about JSPath at `https://github.com/dilatov/jspath`. The following is an example of a filter to show how you can search for a website by name.

```
GET   /federations?filter=.entities{.name="MyWebsite"}
```

- depth—Enables you to specify what kinds of objects you want returned. It's sort of like using an objectclass=object filter in LDAP. The following request shows an example where you might want to get back just a list of organizations that associated with the federation.

```
GET   /federations/1234?depth=federations.organization
```

- sign—Enables you to request that the federation sign the returning JSON object using the private key of the federation, in a format specified by the signing algorithm.

```
GET /federations/1234/sign=true&alg=RS512
```

OTTO Next

OTTO is still under development at the Kantara Initiative. You can read the draft specifications, meeting minutes, and visit the test site:

- OTTO GitHub: https://github.com/KantaraInitiative/wg-otto

- OTTO APIs: https://gluu.co/otto-api

- Core vocabulary: https://gluu.co/otto-vocab

- OpenID vocabulary: https://gluu.co/otto-openid

- SAML vocabulary: https://gluu.co/otto-saml

- Swagger demo site (not guaranteed to be up!): http://otto-test. gluu.org/swagger/

Jagger

Jagger was developed by HEAnet to manage the Edugate multiparty SAML federation. in Ireland, Jagger is an easy way to deploy and operate federation management platform that provides a website for participant administrators to join and update a federation, and for federation administrators to approve and publish SAML metadata. One of the nice features is that it supports the management of multiple federations, making it an excellent choice for a registration authority. It also creates a single circle of trust, containing metadata of all trusted entities via multiple federations. The home page for Jagger is `https://jagger.heanet.ie` (see Figure 10-10).

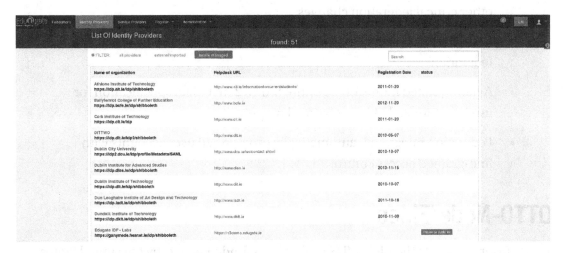

Figure 10-10. *Jagger screenshot showing list of IDPs*

Federation Registry

Developed by the Australian Access Federation in the higher education sector, Federation Registration is a Java platform for hosting a single federation. FR won't get any further support or updates—they have only been doing security updates for some time. Features include:

- A focus on organizations as the key building block for the federation

- Allows for organizations to be service providers only

- A personalized dashboard view of the federation for all users

- A highly refined, multi-browser, HTML5 compliant user interface

- The user interface is fully themeable to suit the look and feel of your organization and is multilingual capable out of the box

- Management for all aspects of SAML 2 compliant identity and service providers SAML 2.x compliant metadata generation

- Additional assistance for Shibboleth IDP and SP administrators, including automated Attribute Filter generation

- Public registration for organizations, identity providers, and service providers that are new to the federation

- A fully customizable workflow engine to handle registrations and other critical federation changes

- Compliance reporting to gain insight into various areas of your federation

- A hand-crafted model of the entire SAML 2 metadata specification for use in automated object relational mapping

- Federation integrated, automatically provisioned user accounts with fine-grained access control

OTTO-Node/Fides

This software, a part of the ERASMUS project, was funded in part by the United States Department of Homeland Security's Science and Technology Directorate. Standard disclaimer: "The content of this book does not necessarily reflect the position or the policy of the U.S. Government and no official endorsement should be inferred."

Fides is a web application that enables a person to register, then register an organization and apply to become a member of the federation. It includes enrollment of an OpenID Provider, using the discovery features of OpenID Connect. A federation administrator manually approves membership applications.

This project included support for creation of "badge assertions," which are JSON-LD data structures defined in the Open Badges 2.0 specification, which can be found at https://gluu.co/open-badges-2-0. In our pilot, we were using badges to convey professional training and certifications that were specific to the emergency responder community. The Fides federation admin can authorize an organization to issue certain types of badges.

Fides also calls the OTTO APIs—for example, when a federation admin approves a new participant, Fides calls the OTTO federation endpoint to make the link.

Fides and OTTO Node code can be found in Gluu's GitHub repository: https://github.com/GluuFederation/otto-node https://github.com/GluuFederation/erasmus/tree/master/FIDES

More information about ERASMUS can be found at https://kantarainitiative.org/trustoperations/kantara-identity-privacy-incubator/erasmus/.

See Figure 10-11 for a FIDES screenshot.

Figure 10-11. *FIDES screenshot showing Federation*

Conclusion

A theme of human history is that we're better together, and federations make this happen at scale. Certainly, as our society becomes increasingly digital, we need more economies of scale in trust management. You can't read every privacy policy for every service you sign up for. Maybe federations can give us more collective bargaining power. Or maybe they can just help our businesses get more done with less money. Either way, this technology is also likely to grow and will make the Internet a safer place for all.

Index

A

G

P, Q

S

W, X, Y, Z

Printed in the United States
By Bookmasters